COMICS AND Sacred Texts

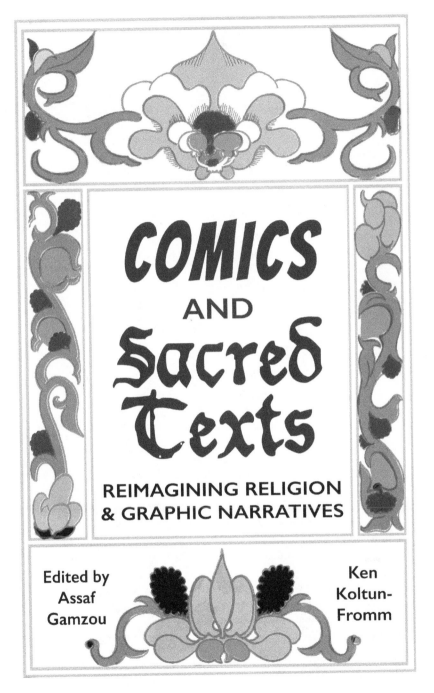

COMICS AND Sacred Texts

REIMAGINING RELIGION & GRAPHIC NARRATIVES

Edited by
Assaf Gamzou
Ken Koltun-Fromm

UNIVERSITY PRESS OF MISSISSIPPI / JACKSON

The University Press of Mississippi is the scholarly publishing agency of the Mississippi Institutions of Higher Learning: Alcorn State University, Delta State University, Jackson State University, Mississippi State University, Mississippi University for Women, Mississippi Valley State University, University of Mississippi, and University of Southern Mississippi.

www.upress.state.ms.us

The University Press of Mississippi is a member of the Association of University Presses.

First printing 2018
∞

Library of Congress Cataloging-in-Publication Data

Names: Gamzou, Assaf, 1984– editor. | Koltun-Fromm, Ken, editor.
Title: Comics and sacred texts : reimagining religion and graphic narratives / edited by Assaf Gamzou and Ken Koltun-Fromm.
Description: Jackson : University Press of Mississippi, [2018] | Includes bibliographical references and index. |
Identifiers: LCCN 2018017931 (print) | LCCN 2018020181 (ebook) | ISBN 9781496819222 (epub single) | ISBN 9781496819239 (epub institutional) | ISBN 9781496819246 (pdf single) | ISBN 9781496819253 (pdf institutional) | ISBN 9781496819215 (hardcover : alk. paper) | ISBN 9781496819475 (pbk. : alk. paper)
Subjects: LCSH: Comic books, strips, etc.—Religious aspects. | Comic books, strips, etc.—Criticism and interpretation. | Superheroes—Religious aspects. | Popular culture—Religious aspects.
Classification: LCC PN6712 (ebook) | LCC PN6712 .C53 2018 (print) | DDC 741.5/382—dc23
LC record available at https://lccn.loc.gov/2018017931

British Library Cataloging-in-Publication Data available

CONTENTS

ACKNOWLEDGMENTS

ALL BOOKS HAVE ORIGIN STORIES, AND THIS ONE BEGAN WITH A SMALL but influential conference held at Princeton University in April 2015. Frames: Jewish Culture and the Comic Book was a two-day event orchestrated by Charlotte Werbe and Marie Sanquer. The conference was extraordinarily rich and diverse, with an accompanying exhibition and papers from prominent and emerging scholars (one of whom, A. David Lewis, is also a contributor to this book). It was there that we first met, and over coffee the next day we sketched out this project.

After receiving strong interest from a call for papers, we quickly moved to establish our own conference symposium on Sacred Texts and Comics at Haverford College in May 2016, hosted by Ken Koltun-Fromm and supported by the Hurford Center for the Arts and Humanities. With an exhibition curated by Assaf Gamzou, the conference offered panels, paper presentations, and workshops from contributors to this volume. We wish to thank the Hurford Center at Haverford College for its support and encouragement, together with the artists featured in the exhibition, Biblical Proportions: Stories from the Testaments in Comics: Shay Charka, Zev Engelmayer, Miriam Katin, Peter Kuper, Strakings and Henry Flint, Chris Ware, and works from Will Eisner, made available through the caretakers of his estate, Denis Kitchen and Carl and Nancy Groper. Ken is especially grateful to his students from "Reading Comics and Religion" and our visiting artist J. T. Waldman, who all helped to shape our understanding of comics and the sacred, and who actively constructed and participated in the symposium. Without the administrative support and contribution from students and artists alike, the symposium could not have been the success that it surely was, and a small but fervent community of scholars owes a debt of gratitude to all involved.

Thanks too are in order for the staff of the Israeli cartoon museum for their support: Galit Gaon, the founder and chief curator, for her vision and support for what sometimes seemed like very strange ideas, and Dikla, Hilla, Amnon, and Michal for their continued work and effort.

We wish to thank the University Press of Mississippi for its continued and valuable support for this project, especially our editor Vijay Shah and editorial assistant Lisa McMurtray. We also received kind help from Carla Speed McNeil, who illustrated "the wormhole" for chapter 4, and Neta Manor, who helped with images throughout the book.

Assaf wishes to personally thank his family: My one and only partner in crime, Michal, and my children, Shelly and Dori: you give meaning to this and any other endeavor I undertake, and force me, every day, to try and be who I want to be for you. Without you this would not be possible, or worthwhile.

. . .

We dedicate this book to Ken's colleague at Haverford College, Robert Germany, who taught us the joys of intellectual creativity, and who died much too young to see the fruits of his glorious labor.

Introduction

COMICS AND SACRED TEXTS

ASSAF GAMZOU AND KEN KOLTUN-FROMM

ROBERT ORSI TELLS A WONDERFUL STORY ABOUT HIS STUDENTS IN HIS US urban religion class. As he recounts his visit to St. Lucy, a Catholic church in the North Bronx, his students become visibly uneasy, even horrified, as they learn how the congregants would use holy water for apparently mundane things. For the water streaming from the Bronx grotto was thought to be the same miraculous water flowing in Lourdes, France, where Mary had revealed herself to a young woman in 1858. Pilgrims traveled to Lourdes to bathe in its salvific springs; so too this Italian Catholic community would turn to the Bronx grotto, built in 1939, for similarly edifying results. Yet not only did these believers drink from the well and pour water over themselves as a kind of protective covering, but "men in shorts and t-shirts filled their radiators with Bronx Lourdes water for protection on the road." When Orsi asked an older woman about the source of this sweet water, she answered in a rather irritable tone, "It's city water—it comes from the reservoir, I guess." Yet it is Orsi's punch-line that tends to rattle his students: "Later I was told by one of the caretakers at the grotto that no one really believed the story about the underground spring; everyone knows exactly where the water comes from and everyone maintains the water is holy and powerful" (3–5).

Orsi, along with colleagues whose scholarship engages the material and lived practices of religious actors, persistently undermines presumptions about religion and the sacred, and so do the comics discussed in this volume, *Comics and Sacred Texts: Reimagining Religion and Graphic Narratives*. Collectively, these essays argue that the sacred appears in unusual and often overlooked places to offer new visionary modes for recognizing the sacred. We claim that *seeing* the sacred is a learned practice, and these collected essays are pedagogical texts designed to frame that learning. We must learn where to look for and how to envision the sacred. In seeing the sacred anew, graphic narratives play a key role in exploring how the sacred appears in image and text. As a visual and textual medium, comics expose the graphic interplay of seeing the sacred and reading about it. In this imagined, visual/textual space, the graphic narratives discussed in *Comics and Sacred Texts* reveal how the sacred appears in narrative and script (section 1), how comics revise and transform notions of the sacred in religious texts (section 2), how comic monsters and bodies out of place reposition sacred boundaries (section 3), and how comics can reveal and infuse everyday, mundane spaces with the sacred (section 4). Together, these four sections open new ways to see and to discover the sacred in a visual medium often ignored in religious studies.

But learning to see the sacred in overlooked arenas also means unlearning old habits of vision. Such poorer accounts of seeing can be found in antiquated models that too easily relegate religion to bounded, dualistic categories of analysis. We read of Émile Durkheim and his famous distinction between the sacred and the profane as "two distinct classes, as two worlds between which there is nothing in common" (54). Or students of religion might appeal to Mircea Eliade and his distinctly Christian reading in which the sacred manifests as a power and force "wholly other" to the profane (124–25). To be sure, Eliade and Durkheim are far more nuanced than these simple formulations would suggest. And more robust theories of religion expand their views by appealing to cultural and linguistic studies. But the tendency is nonetheless instructive: we wish to isolate religion and the sacred from perceived defiled acts and profane things. Religion happens in certain places, far apart from the messiness and materiality of Orsi's car radiators and negotiated, ambivalent lives. And it is not only students who imagine religion in these ways; scholars too locate religion in distinct spheres in order to study and examine it. For if diffuse, religion might be far too textured and elastic for theories and methods to contain it. We all have something to gain from locating, selecting, insulating, and thereby protecting the sacred.

Comics and Sacred Texts helps us to recalibrate our seeing the sacred in places and in forms beyond categorical dualisms and divisions. This graphic capacity to reveal the sacred is not just an accidental occurrence that we discover in some but not all comics. It is not just about subject matter; the graphic form itself is ideally suited to reveal how the sacred appears in uncanny places. By wedding text to image, and at times even transforming image into text and text into image, comics *as a form* challenge hard boundaries and principles. Through texture, line thickness, time configured as space, and the various tricks comic artists use to engage the reader as active co-creators, graphic narratives can inform how readers imagine and reconstruct the sacred as a material, visual experience. This experience, we argue in this book, is not cordoned off from our everyday, mundane lives but instead is interwoven in how we imagine living in a world suffused with language, bodies, and ordinary practices.

Yet comics, much like religion, are also viewed and read through a specific set of presuppositions. Indeed, the term "graphic narrative" itself, along with others such as "sequential art" and "graphic novels," are linguistic attempts to overcome the presumed lowbrow, sexualized, often violent images associated with comics. In this all-too-common discourse, comics are simply male teenage fantasies projected onto superheroes who rescue the poor damsel in distress. We see bright, strong colors driven by paper-thin plots, cheap reads for a generation sunk in visual splendor. But comics offer more than youthful pleasures; they also alert us to the richness of human experience, to the hybridity of the image/text, and to visions of the sacred that interrogate traditional claims about where the holy comes from, and where to discover and experience it. *Comics and Sacred Texts* teaches us to see the sacred anew.

Even as this volume breaks new ground in realigning how and where to discover the sacred, it nonetheless travels along an undercurrent begun in 1972, when Umberto Eco and Natalie Chilton published their pioneering essay "The Myth of Superman." Here, Eco and Chilton analyzed superman's "mythic function," and by extension the superhero genre's literary and social effect (15). Ever since, scholars have debated the mythic and religious meanings of the superhero character, with important articles, anthologies, and full-length manuscripts contributing to an ever-growing field. Works with such energetic titles as Gerard Jones's *Men of Tomorrow: Geeks, Gangsters, and the Birth of the Comic Book* (2005), Danny Fingeroth's *Disguised as Clark Kent: Jews, Comics, and the Creation of the Superhero* (2008), and Arie Kaplan's *From Krakow to Krypton: Jews and Comic Books* (2008), have legitimated and broadened this field of inquiry. One can even discern subfields, such as the effect of Jewish identity on the superhero genre, and works penned by comic artists themselves—the most interesting of which might be Grant Morrison's *Supergods: What Masked Vigilantes, Miraculous Mutants, and a Sun God from Smallville Can Teach Us about Being Human* (2011). Morrison, an accomplished comics writer who has worked within the superhero genre, challenges and broadens Eco and Chilton's concern to tackle notions of sacred myth and religious transcendence beyond the traditional hero. His thoughtful engagement with sacred texts and figures (especially in *Animal*

Man) interrogates the place and scope of the sacred in graphic narratives. In both Morrison and the essays in *Comics and Sacred Texts*, the very notion of what counts as the religious sacred, its very shape and place in human experience, is confronted anew and with critical rigor.

This critical encounter too has strong roots and has recently blossomed into a burgeoning field of academic inquiry. Just in the past decade, we have witnessed publications such as Karline McLain's *India's Immortal Comic Books* (2009), A. David Lewis and Christine Hoff Kraemer's edited volume *Graven Images: Religion in Comic Books & Graphic Novels* (2010), and Samantha Baskind and Ranen Omer-Sherman's editorial work for *The Jewish Graphic Novel: Critical Approaches* (2010). It is no surprise, then, that one can find essays from McLain, Lewis, Baskind, and Omer-Sherman in *Comics and Sacred Texts*. But here their approaches, like others in this collected volume, focus on how to reimagine the sacred in comics studies. We have altogether abandoned the once noticeable apologetic stance toward comic books and instead critically engage comics as vital and reflective texts about religious experience. The hard-earned work of McLain, Lewis, Baskind, Omer-Sherman, and others to open the field of religion and comics has been largely successful; now we hope to reimagine the religious, and what counts as religious, through the tools and perspectives of comics studies.

Comics and notions of the sacred interweave within graphic narratives in nuanced and provocative ways, much as notions of the sacred infused the lived experiences of those religious practitioners whom Orsi examined. Indeed, the sacred often appears in graphic narratives as an everyday, physical, emotive encounter with the material world. Yet this other side of the sacred would still be too easy, too bifurcating, and too one-sided. How do comics reveal new contours and spaces of the sacred? Graphic narratives have distinct advantages in articulating a more fluid, material sacred, and this for primarily three reasons: 1) they can *show* (or, just as importantly, choose *not* to show) what the sacred looks like, revealing the way it weaves through multiple forms, and through the interplay of text and image; 2) comics utilize panels and gutters to both separate and relate human activities and emotions, and so can motivate this both/and mode of engaging the sacred; and 3) in their *showing* and *telling*, in the stutter-step of the paneled narratives, comics offer us a *liminal* experience of reading, engaging, and constructing meaning. It is an experience "betwixt and between time" (Turner 95) that in its form as an *imagetext* both undermines the separation of media and harbors the potential for rethinking how media reveal the sacred. While this liminal quality is not necessarily communal, as Turner originally believed, but instead deeply personal, it still offers a unique space of creative exploration and transcendence.

In these ways graphic narratives motivate certain ways of seeing and experiencing the world. In both content and form, graphic narratives position the sacred as a visual spectacle of transfigurings, sometimes locating it in our everyday, public lives, and sometimes positioning the sacred in distinct, private moments. Panels and page-turn reveals can mark these separations, and the gutter too maps the arena of personal engagement and relational activity. As Scott McCloud and others have argued with such conviction, the gutter remains the space of readerly involvement in the magic of comics. Here, the reader creates the comic, becomes an active participant in its making, and so shapes the movement and structure of the sacred in narrative form. McCloud describes this activity as closure: the comic images may show me the axe raised, but the comic is "not the one who let[s] it drop or decide[s] how hard the blow, or who screamed, or why" (68). This we do as comic readers, and the gutter is the place of our imaginative activity. But comics are more than gutters, and readerly involvement happens in other spaces too. The essays in *Comics and Sacred Texts* show how comic script, narrative trajectories, out-of-place bodies, and revamped religious texts inform our visual experiences of the sacred. We can see how the sacred works in the very way these comics motivate a mode of reading and seeing.

Let us look at two examples of how comics inform new visual dimensions of the sacred. In Will Eisner's *A Contract with God* (1978), we see Frimme Hersh confronting his God (Eisner 24). Eisner frames the story as a dialogue in which we only hear Frimme's voice. That voice has a shape and a pitch, emphasized by the dark background to the speech bubble and the all-capitalized letters. But we do not see this dialogue between Frimme and God; we can only imagine it, as the tenement dwellers do, behind closed doors. Within that frame there is the inner room, where Frimme yells at his God, and the outer, public staircase, where we dwell. Eisner draws us into the tenement, together with its inhabitants, as we eavesdrop on Frimme's private argument. Already we can see how this text informs visions of the sacred: it happens in humble, yet not entirely private, spaces. We listen in on these sacred dialogues, as other tenement dwellers do. But these encounters are not moments of bliss, quietude, or even transformative experiences separate from our ordinary lives. They are violent and confrontational; they are angry encounters with a God who does not talk back. The sacred, in this depiction, echoes relations that tenement dwellers know too well from their everyday lives. The sacred is neither "special" nor unique; it is mundane, almost quotidian in its fervor and desire. This graphic narrative captures the everyday sacred, the sense that the holy is local, almost banal, perhaps even routine. One can easily imagine that some on the staircase had their moments with God too—flashes of anger that mirror their own personal relations as well. And Eisner *shows* us this familiarity in the faces of those on the staircase: they listen not in shock but with nonchalant understanding—note, for example, the folded arms of the father in the stairwell, or the relaxed young person at the top of the staircase, sitting on folded legs as if watching a movie over and over again. Eisner instructs us in how to see the sacred in the everyday relations of city life, and in the detailed accounts of those who observe.

Comics like this one realign our vision of the sacred away from a special moment in time and help to educate us to see the sacred as a familiar visual spectacle that we often fail to see. We tend to look for the sacred, on Eisner's page, inside and beyond the door; but we would learn more about it by noticing the bodily comportment of the stairwell bodies and the graphic violence inscribed in speech bubbles. Yet visions of the sacred do not stop, or even begin, here. The lower frame, which is really no frame at all, takes on a rather different, global view. That dialogue behind closed doors, we now discover, is in fact a very public spat. And in this perspective we do not hear so much as see God's fury; God responds to Frimme's accusation with bolts of lightning that shake the tenement foundations. This too is a natural occurrence, much like the common arguments erupting among neighbors. The sacred moves between the private and natural lives of "the old tenement." It neither is a still, small voice nor an experience on the road to some other place, as Jewish and Christian texts often depict sacred moments. Instead, Eisner's *A Contract with God* envisions a raging, aggressive confrontation between two close friends, one of whom, it appears, has broken a contractual deal. Where does this dialogue happen? It happens behind closed doors, and in and outside the tenement halls. We do not usually see the sacred in these places, or through the eyes of these bodies. This is how graphic narratives can reveal new visions of the sacred.

The comic sacred destabilizes traditional notions of divinity, because it undermines clear chains of authority. The sacred does not come to us, as it were, clean and pure from traditional and authorized sources. We see no gods, church leaders, or rabbis to legitimate the sacred. Eisner offers us bolts of lightning, and even a large carved rock designed to evoke the Ten Commandments, but there exists no divine authority to legitimate these claims. The sacred *appears*; it is not revealed by divine sources. This is an altogether modern sense of the holy, in which experiences of transcendence,

Figure 0.1. Frimme Hersh and tenement dwellers confronting God, *A Contract with God*, page 24, by Will Eisner. Copyright © 1978 Will Eisner. Used by permission of W. W. Norton & Company, Inc.

or glimpses of holiness, replace *the* transcendent or *the* holy. In short, the revealed sacred takes the place of the one who reveals the sacred. Martin Buber once called this phenomenon "the eclipse of God," and he sought to rediscover divinity in relational encounter. For Buber, we rediscover God through our personal interactions with others. In the comics discussed in this volume, personal encounter is all we have; the experience of the sacred altogether replaces the being or beings who are sacred. In a world suffused

Figure 0.2. Hieronymus (Hip) Flask and Elijah Delaney fighting for a stolen ritual statue, *Elephantmen* #2, page 6, by Richard Starkings, Moritat, and Jose Ladronn. Copyright © 2006 Comicraft

with divinity but not with the Divine, we need to relearn how to experience the sacred without traditional sources to legitimate it. This too is how graphic narratives train us to see the sacred in our ordinary experiences. Comics move us to consider the sacred as a visual practice and space, one coupled to everyday and extraordinary moments within our material lives.

Another, very different example of the revealed sacred can be gleaned in the second issue of the series *Elephantmen*. This series tells the story of a dystopian future, where mutant human/animal hybrids are bred for war by an evil all-powerful corporation. The series follows the lives of these mutants primarily in their "civilian life" upon release from the corporation's hold, and we learn how they cope with everyday reality. The second issue in the series is unique, and offers us an opportunity to examine how the sacred in comics works as an imagetext.

The entire second issue jettisons all word and thought balloons. Instead, the creators utilize captions throughout the narrative, but they stand at a distance from the visual images. So while the images depict a physical struggle between a hippopotamus and an alligator, the captions derive from the book of Job and the poem about behemoth and leviathan. By the sixth page the futuristic background has completely fallen away, with captions and bodies all that are left on an almost blank background. Gutters, too, are sparse in these pages, with just a few panels. The effect is startling, drawing to the fore two texts, two apparently incommensurable narratives vying to be read—the biblical verses from Job and the visual bodies. One narrative confronts the reader in black ink, establishing authority by deploying a biblical font in our visual vernacular, and quoting an authoritative text. Yet the other, visual narrative continually undermines that biblical, textual authority. This corrosive narrative in images, one that constantly moves and changes, belongs to an altogether different vernacular register—one of monsters, aliens, future worlds, and transformed spaces. This visual text confronts the reader with bodies—monstrous bodies, with reconfigured boundaries, that compel us to read anew the written, biblical, *sacred* text (Starkings et al. 6). The book of Job now looks different to us, both as a written and as a visual medium.

. . .

The essays in *Comics and Sacred Texts* do this kind of work; they traverse boundaries to envision the sacred in visual script, in imaginative retellings of religious stories, in uncanny bodies, and in the common practices of everyday lives. This pedagogical attempt to revision the sacred, to educate us to see the sacred in new ways, subtends all the essays in this volume. Each section opens with a short introductory page that articulates the claims and challenges advanced in the essays of that section. "Seeing the Sacred in Comics," the first section in this volume, explores how the sacred appears in script and narrative in such diverse works as Craig Thompson's *Habibi*, Keshni Kashyap's *Tina's Mouth*, and Jonathan Hickman's *East of West*. The essays consider how modes of representation resituate the sacred. The second section, "Reimagining Sacred Texts through Comics," probes the relations between traditional religious texts and their comics adaptations. This mode of reading and rereading confronts assumptions about received literature, challenging us to discover anew the links between sacred "source" and comic "translation." We encounter graphic adaptations of the Gospel of Mark, the Hindu Ramayana saga, the book of Samuel, and the book of Genesis through critical comics studies. Sacred texts literally will never look the same again, because comics discipline readers to see the sacred as textual encounter. "Transfigured Comic Selves, Monsters, and the Body," the third section in this volume, examines monstrous bodies that remain out of place. From Japanese *manga* to the Holocaust, and even to Marvel's X-Men, we see how monstrous selves establish boundaries for the sacred. In these comics, bodies out of place delimit what counts as a sacred body and experience. The very last collection of essays, "The Everyday Sacred in Comics," locates this charged landscape within the ordinary and mundane. These essays directly challenge the profane/sacred divide, noting how urban scenes of encounter, and even the everyday act of walking the streets, can all bump up against sacred modalities of experience.

The fundamental claim tying these four rubrics together is simply this: graphic narratives can be usefully described as culturally educational, pedagogical texts able to motivate new modes of seeing the sacred. For sacred texts never come to us as blank slates without engaged modes of seeing or representational language. We learn how to see and read the sacred, and we argue in *Comics and Sacred Texts* that this cultural education happens in the graphic narratives discussed here. Developing a critical study of the comic sacred opens new, panoramic encounters with our daily but extraordinary lives. Our hope and challenge for this volume is to show how comic narratives inform new modes of seeing the sacred in text and image.

BIBLIOGRAPHY

Baskind, Samantha, and Ranen Omer-Sherman, eds. *The Jewish Graphic Novel: Critical Approaches*. New Brunswick: Rutgers University Press, 2008.

Buber, Martin. *The Eclipse of God*. New York: Humanity Books, 1952.

Crumb, R. *The Book of Genesis Illustrated*. New York: W. W. Norton, 2009.

Durkheim, Émile. *The Elementary Forms of Religious Life*. New York: Free Press, 1915.

Eco, Umberto, and Natalie Chilton. "The Myth of Superman." *Diacritics* 2, no. 1 (1972): 14–22.

Eisner, Will. *A Contract with God*. New York: W. W. Norton, 2006.

Eliade, Mircea. *Myths, Dreams, and Mysteries: The Encounter between Contemporary Faiths and Archaic Realities*. New York: Harper & Row, 1960.

Fingeroth, Danny. *Disguised as Clark Kent: Jews, Comics, and the Creation of the Superhero*. New York: Bloomsbury Academic, 2008.

Jones, Gerard. *Men of Tomorrow: Geeks, Gangsters, and the Birth of the Comic Book*. New York: Basic Books, 2008.

Kaplan, Arie. *From Krakow to Krypton: Jews and Comics Books*. Philadelphia: Jewish Publication Society, 2008

Lewis, A. David, and Christine Hoff Kraemer, eds. *Graven Images: Religion in Comic Books and Graphic Novels*. New York: Continuum, 2010.

McCloud, Scott. *Understanding Comics: The Invisible Art*. New York: HarperCollins, 1993.

McLain, Karline. *India's Immortal Comic Books: Gods, Kings, and Other Heroes*. Bloomington: Indiana University Press, 2009.

Morrison, Grant. *Supergods: What Masked Vigilantes, Miraculous Mutants, and a Sun God from Smallville Can Teach Us about Being Human*. New York: Spiegel & Grau, 2012.

Orsi, Robert. "Everyday Miracles: The Study of Lived Religion." In *Lived Religion in America*, edited by David Hall, 3–21. Princeton: Princeton University Press, 1997.

Starkings, Richard, Moritat, and Jose Ladronn. *Elephantmen* no. 2 (August 2006). Portland: Image Comics, 2006.

Turner, Victor. *The Ritual Process: Structure and Anti-structure*. Ithaca: Cornell University Press, 1966.

Part I

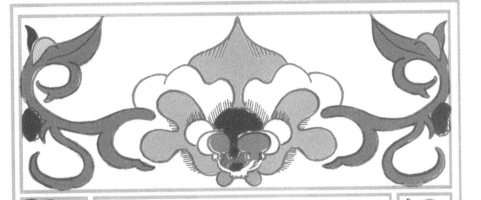

SEEING THE SACRED IN COMICS

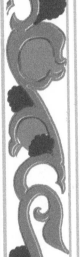

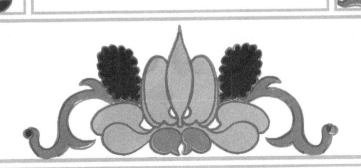

Scholars of religion discover the sacred in many well-traveled arenas of research: in communal rituals, in the sacred literature of religious traditions, in the theological claims made by religious adepts. Religions reveal the sacred in these places and through these modalities. The essays in this section, however, suggest that we can and should look elsewhere for sacred revelations. The sacred erupts in places, and through mediums, that challenge where we should *see* and *encounter* divine presence. The first two essays show how the sacred languages of Arabic and Hebrew *as script* work as sacred mediums and do so through graphic narratives. The third and fourth essays explore how language functions to encounter the sacred within the text itself. Together, these essays argue that we should cultivate the ability to see the sacred in script, language, images, and fiction. The sacred houses a form, a shape, and a graphic visual presence. A Hebrew letter can reveal accounts of the sacred as much as fictional literature might claim sacred status for its invented fantasies. The sacred, in these ways, is not only experienced but encountered as a particular shape and form. By learning to see the sacred as a kind of scripted form, indeed as a graphic narrative in which the shape of the sacred informs its very meaning, we can also rethink how the sacred appears in rituals, literature, and sacred texts.

Chapter One

WRITING THE SACRED IN CRAIG THOMPSON'S *HABIBI*

MADELINE BACKUS AND KEN KOLTUN-FROMM

IN *HABIBI* (2011), A MONUMENTAL WORK OF THE GRAPHIC NARRATIVE imagination, Craig Thompson constructs the oriental sacred through Arabic calligraphy, weaving sacrality into the visual and textual narrative of the imagined, exotic other. The exotic and even erotic forms of calligraphy stylize a natural and imminently accessible sacred that works within an oriental mode of visual exposure. We can see this oriental sacred in the natural landscape, in the mythic and salvific animals, in the Islamic textual traditions of hadiths and Qur'an, and in the material body of Dodola, who captures the young Zam's erotic fantasies. Thompson deploys calligraphy to open Islamic and Arabic culture to the oriental gaze, imagining the sacred within the exotic world of Richard Burton's *Arabian Nights*.

Habibi is the love story of Zam and Dodola, who meet when a young Dodola saves baby Zam as they escape together from a slave market. The two live in seclusion on an abandoned desert ship as brother and sister until Zam witnesses Dodola's rape—a recurring bodily violence as she negotiates for food from desert travelers. Haunted by his own latent sexual desires for Dodola and the shame of visual witness, Zam searches for food and water to spare Dodola from a more physical, abusive shame. But the two are separated—Dodola is sold into slavery once again, becoming the prized catch within the Sultan's harem, while Zam escapes to the city, cuts off his sexual organ to remove his erotic shame, but then gains employment as a eunuch at the sultan's palace. When Zam recognizes Dodola and saves her from execution by drowning, they both escape the palace, adopt a baby girl, and leave the city as parental lovers.

This story of budding romantic love, erotic inhibitions, physical abuse, and the exotic East are fantastical tales within the imagined orient of Richard Burton's *Arabian Nights*. Indeed, Craig Thompson modeled a good deal of his graphic narrative on that text and self-consciously appropriated its orientalist project. Thompson locates his oriental gaze in Wanatolia, a nation of his own creation that over the course of the story develops from slave market to desert wasteland, and from the sultan's harem to the heart of a bustling, commercial city. The geographical and spatial transformation of Wanatolia corresponds to a progressive, ocular orientalism: *Habibi* begins in a premodern, exotic East but transforms over some six hundred pages into a dirty, patriarchal, inhumane Arabia. The exotic orient, however, remains the same, transgressive other—attractive in both its erotic and savage iterations.

Within this space and gaze, Arabic calligraphy takes on the form and function of the sacred orient. Thompson deploys calligraphy as an image/text to naturalize the orientalist discourse as sacred space. Dodola tells stories from the Qur'an, weaving them within the meandering lines of Arabic calligraphy learned from her first husband. Zam literally sees the calligraphic forms as letters, animals, mountains, and bodies. He encounters calligraphy as that material script within nature: a writing of and in the world as the naturalized sacred. In this sense, the comic form is not image alongside text, or even the interplay of these two mediums, but instead is a bridging or bricolage of textual and visual forms. This is how calligraphy has often been employed in Arabic culture (Elias 264–83), and this visual text functions here to present that culture as the oriental other. In *Habibi* calligraphy is the sacred text as comic image/text, braiding together the play of sacred inscription and oriental gaze. Though natural and exotic, the sacred is also elusive and deceptive: it can, like the orient itself, seduce one into hypnotic fantasies of reality. Even the design cover of *Habibi* contributes to this self-deception, for it appears as sacred text itself, and the narrative's sheer girth conveys its authority. The comic form, together with the calligraphic image/text, reveals sacred writing as the exotic, oriental other.

There is by now a vast literature deeply critical of Thompson's oriental framework. Note, for example, Nadim Damluji's blanket condemnation of Thompson's oriental writing, gestured in the very title of the essay "Can the Subaltern Draw?: The Spectre of Orientalism in Craig Thompson's *Habibi*." For Damluji, *Habibi* "is a tragically familiar Orientalist tale" that "fails to escape many classic Orientalist trappings." One finds similar critique from a number of online blogging communities, interviews with Thompson, and book reviews. Even the *New York Times* panned *Habibi* with the pithy title

"The Graphic Novel as Orientalist Mash-Up." Yet as these readers condemn the oriental frame, they consistently praise the stylized calligraphy as largely outside that discourse. Damluji's tribute is quite typical: "First let's discuss what *Habibi* gets right. The good is found foremost in the calligraphy and geometric patterns Thompson employs throughout *Habibi*." Our contention, to the contrary, is that calligraphic geometry is a critical feature of Thompson's oriental gaze. Calligraphy is the vehicle that drives our oriental gaze in *Habibi*; it is both the medium and the message of the comic, and it is meant to be *seen* more than read (Elias 264–70). We see calligraphy visually in the comic's animals (the snake, among others), the exotic landscapes (Wanatolia and the desert wasteland), and bodies—especially in Dodola's sexualized, penetrated form. Calligraphy is a critical feature of the *Habibi* oriental narrative, flowing through the scenic forms as a mode of sacralization.

. . .

Dodola's body and a large, dark snake frame Zam's dark fantasy visually and thematically. Zam dreams he becomes Eve's son Abel and removes Eve's amulet to possess her power. His small black hands caress her naked body—a visual and erotic parallel to the snake winding through the tree (Thompson 137). But Zam's fantasy confronts the reality of an actual snake, one that interrupts his daydream but leads him back to the orientalizing moves of Arabic calligraphy. He shouts at the snake but then watches in amazement as it repeatedly takes the form of various Arabic letters (138). Zam finally realizes that the snake spells out the corners of the *buduh*—an amulet from Dodola to protect Zam in the wilderness, and the very amulet worn in his sexual fantasies. Note too how the *buduh* mirrors the design of the page with nine frames. The *buduh* as comic page sacralizes and legitimates the comic book as sacred text and, by extension, the space of the sacred orient as well. Though the snake marks the transition from dream to reality, it nonetheless subverts that distinction by trafficking in allusions. By sliding within and around fantasy, and transforming into various natural shapes and calligraphic lettering, the snake marks the oriental other as mysterious, subversive, exotic, and enticing. As the serpent transfigures into written script, calligraphy becomes the very shape and form of the oriental gaze.

In *Habibi*, Thompson visually distinguishes Arabic stories with elaborate frames. These darker markings tend to separate Zam's fantasies from reality, but his desert wanderings blur the line between fantasy and reality as the two bleed together into the oriental frame. Thompson constructs this fantastical weaving through the calligraphic form. The beguiling snake transforms into Zam's linguistic guide through the barren desert, leading him to a pure

Figure 1.1. Nine-panel page of Zam confronting snake, *Habibi*, page 138, by Craig Thompson. Copyright © 2011 Craig Thompson

and abundant water source—perhaps an allusion to the well of Zamzam, the desert water source discovered by Hagar according to Islamic tradition. Zam believes the serpent is a magical being in its transformative capacity to become script. Calligraphy *moves* Zam between fantasy and reality: we see it on Zam's magical amulet, written into the landscape, and inscribed into animal flesh. This is not a kind of tattooing that inscribes the flesh from without (Elias 268–69); this is a tattooing from within, as it were, from the very core of the natural world. Reflecting back Zam's facial expression, the riverwater dissolves into flowing, Arabic script as Zam dips his finger into the watery substance (Thompson 141). Calligraphy grows and dominates the page spread, capturing Zam's and the reader's attention. Thompson uses calligraphy and Islamic sacred stories to construct this oriental world, one both mysterious and seductive. It is no wonder, then, that Zam fails to recognize the enormous dam enclosing the water stream. He is lost in the magical realism of calligraphic forms and fantastical, natural shapes. His gaze, like ours, has become oriental.

Zam's gaze becomes the reader's own, so his, like ours, moves between fantasy and reality. In that movement, bodies reveal gender distinctions. Zam's encounter with naturalized calligraphy—in the snake, in the river, and in Dodola's body—ascribes masculine power and control to sacred script and black ink. This sense of controlling force has lasting significance for Zam's sexual identity. Stories from the Qur'an and hadiths work on Zam like spells. In Zam's desert fantasy the dark, threatening body of the serpent represents Zam's sexual desire for Dodola. We see the snake as a phallus, both in Zam's dreams and in his waking state. Note, for example, how the reader enters into one of Zam's fantasies, where Thompson weaves the snake through this verse from the Qur'an (28:30):

> And when he came up to it, a Voice cried to him out of the bush from the right side of the valley in the sacred hollow. "O Moses I truly am God, the Lord of the worlds. Throw down now thy rod." And when he saw it move as though it were a serpent he retreated and returned not. "O Moses," cried the Voice, "draw near and fear not, for thou art in safety." (Thompson 308–9)

Thompson visually withdraws this story from the *Habibi* narrative by stylizing the two frames on the page spread. These ornamental frames contrast sharply with the bottom, rigid frame that reveals Zam drinking from the river. In the stylized sequence, we see Moses's rod transform into the snake

Figure 1.2. Zam recognizing calligraphy in the water, *Habibi*, page 141, by Craig Thompson. Copyright © 2011 Craig Thompson

as he gazes upon the burning bush. Zam's small figure appears in the crook of the curved snake, and as the voice of God tells Moses, "draw near and fear not, for thou art in safety," the snake lowers Zam into the water. Zam emerges from his fantasy in the straight, rigid frame besides the reservoir. The next page draws back from this more immediate scene, revealing the serpent behind and protecting the boy. Zam expresses his gratitude ("You saved me, snake!"), but Thompson has done more here than bring Zam to water: he has woven sexual prowess, qur'anic tales, and gendered nature into Zam's fantastical reality. The qur'anic text situates and glosses Zam's sexual desires

Figure 1.3. Zam's fantasies of the snake, *Habibi*, page 309, by Craig Thompson. Copyright © 2011 Craig Thompson

as sacred inscription, blurring distinctions between fantasy and reality as well as sacred and profane. By writing Zam into holy scripture, Thompson represents the sacred as a male, sexual, and material yearning for water as the feminine gift of life.

These tropes of sexuality resurface when the serpent rescues Zam yet again near water—this time at the sultan's forbidden watering hole. As the snake attacks the sultan's guards, allowing Zam precious time to escape, his head is removed in one swift motion. Thompson depicts this brutal death as a foreshadowing of Zam's own castration: this very same image of the snake's beheading reappears some twenty-three pages later when Zam undergoes his cutting. The snake emerges from calligraphic form with its mouth open to consume a pure white orb, and the snake's beheading stands in for Zam's own. But in the gutter—in the scene readers do not see yet cannot help but imagine—Zam now takes the place of the snake, with his phallus "sliced off in one swoop with a sharp razor" (335–36). The razor at once silences Zam (he refuses to speak in the palace) and emasculates him. Even more, he envisions Dodola as performing similar acts of self-mutilation: in a somewhat bizarre panel, Dodola removes her breasts and hands them to Zam for nourishment—much like Saint Agatha's presentation of her breasts on a plate. Sexual impotency and transgression, gender bending, nature as sacred writing—all this encodes *Habibi* as the magical orient of desire, fantasy, and anxiety.

. . .

Thompson writes calligraphy into the landscape as the oriental sacred, infusing it with the magical dimensions of Islam, and rooting it in a neverland mysticism of *Arabian Nights*. He presents the sacred as exotic and material script, but also as a form of writing that disarms and deceives. Each page of *Habibi* is painstakingly illuminated, and Thompson warmly embraces the artistic possibilities of an ancient and venerable Arabic tradition of calligraphy. At times he uses calligraphy to approach Islam with reverential respect, illustrating, for example, Muhammad's ascension to heaven—together with other stories from the Qur'an and its commentaries—with thoughtful attention to detail. Yet alongside this deference Thompson also sexualizes Dodola's body through calligraphy. Her sexual encounters, which are often violent or unwanted, travel within the orbit of magical stories about talismanic squares and occult numerology, all inscribed by Arabic calligraphy. Thompson frames Dodola's rape within calligraphic forms, drawing her body as fluid water. Like the pure water Zam discovers at Wanatolia's dam, Dodola's body is sacred as calligraphic script. The water ripples with calligraphic forms, just as the snake, which attracted Zam to the dam, transforms into one of the letters in the talismanic square. With Dodola's body inscribed with calligraphic ink, Thompson effectively feminizes body and water—both permeable substances are subject to the visual and physical violence of the male gaze.

Calligraphy allows Thompson the space to expose and conceal his authorial hand; it weaves through his comic in ways that foreground both art and artistry, but in a mode that leads a reader to see calligraphy as naturally embedded in a sacred, oriental order of things. Thompson dazzles with his artistry—commentators even complain of his artistic swagger—in order to draw the reader into his calligraphic wanderings. Those wanderings naturalize calligraphy as sacred order, and so legitimize and reinforce an oriental vision as *natural*; the oriental comic is both artifice and embodied. Thompson highlights his own creative force, as Hilary Chute and Jared Gardner have theorized for comics in general (Chute 17; Gardner 73). But he also situates the oriental gaze as a discovered, natural, and sacred order *in* landscape, and *in* Dodola's enchanted, sexualized body. Calligraphy works to turn Dodola's body from constructed fantasy to sacred nature. We do not merely see her body as embodied script; her body becomes a landscape delimited and defined by calligraphy.

Magical jinn, Dodola's erotic body, and calligraphic writing all frame Zam's visual world. But the reader engages that world through Zam's eyes; his vision becomes the reader's oriental gaze. We see this, for example, when Zam searches for life-preserving water in the desert. He sees magical beings (jinn), images of Dodola's naked body, and the curves of nature that transform into Arabic calligraphy and bodily, erotic shapes. The hills of the desert become Dodola's thighs, which Zam peers through as his sexual fantasies interact with her frame, the landscape, and calligraphy (Thompson 166). This all forms the oriental horizon of vision for both Zam and the reader. Desert spirits frame his sexual awakening, and calligraphy materializes—in shape, form, and substance—his attraction to Dodola. The desert landscape too becomes the stuff of oriental magic as it is manipulated by travelers and exotic jinn. Indeed, the desert as bland and unbridled landscape is the oriental backdrop to Zam's fantasies about Dodola. She appears as Eve fully nude, shrouded by spirits and lush wilderness, as his search for water leads into sexual illusions.

The authorial posture is one that hides authorial creation by feigning a world already magical and sacred. In *Habibi* we see bibliomancy, geomancy, and letterisms as representative of a natural, material Islam already there, ready to be discovered by the oriental gaze. To be clear, we know that Thompson has put all this before us, but he does so by simulating an oriental view that fantasizes a world discovered rather than made. Thompson pulls on these magical and pre-modern elements of Islam to enhance our encounter with the religious as exotic other. We see Thompson diagramming magic squares, the *bismillah*, and Zam's *buduh*. He builds a world where enchantment is built into the landscape. Talismans and amulets, like Zam's *buduh*, have a long history as prophylactic objects, with particular efficacy in the premodern period, and with power rooted in holy texts and prayers (Savage-Smith 129). The flow and fluidity of sacred script, its rhythm and pace, dominate entire pages and simultaneously draw our eyes to minute details. In *Habibi* calligraphy is not just confined to the Qur'an or even to Zam's *buduh*; it moves through the book like water. Calligraphy fuses nature and the sacred.

Thompson harnesses the religious power of divine script and channels it through an embodied landscape. The four corners of Zam's *buduh* (b, d, w, and h) correspond to four archangels, four natural elements, and the four cardinal directions. Azrael, Raphael, Michael, and Gabriel, as the four guardians of Eden, represent earth, air, fire, and water (130). These natural elements create a celestial, religious space grounded in the environmental realities of Wanatolia. Written into *Habibi* is a critique and commentary on environmental destruction. The environment is pure where we see calligraphy as water; it is defiled when water becomes political capital. But Thompson's critique is also a gendered one, for he feminizes the landscape through Dodola's body. He uses calligraphy to penetrate and possess the barren Arabian landscape and Dodola's curved body. Indeed, body and landscape together become a fluid medium, one that acts and moves like water. Thompson positions his reader to gaze at, and so penetrate Dodola's liquid body. To push this metaphor a bit further, we could say we swim in it, and so in part remake the curvature of her embodied frame.

Arabic calligraphy is deeply tied to the order and logic of Thompson's oriental world. This is particularly so in panels of the barren desert landscape. The rolling mountains of sand become visually pregnant with calligraphic script through Thompson's hand and Zam's gaze. The landscape is the locus of the sacred: "the desert," Zam exclaims, is "God's domain" (630). But when Zam and Dodola pass through the city bursting with people, garbage, drought, and illness, there is no space in this brutal landscape for calligraphy to mark the sacred. In the vast openness of the desert, Thompson draws the curves of the earth with the curves of Dodola's scripted body; yet in the city Zam and Dodola remain alone in their bodily inscription. The landscape becomes the profane other through the absence of calligraphy, even if the sacred still resides in and through Dodola's body. This twinning of body and landscape—at once unified in the desert but torn asunder in the city—marks Zam's and Dodola's bodies as exotic objects. The cityscape, however, contains an oriental Islam configured as barbaric and irrational. Although we recognize modern elements in the fantastical city of Wanatolia, the sultan's palace draws us back to the oriental premodern *Arabian Nights*. What little control Dodola retained over her body in the desert, she loses completely in the sultan's harem. As his "prized catch" she is repeatedly raped by the sultan and bears him a child. The sultan is a large, hairy, sexually insatiable, violent, and opium-impaired ruler. He is the oriental model for Middle Eastern patriarchy and backwardness, and he consumes and offends Dodola's sacred frame again and again.

. . .

Readers encounter the sacred through Dodola's calligraphic body. She engenders religious knowledge in *Habibi*; she reads and writes sacred stories, and weaves fantasies both religious and cultural—much like Shahrazad in *Arabian Nights*. Dodola is a permeable figure, and her naked body is persistently violated by Zam, desert travelers, and spiritual forces. As sacred, visual body, she both controls and is subjected to the power of calligraphy. Dodola's first husband, a scribe, introduces Dodola to sexual and religious knowledge at age nine. He copies manuscripts from "the Qur'an, the hadiths, One Thousand and One Nights, and the works of the great poets" (Thompson 15). This easy conflation of sacred scripture, imaginative poetics, and oriental fantasy literature is rhetorically alluring. The stories of the *Arabian Nights* have a variety of ethnic origins and were circulated orally before they were written down in the thirteenth century (Burton xiv). In the nineteenth century, European colonists adopted and reworked the *Arabian Nights* for a Western audience, and Richard Burton's translation became the most popular text for Westerners to encounter "authentic" Arabian culture. Thompson borrows heavily from Burton's overly sexualized and violent imagining of the orient and represents it together with qur'anic and poetic texts. Bridging these diverse genres through calligraphy does more than reinforce the orientalist vision of Arabia as unbridled violence and sexual promiscuity. It also situates the orient *within* sacred texts, and so within qur'anic verse and the Islamic poetic traditions. Orientalism goes all the way down, as it were, and we see that foundational oriental gaze in Dodola's body.

Dodola's only recourse, her one great source of power, is the subversive capacity of calligraphy to wind its way between fantasy and reality—bending time and space to create a transcendent sacred order. In her desperate attempt to escape the sultan's gross sexual needs, Dodola takes shelter in the palace stables among horses and exotic birds. Deep in an opium stupor, the sultan envisions Dodola as the *buraq*—a mythical horse in the hadith literature described as part horse, woman, and bird (Thompson 282). Although impaired, the sultan's gaze becomes the reader's own, transforming Dodola's sexualized body into a mythic object. Here we see how Thompson writes Dodola into Islamic lore, but the sacred remains a sexual and masculine space of domination. The sultan is only aroused by this mythic site, and must possess her sexually. This hypersexuality continues in other frames as well,

Figure 1.4. Dodola as *buraq*, *Habibi*, page 282, by Craig Thompson. Copyright © 2011 Craig Thompson

and Thompson links the riding of horses to the sultan's own grotesque riding of Dodola. The sacred is masculine, sexual domination in these frames. And where the sultan's desires (and even Zam's snake) reflect male potency and ownership of space, Dodola's frame remains a weak, impotent, penetrated vessel. She retains little agency or ownership over her own body when descripted from sacred calligraphy. Without that holy script to frame her body, she becomes a mere receptacle for male aggressive fantasies. And the comic works to implicate readers in this male gaze as we project Dodola's sacred sexuality onto an illusive mythic potency. As her body transfixes and beguiles the sultan, so too she captures the reader in this oriental moment. The sudden and almost effortless shift between Dodola as sacred *buraq* and Dodola as naked, violated body—violated by the reader's vision as much as by the sultan's penetration—highlights the conflicting readings of her sexualized body.

Dodola can regain her bodily integrity, paradoxically, only through a male gaze that scripts her body with calligraphic form. Like the desert landscape, calligraphy remaps Dodola's body, and we read sacrality through her. As iconic and sacred image/text, calligraphy both objectifies and empowers Dodola. She embodies script, and through Zam's (and the reader's) gaze, she becomes a sexualized object; but she comes to own and to command her body through calligraphy, allowing her to embody a sacralized and protective script. Although at the mercy of the sultan, Dodola never fully submits to him and practices her independence through fantasy, sacred stories, and the study of the occult. She actively scripts what has been inscribed on her body by the male gaze.

As the desert snake leads Zam to water, so too calligraphy guides Zam to Dodola in the sultan's palace, creating a surface of sacred writing over and within a narrativized world. The sultan's collection of women, Dodola among them, parade through the gardens in a rare moment of semipublic viewing (though still completely veiled but for the eyes). We see Zam peering over the rose bush hedge as his gaze becomes ours—we all see Dodola in the center of an eye-shaped panel shrouded by roses (Thompson 395). In his haste to reclaim her, Zam attempts to scale the palace wall but is prevented by two separate palace employees. Dodola's eyes follow Zam as two guards prevent this boundary crossing and he returns to his menial tasks.

Dodola is embodied as calligraphy, an inscribed physicality reinforced by Zam's and the reader's visual penetration of her written surface. It is a kind of tattooing that goes all the way down, penetrating to a depth that reads from the inside out. In a desperate attempt to see her once more in the palace, Zam climbs atop the roof and peers through the lattice into the sultan's garden.

The lattice swirls and curves, taking visual cues from Thompson's calligraphic style, and as Zam peers through it, his eyes become the eyes we see in the *bismillah* (403). Thompson draws a series of vertical panels of Dodola's face and then leads the reader's gaze to the full panel on the opposite page with Dodola in full silhouette (405). Created with Islamic calligraphy—some of it recognizable, some of it mere doodles—Dodola's body is the passive receiver of sacred script. She no longer tells the stories with language; that language now works on and through her. This bodily inscription winds through and creates her frame, accentuating and objectifying her sexualized figure as sacred text. As Zam's gaze becomes the reader's own, calligraphy transforms the material body into a gendered, erotic, and sacred text. We visually consume Dodola's body through calligraphy, and we see the word—the sacred script—become flesh.

Dodola embodies sacred calligraphy through the male gaze, but she also literally consumes calligraphy as prophylactic against the filth and disease of the modern city. Zam and Dodola escape from the palace by means of a water system that funnels pure, clean water from the desert oasis to the palace but spews waste to the rest of the city. Doused in this toxic sewage and approaching death, Dodola limply drapes herself over Zam's arms as he carries her to safety, far from the deathly waters. Thompson illustrates the septic waters in grotesque detail, taking on the comic form and style of feces. Dodola's condition is so severe after drinking the noxious refuse that even Zam cannot nurse her back to health, and so he must seek (with the fisherman Noah's help) a medical healer. The shrouded, enchanted doctor arrives with magical implements for healing that work a material encounter with calligraphy as prophylactic. Cloaked in mystery and occult knowledge, the doctor mixes ink with water to create a magic bowl of healing. After dissolving the sacred calligraphy, the doctor hands the curative liquid to Dodola as protective, palliative script. By ingesting the letters into her material body, Dodola gives witness to the power of sacred writing as prophylactic, magical cure. The alchemy works to revive Dodola, who now embodies not only the form but also the magical substance of oriental script (472–75).

Magical bowls and squares existed throughout Arabia in the pre-Islamic period (Silverman 19). Even as some forms of Islam reject magical readings of the Qur'an, the practice has continued as a material and protective encounter with the sacred. Writing boards are a magico-religious tradition that transfers the sacred power of Arabic calligraphy to material and consumable form. Travis Zadeh cites Islamic scholars from the fourteenth century who argue that "the act of writing verses of the Qur'an in ink, immersing the paper in

Figure 1.5. Dodola as embodied script, *Habibi*, page 405, by Craig Thompson. Copyright © 2011 Craig Thompson

water, and then drinking the water, was also a tradition accepted by many in the early community" (Zadeh 464). The "charismatic and medicinal qualities of the Qur'an," including writing on a bowl, were more than isolated incidents in medieval Islam. Magic bowls and writing boards served functional rather than aesthetic purposes, and in *Habibi* we see the calligraphy inscribed by the healer is less ornate than the flowing script Thompson usually employs. The calligraphy used for prophylactic purposes is a "symbolic act of soliciting the spiritual assistance of God using a message that is destined not for human eyes but for those of God" (Silverman 20).

Yet as Dodola imbibes the sacred script, it takes on aesthetic significance, and moves from the purview of God to the reader's gaze. Dodola's body

Figure 1.6. Dodola ingesting curative script, *Habibi*, page 475, by Craig Thompson. Copyright © 2011 Craig Thompson

becomes a sexual vessel for calligraphy that serves orientalized, aesthetic ends. The calligraphy embodied by Dodola reflects the calligraphy found in Zam's amulet, rather than the mystical script enveloping her. Dodola's body projects and is projected onto sacred writing that controls her. We have already seen one form of this magical substance in Zam's amulet as magical square. Yet Zam's encounter with magic always remains external to his own body; he interacts with the sacred as an embodied other. But this is not the case for Dodola: she absorbs the sacred into her flesh and becomes that material substance. Calligraphy becomes sacred through her body as sexualized image. Still, Dodola does not ingest the prophylactic writing on her own; she requires Zam's male and powerful hand to do this for her (Thompson 475). Male bodies control access to the sacred, even if the sacred resides in the feminine. And that gendered figure becomes a sexualized body when Thompson positions Zam's gaze as the reader's own. Thompson effectively colonizes Dodola's body through calligraphy, establishing her sexualized form as the material object of the oriental gaze.

The sexualized snake in Zam's fantastical imagination genders calligraphy as masculine and guides Zam toward bodies of water and the body of Dodola now marked as feminine. Dodola is the literal and figurative center of Zam's and the reader's gaze, and her presence lingers through calligraphy. As he cleans alone in the highly stylized yet vacuous palace, Zam uncovers a sacred presence. In this palace the walls have eyes, and Zam finds himself being watched by sacred calligraphy embedded in the wall behind him (397). Dodola's eyes, framed by her veil and captured in Zam's imagination, follow him inside. As Zam turns to discover the *bismillah* on the wall, it transforms into an image/text where the text renders a visual eye at its very center. Thompson draws the calligraphic form of the *bismillah* as image, for Dodola's eye is literally written over the text, and we *read* Dodola's eye in the calligraphic image. As Jamal Elias has argued, Arabic calligraphy is often meant to be seen rather than read (Elias 264–70), and this is clearly the case in Thompson's graphic novel. In the spread's final panel, Zam reaches to touch the wall, and when we turn the page, we find Zam's face encased in a diagram of the *bismillah*. Here we see how embodied calligraphy, now etched into the very materiality of this exotic world, becomes, literally, the focal center of the oriental gaze.

Zam's gaze becomes reoriented to calligraphy after visually consuming Dodola, and Zam is the center, becoming the eye of the calligraphic image in the palace. This sense of embodied vision, where the eye takes on the form and style of Arabic calligraphy, implicates Zam's and the reader's gaze as both sacred and masculine. But it is a penetrating vision, one that embodies Dodola as calligraphic form. As Zam's gaze becomes our own, we sacralize Dodola's body as embodied script.

. . .

Thompson weaves calligraphy through these disjointed narratives of bodies, landscapes, and magical animals to create a story of enchanted love. We have traced the modes by which calligraphy interweaves and frames these narratives, but Thompson positions them as leitmotifs for the larger, more unified story of Ishmael and Isaac—two brothers who come to represent the Islamic and Christian traditions (the Jewish tradition is all but silenced here). Their near sacrifice by father Abraham works as a guiding frame to read Dodola's and Zam's own sacrificial lives. Dodola is at once the sacrificed and the sacrificer, and like Abraham she unites divergent religious histories. Her embodied sacrality joins the traditions, and Thompson creates one seamless, romantic landscape by writing sacrality into her.

This claim to unity within diversity is a feature of the oriental gaze, and part of Thompson's desire to unify divergent religious traditions. The hand of Abraham holds each child in submission as intertwining trees sprout behind them, and we see two streams of what could be blood, ink, or water emanating from Isaac and Ishmael respectively (Thompson 645). Thompson knows, of course, that the father does not sacrifice his son in the Muslim and Christian traditions, and so he depicts the angel Gabriel intervening by offering a ram in exchange for each boy. Yet here too calligraphy unites traditions and narrative stories as the trees behind the sacrificial altar visually echo the sacred, oriental landscape drawn throughout *Habibi*. Islamic calligraphy functions here to unite Ishmael and Isaac, and through them join Islam with Christianity. Thompson cites the Qur'an, chapter 31, verse 27, to heal a broken world through sacred script: "If all the trees on earth were made into pens, and the ocean supplied the ink, augmented by seven more oceans, the words of God would not run out." We see the tree branches reaching toward heaven as they mutate into calligraphic lettering, dripping ink into a pool of the night sky. The word of God flows through the trees into both Isaac and Ishmael, becoming blood that develops into two distinct faiths. Thompson offers the stories of Ishmael and Isaac as corrective to what he sees as the American tendency to divide Christianity from Islam in order to vilify the latter. Sacred script heals a divided world by drawing the perceived other into the self, inscribing the one body as a unity of complementary opposites. The sting of the other has been removed; this is how we create and establish the oriental gaze.

In an interview with *Guernica* magazine, Thompson admits that underwriting *Habibi* is a strong "sense of American guilt and awareness of our tacit participation in exploiting cultures elsewhere in the world" (Armstrong). Drawing Islam as a visual partner to Christianity, where both share foundational stories and the religious art of writing, Thompson can make Islam palatable to a Western audience. But this form of recognition has its cost: Islam becomes acceptable only through the oriental gaze mediated by Islamic calligraphy. That gaze weaves through landscapes and bodies to exoticize and sexualize the other, and to command a male performance of domination over female sites of impotence. By locating the sacred in script, in the sexualized body of Dodola, in barren desert landscapes, in exotic animals, and in the romantic unity of religious traditions, Thompson draws Islam within a recognizable orientalist discourse. In these ways, calligraphy functions as the orient itself.

The locale of oriental reproduction, we submit, lies in Dodola's written body, as the divergent paths represented by Ishmael and Isaac weave through her sexual and reproductive organs. Thompson visually ties the calligraphic trees and inky blood of Ishmael and Isaac to two reproductive streams flowing from Dodola's vaginal source (Thompson 267). Just as Abraham is the father of Islam and Christianity, so too Dodola is the source of sexuality and healing script. Through Dodola's body Thompson writes sexuality into Islam and conflates her sexual prowess with religious authority. Dodola creates the oriental world through her body, and her power flows from her sexed body as ink flows from a pen. Zam's gaze orientalizes the natural and embodied world through and in the calligraphic image/text. That oriental vision, we have argued throughout this chapter, is a consumptive gaze directed at Dodola's body and the magical landscapes of desert and city. Thompson draws his romantic fairy tale with sacred texts and scripts, reducing their complexities to a series of curved shapes that constitute Dodola's orientalized frame. We read calligraphy in and through the barren landscapes and the flowing waters, yet it is Dodola's sexualized body that engenders Thompson's sexual, romantic, and sacred tropes. Gazing at Dodola is a mode of oriental consumption, one mediated and produced by the sacred script of Arabic calligraphy.

BIBLIOGRAPHY

Armstrong, Meakin. "Fundamentals: An Interview with Craig Thompson." *Guernica: A Magazine of Art & Politics* (September 15, 2011); https://www.guernicamag.com/interviews/thompson_interview_9_15_11/. Accessed August 17, 2016.

Burton, Richard. *The Arabian Nights: Tales from a Thousand and One Nights*. New York: Modern Library, 2004.

Chute, Hillary L. *Disaster Drawn: Visual Witness, Comics, and Documentary Form*. Cambridge: Harvard University Press, 2016.

Creswell, Robyn. "The Graphic Novel as Orientalist Mash-Up." *New York Times*, October 14, 2011. http://www.nytimes.com/2011/10/16/books/review/habibi-written-and-illustrated-by-craig-thompson-book-review.html?pagewanted=all&_r=1. Accessed August 17, 2016.

Damluji, Nadim. "Can the Subaltern Draw? The Spectre of Orientalism in Craig Thompson's *Habibi*." *The Hooded Utilitarian*, October 4, 2011. http://www.hoodedutilitarian.com/2011/10/can-the-subaltern-draw-the-spectre-of-orientalism-in-craig-thompsons-habibi/. Accessed August 17, 2016.

Elias, Jamal J. *Aisha's Cushion: Religious Art, Perception, and Practice in Islam*. Cambridge: Harvard University Press, 2012.

Gardner, Jared. *Projections: Comics and the History of Twenty-First-Century Storytelling*. Stanford: Stanford University Press, 2012.

Savage-Smith, Emilie (ed.). *Magic and Divination in Early Islam*. Burlington, VT: Ashgate, 2004.

Silverman, Raymond. "Arabic Writing and the Occult." In *Brocade of the Pen: The Art of Islamic Writing*, edited by Carrol Garrett Fisher and Ulku Bates, 19–30. East Lansing: Michigan State University Kresge Art, 1991.

Thompson, Craig. *Habibi*. New York: Pantheon, 2011.

Zadeh, Travis. "Touching and Ingesting: Early Debates of the Material Qur'an." *American Oriental Society* 129, no. 3 (September 2009): 443–66.

Chapter Two

GOD'S COMICS

The Hebrew Alphabet as Graphic Narrative

SUSAN HANDELMAN

IN HIS AUTOBIOGRAPHY, *ALL RIVERS RUN TO THE SEA*, THE LATE ELIE WIESEL describes learning to read Hebrew as a child:

> My first teacher, the Batizer Rebbe, a sweet old man with a snow-white beard that devoured his face, pointed to the twenty-two holy letters of the Hebrew alphabet and said, "Here, children, are the beginning and the end of all things. Thousands upon thousands of works have been written and will be written with these letters. Look at them and study them with love, for they will be your links to life. And to eternity."
>
> When I read the first word aloud—*B'reshit*, "in the beginning"—I felt transported into an enchanted universe. An intense joy gripped me when I came to understand the first verse. "It was with the twenty-two letters of the *aleph-beth* that God created the world," said the teacher, who on reflection was probably not so old. "Take care of them and they will take care of you. They will go with you everywhere. They will make you laugh and cry. Or rather, they will cry when you cry and laugh when you laugh, and if you are worthy of it, they will allow you into hidden sanctuaries where all becomes. . . ." All becomes what? Dust? Truth? Life? It was a sentence he never finished. (10)

The old rabbi brought the letters to life for the young boy. They became embodied characters, full of movement and emotion, anthropomorphic guides beckoning on to hidden worlds . . . like characters from "comics," one could even say. But this wasn't just a clever pedagogical trick to engage a young child. The rabbi was teaching Elie one of the deepest ideas of Jewish rabbinic tradition: the letters of the Hebrew alphabet are not neutral marks on a page, but living cosmic forces, building blocks of the universe, whose specific graphic forms, combinations, and sequences continuously channel God's creative energies.[1]

When I was a child like Elie and didn't know Hebrew, I used to look at an inscription of the biblical verse "How goodly are your tents, O Jacob" (Num. 24.25) sculpted in large, black, one-foot Hebrew letters, high above our heads on a beam over the synagogue pulpit. I didn't know then what verse it was or what the letters meant, nor did I understand the synagogue service. But the Hebrew letters transfixed me, danced and moved and beckoned me to other realms. They do so even now, after many decades of Hebrew study. In rabbinic tradition the graphic shapes of the letters have their own life; they tell "other stories" than the ones we are familiar with on the Bible's literal narrative level. In these depths I meet them anew again and again; it is where *the words become images, and the images, words.*

I would like in this chapter to probe the Jewish visual imagination of the sacred through a discussion of the Hebrew alphabet as "graphic narrative." How does the relation of text and image become deconstructed and redefined in classical rabbinic writings on the Hebrew alphabet and the forms of the letters? What reciprocal dialogue can we start between "comics" and "Torah," between theories of graphic narrative and rabbinic interpretation? What might a "theology of graphic narrative" look like? Even after decades as a professor of literature, I still ask myself: what is this magic of marking and writing, of seeing these black marks on a white page, that allows me to transfer my thoughts to you across time and space? We usually look "through" rather than "at" those marks, reading quickly for "meaning." Like the complex interplay of word and image in comics panels, the rabbinic focus on the graphic shapes of the Hebrew letters of the Torah forces us to slow down our reading. "Torah" is the word Jews use to refer to the entire corpus of the Bible (the "Written Torah") plus the thousands of years of oral and written interpretation of it (the "Oral Torah"). Like comics, Torah text then becomes "multi-modal," with parallel tracks of text and images colliding and interacting, sounding and resounding.

. . .

How to begin, then? "All beginnings are difficult," say the ancient rabbis (*Mekhilta*, Ba-hodesh 2). Indeed, whether it's learning how to read, or beginning writing an essay, summoning an image, drawing a comics panel, or creating a cosmos. But everything is already implicitly there, in the beginning. So I'll focus my discussion on the first letter of that first word of the Bible that Elie Wiesel learned to read—the Hebrew letter *beit* of the word *b'reishit* [בראשית]. *Beit* is the second letter of the Hebrew alphabet: the first is *alef* [א], and then comes *beit* [ב]. We'll explore these two letters independently and then in sequence as "graphic narratives" about beginnings.

Before proceeding, a few remarks are needed about the Hebrew language and biblical text. Hebrew is constructed around three-letter consonantal roots and written with twenty-two consonantal letters. Those twenty-two letters of Hebrew share with other ancient Semitic languages the pictorial-graphical symbols that are at the origin of *all* alphabetic writing. *Alef* and *beit* are the ancestors of the Greek *alpha* and *beta* and the Latin letters "A" and "B," in which you are reading me now. Unlike Latin, however, Hebrew does not have vowels, and so reading Hebrew is like playing Scrabble. If you saw the two consonants "ct" and needed to decipher the word to which they referred, you could try various vowels: "cut," "acute," "act," "coat," "cat," "cot." The hand-written Torah scrolls, passed down since ancient times and composed according to strict Jewish legal prescriptions, also have no upper and lower cases, no sentence endings or pauses and no numbers separating chapters and verses. These scrolls contain an unpunctuated, unvocalized string of letters read from right to left—a visual feast, but how do you know what the letters and words mean, and how to combine them? On the one hand, the lack of vowels and punctuation opens the text up to many dimensions of meaning, to alternate narratives and various ways of reading every letter sequence. But that openness also risks incomprehensibility and distortion. During the Middle Ages, rabbinic scribes called *masoretes* (from the Hebrew word for "tradition") added a system of diacritical marks and annotations in order to pass on the normative community's traditional understanding of the text and boundaries for interpretation. Figure 2.1 depicts the first line of the book of Genesis, the way it appears printed in rabbinic Hebrew Bibles since the fifteenth century. Elie Wiesel was most likely looking at just such a printed page of the first verses of Genesis when he learned to read with his

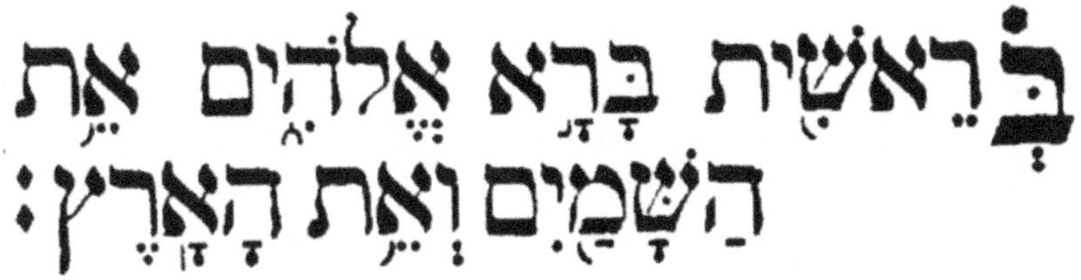

Figure 2.1. Genesis 1:1 (Hebrew: Bereishit בראשית) in the traditional Hebrew script. "Bereishit" from page 2 of the Rabbinic Bible (Hebrew: Mikraot Gedolot מקראות גדולות), Jerusalem 1931 printing. In the public domain

teacher. Jews use these printed texts for study, but they are not permitted for the official, ritual, chanted reading of the Torah in the synagogue, where only the handwritten, unpunctuated scrolls can be used.

Some of the little added dots and lines around the letters are called vowel points, *nekudot*; others mark chapter and verse; others are cantillation marks, called *te'amim.* Like the soundtrack of a film, the marks for chanting add sense and dramatic impact to the verses. Or, to use another metaphor, the masoretic diacritical marks are like a set of "stage directions," telling the actors how to move, talk, and animate the script. Jewish mystical traditions refer to the letters as "bodies" and to the vowels and chant marks as the "souls" that breathe and sing the letters to life. From the point of view of graphic narrative, these marks parallel devices comics artists use called "emanata"—the lines and squiggles and icons around an object or a character, revealing what is going on in the character's head—or the words the comics artist uses to add sound dimensions to a silent object on the page, such as "BOOM! or "THWACK!" In sum, the meaning of the Hebrew letters comes both from active seeing and from performance. The root of the Hebrew word for "reading" is also the root for "calling": *kara* קרא. The reader/viewer/chanter calls the meaning of the silent letters into being, reciprocally participating in their life. As Elie Wiesel's teacher told him: "Take care of them and they will take care of you. . . . [T]hey will cry when you cry and laugh when you laugh. . . ."

Now, let's take a breath—or, to use the technical term for one of those masoretic diacritical marks, an *etnachta*, a "pause." The *etnachta* looks like a little upside-down horseshoe ֑; it signals to the person reading or chanting where to stop for a moment. That pause helps establish grammatical structure and meaning in an unpunctuated text. But it's something *every* speaker, singer, artist or writer needs to do: incorporate moments of pause, breath, blank space into the onrushing flow of letters, images, sounds, words. There is an especially interesting rabbinic law, among the thousands about how to handwrite a Torah scroll: the letters can't touch each other (*Menakhot* 29a). If even one letter touches another letter slightly, the *entire scroll* is invalidated. Rabbinic law prescribes other types of empty space, including spaces *inside* the letters, between words, between different biblical sections, special spacing for poetic passages, and even for the white character of the parchment upon which the black letters are written. On a deeper level, as we'll see below, in those "hidden sanctuaries" of Jewish mysticism to which Elie's teacher alluded, the empty spaces and white background upon which the black letters are written, and the spaces inside of the letters, are seen as more charged with meaning, more significant, and on a "higher" level than the black letters.

Those blank spaces parallel the function of "negative space" in art and of what in comics is called "the gutter," the crucial white space between panels. Scott McCloud, in his classic book *Understanding Comics*, argues that the gutter is what makes comics distinctive, different from film and other media. As he stresses, it also requires the reader to be an active participant. She or he has to create meaning from the sequence of two juxtaposed images or panels and the blank space between them to create "closure," to fill in the gaps; that is part of the pull and magic of comics. It parallels the way the reader of a Hebrew Torah scroll has to actively fill in the gaps of the consonantal text, give it sense, and become pulled into its intonation and rhythm. Writes McCloud, "If visual iconography is the vocabulary of comics, closure is its grammar, and since our definition of comics is the arrangement of elements—then, in a very real sense comics *is* closure" (67).

McCloud's definition of comics has been challenged by other comics theorists, and the academic debate about how to define them is endless. But I'm choosing to use the word "comics" here the way McCloud understands it: "juxtaposed pictorial and other images in deliberate sequence to convey information and/or produce an aesthetic response in the viewer" (9). Comics also involve a special relation and tension between word and image. The visual culture theorist W. J. T. Mitchell broadens the definition even further:

> [C]omics is a transmedium, moving across all boundaries of performance, representation, reproduction, and inscription to find new audiences, new subjects, and new forms of expression. . . . Comics is also transmediatric because it opens audiences onto a deep history that goes back before mass media, perhaps even before writing and drawing, to the fundamental moment of the mark, the graphic sign. . . . (259)

Those primal gestures of marking underlie the origins of alphabets. So let's now narrow our focus down again to the juxtaposed graphic images of *alef* and *beit* in the word *b'reishit*. The Hebrew letter "*beit*" [ב] begins the word *b'reishit* (בראשית) and is the second letter of the Hebrew alphabet (*alef-beit*). In the rabbinic scheme in which each Hebrew letter also has numerical value, *beit* has the value of "two." About *b'reishit*, the word that "begins the beginning," the rabbis ask a simple but profound question: Wouldn't it have been more appropriate for the Torah to begin with the *first* letter of the alphabet, the *alef* [א], since we are dealing with beginnings? Here is a famous midrash (rabbinic form of exegesis), which adds graphic analysis of the letter *beit* to the answer. It comes from the collection known as *Bereishit Rabbah*, a set of commentaries on the book of Genesis compiled from generations of popular rabbinic interpretation and redacted sometime around the fifth century CE:

> R. Yonah said in R. Levi's name: Why was the world created with a *beit*? Just as the *beit* [ב] is closed at the sides but open in front, so you are not permitted to investigate what is above and what is below, what is before and what is behind [the metaphysical secrets of creation, time and history].... You may speculate from the day that days were created, but not on what was before that. . . . And why not with an *alef*? Because it connotes cursing [the word *arur* ארור]. . . . The Holy One, blessed be He, said, "I will create it with the language of blessing, and would that it may stand!" (*Ber. Rabb.* 1:10)

The rabbis are connecting the graphic shape of the *beit* to deeper philosophical and epistemological questions about creation, and how much we can penetrate God's secrets. (We'll examine why they connect those issues to the "blessing" of the *beit* and "curse" of the *alef* later.) The midrash then elaborates a "graphic dialogue" between the *beit* and *alef*:

> Why [did creation start] with a *beit*? Just as a *beit* has two projecting thorns [*oketzim*] one pointing upward and the other below and behind, so when we ask it, "Who created you?" it intimates with its upward point and says, "He who is above created me." And if we ask further, "What is His name?" it intimates to us with its back thorn, and says "The Lord is His name."

The *beit* is graphically coming to life and speaking like a "cartoon" character. Where are those "thorns," and how are they pointing? Look at an image of the *alef* and the *beit* on the following page to see how the forms and sequence of these two letters convert into a graphic narrative relating and enacting a complex metaphysical process. In figure 2.2, in which the letters are handwritten by a contemporary Torah scribe according to traditional Jewish law, the *alef* is on the right and the *beit* on the left, just as they appear in the order of the Hebrew alphabet, which is read from right to left.

Look at the top thick horizontal line of the *beit*, called the "roof" in scribal language, and then move your eyes back to the far right where it intersects

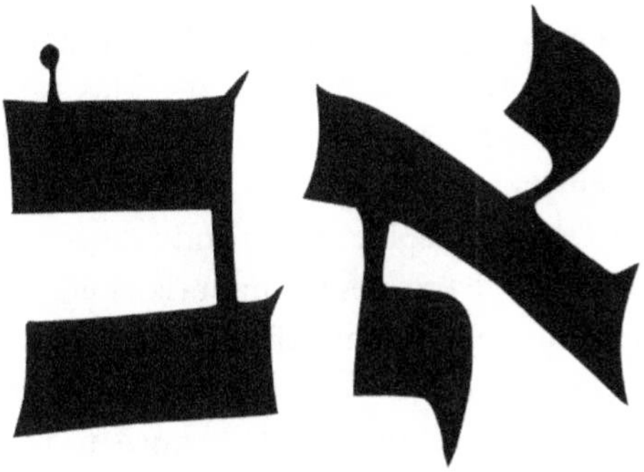

Figure 2.2. The first two letters of the Hebrew alphabet written right to left in a font rendered digitally based on hand-drawings of the traditional Hebrew scribal script (Hebrew: Ktav Stam כתב סת"ם). Alef Beit, by Izzy Pludwinski. Copyright © 2017 Izzy Pludwinski

at the top corner with the vertical line. At the far top right of the intersection, attached to the top right end of the line is a tiny diagonal, thorn-like protrusion, pointing backwards. The protruding point is called an *oketz* or *kotz* ("thorn") in rabbinic scribal terms. There are other names for the various separate strokes and parts that compose the letters, such as "heel," "neck," "arm," "leg," "face," and so forth. They direct and express the life of the strokes that create the letter, their movement and "intention." Now look at the bottom of the vertical base line composing the *beit*, and to the right, to its "back" and "heel." There you see a second large, protruding thicker thorn, also pointing up and backwards. Looked at this way, the "back" of the *beit* has also come alive and is pointing *backward* toward the *alef*.

These two protruding thorns on the tail of the *beit* pointing back at the *alef* are the *beit*'s answers to the eternal questions: Who created the world—and how? "Look back and above," the *beit* is graphically saying to us, according to the midrash: "Look back to the *alef*, and you will see the One, and you will also find out God's name." *Alef* is the first letter of the word *adon* ("Lord") and also of the word *aluf* ("leader, general"). As the first letter of the alphabet, *alef* also has the numerical value of "one." The rabbis are interpreting not only the shapes of each individual letter-image, but the sequence, juxtaposition, and spaces between them, parallel to the way we would begin to construct and analyze a set of comics images or panels. The answer to all the questions, "What's above; what's below; what came before; what's behind?" is: "*Alef, Beit*."

Jewish mystical sources explain that answer more deeply by probing further into the life, forms, and meanings of the letters. Among the most important sources is the *Sefer ha-Bahir* (Book of Illumination), one of the earliest and most foundational Kabbalistic texts.[2] This short, enigmatic book is a redaction of many ancient traditions and part of the literary emergence of Kabbalah in Spain and Provence in the thirteenth century CE. The *Sefer ha-Bahir* also analyzes the graphic shapes and interactions of the *beit* and *alef*. It plays on and radically revises the midrash's interpretation of the *beit* as forbidding us to inquire about the primordial secrets of creation. It takes us right into those hidden realms where the *alef* and *beit* graphically interact like comics panels and create the world. It shows us how this seemingly "simplistic 'comics question'" about which letter should begin the Torah is really a deeper hermeneutic dilemma. For here, *beit* is a "beginning that is second." How is it that *alef*—the first letter, with the value of one—is *not* the beginning? What does it mean that *beit*, the second letter, represents beginning? What, indeed, is "beginning"?

Here is one of the key passages from the *Sefer ha-Bahir*:

> R. Rehumai said and expounded:
>
> Why is the letter *alef* at the head [*ba-rosh*]? For it preceded everything, even Torah.
>
> And why is *beit* next to it? Because it was first [*tehillah*].
>
> And why does it [the *beit*] have a tail? To point to the place from which it came, and there are some who say, that from there the world is sustained. [§17–18]

It sounds like a Zen koan; this text is fragmentary and, like many other Kabbalistic writings, intended to be cryptic, so only the worthy few could understand and pass on the deepest "secrets" of Torah. These texts also deal with religious intuitions beyond syllogistic reason and leave much "gutter"—"white space"—for the reader to decipher. About the gutter in comics, Scott McCloud further writes, "The comics creator asks us to join in a silent dance of the seen and the unseen. The visible and the invisible" (92). That's also a fine way to describe how these Kabbalistic texts are constructed. So prepare as well for some intense effort to understand as we go along.

Elliot Wolfson interprets this passage to mean that *alef* is first, as the "head" [*rosh*] or "foundation," but that it is not the "beginning" [*tehillah*] (135). (There is also a play on the word "*b'reishit*," which has within it letters for the Hebrew word for "head," *rosh* [ראש]: *reish*, *alef*, *shin*.) *Ba-rosh* means "at the head." The passage is telling us that *to know alef we have to start with beit, which points to what came before.* That is what R. Rehumai alludes to in the enigmatic passage, "And why does it [the *beit*] have a tail? To point to the place from which it came. And there are those who say, that from there the world is sustained." We need another *etnachta* here! To help grasp this Kabbalistic distinction of a "beginning" point from the "head" (in the sense of "absolute origin and fount of everything"), think for a moment of how you would determine the "beginning" or "origin" of anything. We often never know the exact beginning point of any journey—be it intellectual or existential—until we are well on our way and look back. And even then, it's not so easy to tell. When did I "begin" to write this essay? When I actually sat down the first day to compose it at the blank screen? When I typed the first word or when I finally got the idea, after trying many other beginnings, to start it with the quotation from Elie Wiesel? Or was it months earlier, when I started the research? Maybe it was when I saw the proposal for this volume of essays. Or even before that, when I started to become interested in graphic narratives, or a few decades ago when I started to study rabbinic texts and learn Hebrew? Or even earlier, when. . . . ? At what temporal moment did I "begin" it? And beyond that, what was its ultimate creative foundation or "origin"?

The question of beginnings is an infinite regress, pointing endlessly back to some ultimately hidden, ungraspable "origin" ("head"), including the "beginnings" of our birth and the birth of our cosmos. As recent science has taught us, even what we can see and measure of the vast universe and its billions of galaxies is only a fraction. The bulk is composed of dark matter that's invisible. I'd like to think of the *alef* in the *Sefer ha-Bahir* as representing a kind of "dark matter," another metaphor for the ungraspable divine origin of the universe. It may be unknowable, but what we *can* see of the universe points back to it. Thus, the *beit*'s tail is pointing back, as it were, from "beginnings" to "origins" in the divine infinite abyss.

The *Sefer ha-Bahir* further interprets the boundaries of what can be seen and understood about the world in the graphic interplay of *alef* and *beit*:

> Why is the letter *beit* closed on all sides and open in the front?
>
> This teaches us that it is the house (*bayit*) of the world. Thus the Holy One Blessed be He is the place of the world and the world is not His place.
>
> Do not read *beit,* but *bayit,* as it is written, [Proverbs 24:3] "With wisdom [*hokhmah*] the house [*bayit*] is built, with understanding it is established. . . . [§14]

The *beit's* shape, as in the midrash, is "closed on three sides and open in front." In its origins in seventeenth-century BCE ancient pre-Canaanite script, the *beit* indeed is an abstracted pictograph of a house, drawn with open door and surrounding walls; and *bayit* means *house* in the cognate Semitic languages. In our midrash and the *Sefer ha-Bahir*, the name *beit*, *bayit*, house, alludes to God's creating the *house* of the world. This is where time and space "begin," and so there is an open space in front for new possibilities, for historical development—but God is also the surrounding, and protecting the "house" of the *beit*. Here the very "blessing" of God, [*brakha*], fills the world, connecting it to the *Ein Sof* of God (lit. "without end," the Kabbalistic term for the abyss of "divine infinity"). In the graphic language of our "Kabbalistic comics panels," *alef*, the primordial ungraspable origin "beyond," makes a connection to the *beit*, the beginning of space and time. The *beit* then builds, makes a place, a home for creation in space and time. God creates time and space, surrounds, fills, and sustains the world but is still always beyond. God is "the place of the world, but the world is not His place": *Alef, Beit.*

The *Sefer ha-Bahir* then takes us deeper into an analysis of how relations between open white spaces and black letters represent and enact the Divine creative flows emanating from God's infinity, and how they connect to and sustain finite creation. It shifts our perception and animates the letters further by making parallels between their forms and the shape of the human body:

> What does the *beit* resemble? [ב] It is like a man, formed by God with wisdom [*hokhmah*]. It is closed on all sides but open in front.
>
> The *alef*, however, is open from behind. [א]
>
> This teaches us that the tail of the beit is open from behind. If not for this, man could not exist.
>
> Likewise, if not for the *beit* on the tail of the *alef* the world could not exist.

Aryeh Kaplan, commenting on this enigmatic passage in his own translation of the *Sefer ha-Bahir*, interprets the front "opening" of the *beit* (the white open space on its left side between the two edges of the thick horizontal black) as the openings of the "two main organs of human expression and generation, the mouth and the sexual organ," which are also "open" in front (Kaplan 99). And indeed, if these human orifices were sealed, a person could not exist. So, too, if the divine generative flow should cease, the world could not exist. This is just a glimpse of a topic for which we have no space here: the way Kabbalistic texts speak simultaneously on many levels, especially of

Figure 2.3. The Hebrew letter *beit* highlighted in gray and circled inside the letter *alef* in a font rendered digitally based on hand-drawings of the traditional Hebrew scribal script (Hebrew: Ktav Stam כתב סת"ם). Beit, by Izzy Pludwinski. Copyright © 2017 Izzy Pludwinski

correspondences and mutual influences among different parts of the cosmos. The main point is that what's described about the human being is another allusion to and reflection of intra-divine processes and the divine supernal creative attributes, emanations known as *sefirot*. These are different "faces" and "dynamic configurations" of the Divine, to which the letters are also related. But what does the *Sefer ha-Bahir* mean with that cryptic phrase about a *beit* "on the tail of the *alef*"? The text mentions *two* tails: the tail of the *beit*, and the *beit* "on the tail of the *alef*." We've seen the first, but where is the second?

We have to move to a more complex visual level now. We've been looking at *alef* and *beit* as two separate letters but are now directed to see how one letter can contain *within itself* other letters and can also become multidimensional. Look back again at the *alef*. Meditate on it playfully; dissolve the letter itself into different shapes, forms, lines, curves, components. Try to see it sculpturally in three dimensions and not just flat on the page. Here is a further hint: another great thirteenth-century Provencal Kabbalist, R. Asher Ben David, writes of the *alef*: "If you flip her in all directions, you shall be able to build each and every letter from her" (qtd. in Fishbane 496). Did you see the *beit* on the "tail" of the *alef* graphically illustrated in figure 2.3 above? The *beit* is upside down, drawn in gray, and circled to make it easier for you to identity.

The "tail" of a letter is sometimes also called the "leg"; here the *beit* is the lower "left leg" of the *alef*. The key point, once again, is how the letters are interpreted as graphically conveying and enacting the Divine flows and emanations that create and continuously sustain the world. Meir Sendor interprets our passage as follows: "Given the right-to-left flow of Hebrew writing, letters that have curves that cup spaces above and to the right are receiving from levels 'above' themselves. Letters that have curves that cup spaces below and to the left are emanating to levels 'below' themselves." With that in mind, the letter *beit* on its own, as we saw before, is closed on three sides and open to the left. This means that it emanates to levels of existence "below," to our "home" world of space and time and finitude. Yet for the world and the whole cosmos on its many other physical and metaphysical levels to exist and endure, the world also has to receive Divine flow from a higher level than that, from "Above." That is the function of the *alef*—and *not just* when it precedes the *beit* in linear sequence. The *alef* also contains *within* it, as Sendor puts it, "an incipient *beit*, a *prefigured beit*, in its backwards upside-down tail." In this way, he continues, the *alef* "has a curve cupping a space to the right, symbolizing and enacting the receiving of emanation from Above." That sustains the entire cosmos and system of Divine creative flow as Kabbalah constructs it.

In sum, "If not for the *beit* on the tail of the *alef* the world could not exist." Aryeh Kaplan further interprets the "*beit* on the tail of the *alef*" to mean: "[E]ven the most brilliant light, is utter darkness when compared to the infinity of God" (99–100). That visible/invisible *beit* within the form of the *alef*, in other words, is part of the metaphysical paradox of the infinite and finite, the ungraspable origin, the Divine abyss giving birth to the finite, to shape, form, space, and time.

. . .

We have now looked at the meaning of the "negative space" *inside* and *between* the letters. The *beit* and *alef*, the *Sefer ha-Bahir* has observed, "open from behind," but in different ways. We also saw before in the midrash how the *beit*'s tail opens from "behind" with its little thorns pointing back to the hidden origin, *alef*. The *alef* opens too, but in another multidimensional way. Look at the two independent letters again: the *alef* has many more "openings" than does the *beit*. In fact, the *alef* is unique among all the letters of the Hebrew alphabet in being "open on all sides." Moreover, when the *alef* is pronounced *verbally*, it sounds like "ahhhhhh"—a simple opening of the mouth and vibrating expiration from the throat, like the sound of the letter "a" in English. *Beit*, in contrast, is pronounced with closed lips, making a short, clipped "b" sound. "Likewise," says the *Sefer ha-Bahir*, "if not for the *beit* on the tail of the *alef* the world could not exist." In another sense, the *beit*'s boundaries make *our* world possible. We couldn't live in a world that was wholly *alef*, so utterly open and permeated by the Infinite. We would be nullified out of existence or go mad. That would not be a "blessing" but a "curse." Those who speak in the name of "Absolute Truths," which they claim to solely possess, bring curse and cruelty to the world, not blessing. They have no room for the other, for plurality, for "*beit*." Therefore, *our* world and *our* Torah (as opposed to other levels of Torah and other metaphysical worlds) begin with the *beit* of *b'reishit*. *We* live and flourish in the world of duality, of time, space and division, not absolutes. Yet somehow, and this *is the critical point* and the great mystery of the universe, there is a level in which the *alef* connects and contracts and flows to the *beit* in order for there to be a world at all; a way in which *alef* contains all the letters, as the Kabbalists affirm, and is the kernel of everything, the origin. Without the continuing, oscillating relation of *alef* and *beit*, the world could not exist. This relation is enacted in the black and white spaces *between* the letters and words, and *inside* the letters, in multiple dimensions.

The *Sefer ha-Bahir* still leaves us many "gutters." But even if you can't quite grasp all the explanations above, it also teaches that these deeper meanings are enacted in the potency of the letters' "graphic narratives"—just by our looking, even without our being consciously aware of or understanding them. The letters and white spaces are "living" Divine agents; the metaphysical-cosmological creative process is enacted and embodied, as it were, every time we gaze at or write the spaces and letters. Doing so is a channel for us to absorb and unite with God's light, even if we have no cognitive grasp of their textual meaning. At the same time, these midrashic and Kabbalistic texts also teach us to *look and read anew*, to play with the letters, to "become scribes" of the Torah as well, as it were.

. . .

Time for a final *etnachta*. Isn't all this, one could object, a kind of giant Rorschach game, where the rabbis are just reading into lines and blotches what they want to see? Well, yes, in a way, because as the rabbis themselves say, the way that you look at and draw the letters, vocalize and chant them brings them to life, creates them, activates their potential divine forces. Writing them, reading them, meditating upon them, composing and recomposing them, makes you participate in their creative energies, connects you to God. The letters come alive; *they create you as you create them*. As the Batizer Rebbe taught the young Elie Wiesel: "Take care of them and they will take care of you. They will go with you everywhere. They will make you laugh and cry. Or rather, they will cry when you cry and laugh when you laugh. . . ." The most fundamental religious, philosophical, and existential questions are in the *alef* and *beit*, though they look like a simple two-panel comic. It's as complicated, and as simple, as the first thing a child learns: "*Alef, Beit.*" But everything is there.

Children themselves are a living form of "*b'reishit*." They are the *beit* pointing back to the *alef*—the parents, the origin from whom they came. Like the *beit*, children also "open to the front," moving the world forward into the future. Parents come together and give birth to the next generation, and as the generation ages, children—the next generation—begin the world anew. Or, as the contemporary Jewish philosopher Emmanuel Levinas once explained: fecundity, the ordinary power of human procreation is not just a biological fact, or blind drive of Eros. It is, in his words, an "ontological category," a relationship between the "same" and the "other" beyond formal logic. A child is part of the parents and also entirely other, living beyond their death into the future, renewing time, and so related to the infinite time of "ever-recommencing being" (Levinas 227, 267). The birth of a child, that is, enacts the power of "infinity" in the "finite"—or, *alef* and *beit*.

But we do not need a complex philosophical analysis to know how children renew creation. They see things differently: children look at everything for the first time without preconceptions, see the animation in all things. Learning the alphabet, they do not see "through" the letters, as practiced adults do, but grasp the letters in all of their living visuality and personality. So there's a special connection among children, comics, letters, seeing the world differently—and the kind of "sophisticated second innocence" an adult attains when looking at images, words, and things "like a child." Comics and graphic narratives have also struggled to be taken seriously and not be seen as simplistic pleasures for barely literate children and unsophisticated adults. But comics artists have always known that behind the deceptive simplicity of their text and image panels are complex resources to express the deepest problems of life. It has taken a long time for academic theorists to catch up, but today we're inundated with texts applying complex semiotic, narrative, and aesthetic theories to comics. In response, in this concluding section, I'd like to elaborate on a few broader connections between comics and religion.

R. Marc Kujavski formulates the larger question at stake in the Kabbalistic interpretations of the visuality of the letters as this: How does a form enclose the infinite, and how does the infinite break out from the inside?[3] This question of form has been my angle here throughout in relating comics to the Hebrew letters. There are numerous academic theorists whom I could cite on the formal aesthetics of comics and theories of the image. But it's the comics artists themselves, I think, who feel most keenly and articulate most eloquently the life of lines, and the relation of the visible and invisible in form—particularly those who write about the nature of their art such as Art Spiegelman, Scott McCloud, Ivan Brunetti, and Lynda Barry. I'll focus briefly here only on Barry, who describes herself in one of her books as follows: "b. 1956 Richland Center WI. Worked as a painter, cartoonist, writer, illustrator, playwright, editor, commentator and teacher, and found they are very much alike" (Barry, *What It Is* 138). In three of her graphic narratives, *Syllabus: Notes from an Accidental Professor* (2014); *What It Is: The Formless Thing Which Gives Form* (2008); and *Picture This: Learn How to Art with the Near-Sighted Monkey* (2010), she becomes a kind of secular version of Elie Wiesel's first teacher, the Batizer Rebbe. In these books she lovingly initiates us into the mysteries and interactions of lines, form, letters, and images. Much of the material is based on her traveling workshop, "Writing the Unthinkable," and courses she taught at the University of Wisconsin as an artist-in-residence. She examines, among other things, the nature of creativity and memory, and the relation of images and words. She provides exercises for hand-drawing to activate parts of the brain and access a realm we can't get to just through "thinking." These works also contain poignant personal and autobiographical stories about her difficult childhood and development as an artist, all drawn as comic pages. They are laced with mischievous humor; images of a "magic cephalopod" and a cigarette-smoking, nearsighted monkey with bandana, house coat, and slippers appear and reappear as her alter egos and avatars.

But I cite Barry here above all because she so exquisitely senses the invisible shimmering through the visible in the life of lines. "By image," she writes, "I don't mean a visual representation. I mean, something that is more like a ghost than a picture; something which feels somehow alive, has no fixed meaning and is contained and transported by something that is not alive—a book, a song, a painting—anything we call an 'art form'" (Barry, *Syllabus* 15). As the image emerges, she adds, "Liking and not liking can make us blind to *what's there*. In spite of how we feel about it, it is making its way from the unseen to the visible world, one line after the next, bringing with it a kind of aliveness I live for: right here, right now" (23). These words, I'd like to suggest, are another way of describing the emergence of *alef* and its connection to *beit*—on both the personal and cosmic levels. In *What It Is*, she further defines an image as "the formless thing which gives things form" (8) and notes the reciprocity in the creative process between form and formlessness.

Writing and drawing are ways of picturing the world, "formed by our own activity, one line suggesting the next" (Barry, *Syllabus* 136). There is play and movement and soul. Or, as she writes in *Picture This,* an image is "the pull-toy that pulls you, takes you from one place to another"; it is "the soul's immune system and transit system" (122). And like our *beit*, an image is "a place, not a picture of a place but a place in and of itself. You can move in it. . . . It seems not invented, but there for you to find" (Barry, *What It Is* 88).

Though I am quoting her verbally in writing here, my citations are missing the colors, fonts, and images in which her words are drawn and embedded on each complexly textured page. Artists like Barry take us beyond the academic, intellectual conceptions of our brains, which reflect only a part of our being. They make us feel the aliveness in the lines, and what we "live for." It is what Ben Shahn called the "Love and Joy about Letters" in the phrase he used for the title of his autobiography. Shahn was profoundly marked by learning the Hebrew alphabet as a child, drawing the letters again and again with great passion and joy. That aesthetic experience became the foundation of his artistic career, where letters appear and reappear in many guises. Barry and Shahn immerse us in the image-text, teaching us how to create, meditate on, and participate in the love, joy, and "life" of lines.

I'd like to suggest a final connection between comics and the sacred: the artist's, the child's, and our love and joy in letters parallels and comes from God's own pleasure, joy, and "primordial drawings"—from "God's comics," as it were, as described in the *Zohar* ("Book of Radiance"), one of the central books of Jewish mysticism. Like the *Sefer ha-Bahir,* the *Zohar* is part of the literary flourishing of Kabbalah in the medieval period but was redacted from many older and ancient sources. In its opening pages, commenting on the first words of Genesis, the *Zohar* tells us: "[W]hen the blessed Holy One wished to fashion the world, all the letters of the Alphabet were hidden away. For two thousand years before creating the world, the blessed Holy One contemplated them and played with them" (1:2b). And before that were even more primordial "drawings" by God in the very first stage of creation:

> At the head of the potency of the King, He engraved engravings in luster on high. A spark of impenetrable darkness flashed within the concealed of the concealed, from the head of Infinity—a cluster of vapor forming in formlessness, thrust in a ring, not white, not black, not red, not green, no color at all. As a cord surveyed, it yielded radiant colors. Deep within the spark gushed a flow, splaying colors below, concealed within the concealed of the mystery of *Ein Sof.* It

> split and did not split its aura, was not known at all, until under the impact splitting, a single, concealed, supernal point shown. Beyond that point, nothing is known, so it is called *Reishit, Beginning*, first command of all. (1:15a)

This is a remarkable passage of poetic beauty, of words and images melding . . . and of deep mystery. It takes us far beyond our academic modes of cognition into a realm to which only the great mystics have access. But these mystics have expressed their experience in a way that somehow allows us to feel and sense a bit of that ultimate unknown. They tell us of the life and joy and desire to create as it wells up in God. And this, I think, is the ultimate source of creative pleasure in all of us, artists and academics, rabbis and readers, parents and children. For we ourselves, finally, are the letters, and the letters are us. We are "God's comics."

I have done a vast amount of reading and research, struggled with the white empty spaces facing me as I formed letters, words, lines, paragraphs, trying to give birth to this essay from nothingness. Nevertheless, here at the end, I feel that all I've given you is the *beit*, and not the *alef*—that we haven't really even begun to understand at all. Still, I hope there is a trace of *alef* glimmering through.

NOTES

1. By "rabbinic tradition" I'm referring to thousands of years of materials. There are exoteric and esoteric traditions, legal and homiletic materials, stories, and folklore. Discussions of the forms and meanings of the Hebrew letters interweave throughout all these traditions. I cite only a few here and do not give further references due to space limitations. The Batizer Rebbe in the epigraph paraphrases a saying from an ancient Kabbalistic text, the *Sefer Yetzirah* 2:2 ["Book of Creation"] that describes this primordial life of the letters before creation. God then plays Scrabble, as it were, combining and recombining the letters in various permutations. Those form the words of our opening verses of Genesis: "And God said. . . . And there was"—a set of performative-creative speech acts, whose letters can then also combine and recombine in endless ways to create all things. There are also many Jewish spiritual practices of meditating on the letters and their combinations in Kabbalah and Chassidic traditions to alter consciousness, create ecstatic experience, or unite with the Divine.

2. Translations of the *Sefer ha-Bahir* are mine. Citations are based on the section numbering in the Hebrew edition listed in the bibliography.

3. I am grateful to Rav Marc Kujavski for his 2009 seminar on the Hebrew letters, which surveyed many Kabbalistic sources and influenced my thinking. I also deeply thank Ora Wiskind Elper for helping me think through and research these issues and for her astute feedback on drafts of this essay.

BIBLIOGRAPHY

Barry, Lynda. *Picture This: Learn How to Art with the Near-Sighted Monkey*. Montreal: Drawn & Quarterly, 2010.

Barry, Lynda. *Syllabus: Notes from an Accidental Professor*. Montreal: Drawn & Quarterly, 2014.

Barry, Lynda. *What It Is: The Formless Thing Which Gives Form*. Montreal: Drawn & Quarterly, 2008.

Bereishit Rabbah. Translated by H. Freedman and Maurice Simon. Vols. 1–2. London: Soncino Press, 1939.

Fishbane, Eitan. "The Speech of Being, the Voice of God: Phonetic Mysticism in the Kabbalah of Asher Ben David and His Contemporaries." *Jewish Quarterly Review* 90, no. 4 (2008): 485–521.

Kaplan, Aryeh (trans.). *The Bahir: A Translation and Commentary*. Northvale, NJ: Jason Aronson, 1995.

Kujavski, Rabbi Marc. Matan, the Sadie Rennert Institute for Women's Torah Studies in Jerusalem, July 2009. Seminar.

Levinas, Emmanuel. *Totality and Infinity: An Essay on Exteriority*. Translated by Alphonso Lingis. Pittsburgh: Duquesne University Press, 1969.

McCloud, Scott. *Understanding Comics: The Invisible Art*. New York: HarperCollins, 1993.

Mitchell, W. J. T. "Comics as Media: Afterword." In *Comics & Media*, special issue of *Critical Inquiry* 40, no. 3 (Spring 2014): 255–65.

Sefer ha-Bahir [*Book of Illumination*]. Margulies ed. Jerusalem: Mossad Ha Rav Kook [Rabbi Kook Institute], 1978.

Sendor, Rabbi Dr. Meir. "Tail of the *Alef*." Received by Dr. Susan Handelman, January 17, 2017.

Shahn, Ben. *Love and Joy about Letters*. New York: Grossman, 1963.

Wiesel, Elie. *All Rivers Run to the Sea*. New York: Schocken Books, 1996.

Wolfson, Elliot. "Before Alef/Where Beginnings End." In *Beginning/Again: Towards a Hermeneutics of Jewish Texts*, edited by Aryeh Cohen and Shaul Magid, 135–61. New York: Seven Bridges Press, 2002.

The Zohar: Pritzker Edition. Translated by Daniel C. Matt. Stanford: Stanford University Press, 2003.

Chapter Three

THE INEFFABILITY OF FORM

Speaking and Seeing the Sacred in *Tina's Mouth* and *The Rabbi's Cat*

LEAH HOCHMAN

WHAT IS THE SACRED? AND HOW CAN IT BE REPRESENTED? THIS CHAPTER looks at the ways two graphic novels—*The Rabbi's Cat* by Joann Sfar and *Tina's Mouth: An Existential Diary* by Keshni Kashyap—illustrate awe, sanctity, and ineffability. Though each work describes a very different conception of the divine—one Jewish, the other Hindu—together they provide an opportunity to investigate attempts to represent physically seemingly aniconic conceptions of sacrality. In exploring how each narrative exposes its respective understanding of the sacred, I look at the way the interplay between word and image suggests multiple, concurrent, and layered definitions of divinity and how it creates a multilayered conversation that invites the reader to participate in each author's exploration of the sacred. As the protagonists of each novel explore the contours of what forms of holiness are (and are not) acceptable and accessible, their respective stories force us to question the conscious and unconscious boundaries that outline the ineffable.

Kashyap's novel *Tina's Mouth: An Existential Comic Diary* unfolds as a diary written as part of a semester project in a philosophy class taken by the fifteen-year-old eponymous Tina. She is the only Hindu American in a largely white, private high school and takes up the assignment both to chronicle her daily activities and to express her growing confusion as her social circle changes and her friendships experience the effects of shifting priorities. The diary offers her the chance to explore her own identity; hand-drawn in black ink, entries illustrate Tina's experiences in conversations and interactions with classmates, family, friends, and strangers. Contextualizing frames are largely absent; instead, images integrated with Tina's words reach across each

Figure 3.1. Tina Malhotra's retort, *Tina's Mouth: An Existential Comic Diary*, page 21, by Keshni Kashyap, illustrations by Mari Araki. Copyright © 2011 Keshni Kashyap

page bound by few borders. Sometimes the words of the diary itself act as makeshift frames for the images they accompany. Indeed not only is the text an integral part of each illustration, but the diary itself forces a continual dialogue between word and image. This interrelationship implores the reader to read the words as picture; their embellishments illustrate Tina's thoughts without need for a separate or objective narration. When Tina records the questions and misconceptions her classmates have about Hinduism, for example, the text explores the flexibility of language by breaking up the straight-line structure of her sentence and decorating each word to reflect her perception of its connotations and impact. Her nonverbal retort—a middle finger in the middle of a spiral of words encircling her body—invites the reader to engage and share her feelings of defense and agency.

Such interplay reflects one of the great joys of graphic novels. The dynamic relationship between complementary and competing visual and written narratives forces a kind of interlocution. The reader must integrate words from a type of visual dialogue in order to unpack the multiplicity of its meaning. The requirement of that kind of agency—one needs to employ visual literacy to read the page—suggests a graphic articulation of what Mikhail Bakhtin named *heteroglossia* (multi-languaged-ness), that is, the multiple contemporaneous literary exchanges that operate in different spheres—author and character, for instance, and reader and protagonist, and author and reader (Bakhtin 261). Each sphere is both autonomous and inextricably linked to the other linguistic spheres. Though a reader will experience words and images differently, the positioning of text and drawing fosters multiple concurrent conversations that enforce a visual form of literary heteroglossia. For Bakhtin, "the language of a novel is a system of its 'languages.'" Those languages "figure into the style of the whole . . . and participate in the process whereby the unified meaning of the whole is structured and revealed" (262). In the graphic novel, that unified meaning originates in the meeting of word and image and sparks a nonliterary third expression of meaning; it creates a separate, universalizing narrative that is greater than the sum of its parts. This unified entity—word plus image, picture plus text—catapults the representative power of the graphic novel to a conceptual level that allows it to describe and illustrate seemingly inexpressible ideas. Together the graphic image and the text function to construct meaning beyond the indescribable; their joint effort to project meaning empowers the reader to dissemble linear or specific (*monoglossic*) meaning. Bakhtin emboldens the novel to take authority over its own multiplicity. Rather than being a passive receptacle that holds recorded words, the "novel orchestrates all its themes, the totality of the world of objects and ideas depicted and expressed in it, by means of the social diversity of speech types [heteroglossia] and by the differing individual voices that flourish under such conditions" (263). The seemingly separate unities of art and language that operate in a graphic novel do so both separately and together; unified they have an even greater impact and influence over the reader's experience. The heteroglossia of the graphic novel expands the frames of reference of both fields, which in turn allows the reader to envisage multiple, simultaneous interpretations if not also to conjoin each with personal interjection.

The effect is something of a supercharged heteroglossia: visual fields of the illustration activate associations and connotations that operate outside of the purely linguistic (e.g., Tina's middle finger illustrates an emotional response that explicitly articulates anger and rejection without using any words) and augment the conceptual association of any accompanying narration. In other words, illustrating Hinduism as a spiral of naive or ill-informed projections that trap Tina inside them artfully imparts far more information to the reader about Tina's intimate feelings than would a straight description. Her nonverbal, emotional response serves the storyline as much as the data printed on the page.

Indeed this power to shape an image for the purely conceptual endows graphic narratives with the unique potential to take up the challenges inherent in illustrating notions of the sacred. Such a challenge is particularly acute in the case of Judaism and Jewish notions of sacrality that eschew visual representations of the divine. It was Immanuel Kant who famously described this difficulty in concrete terms:

> Perhaps there is no more sublime passage in the Jewish Book of the Law than the commandment: "Thou shalt not make unto thyself any graven image, nor any likeness either of that which is in heaven or on the earth, or yet under the earth, etc." This commandment alone can explain the enthusiasm that the Jewish people felt in its civilized period for its religion when it compared itself with other peoples, or the pride that Mohammedanism inspired. The very same thing also holds of the representation of the moral law and the predisposition to morality in us. It is utterly mistaken to worry that if it were deprived of everything that the senses can recommend it would then bring with it nothing but cold, lifeless approval and no moving force or emotion. It is exactly the reverse: for where the senses no longer see anything before them, yet the unmistakable and inextinguishable idea of morality remains, there it would be more necessary to moderate the momentum of an unbounded imagination so as not to let it reach the point of enthusiasm, rather than, from fear of powerlessness of these ideas, to look for assistance for them in images and childish devices. (156)

Leaving an analysis of Kant's misreading of postbiblical Judaism for another date, one can still extract from his analogy to moral law a rejection of the visual to express the ineffable. The deep antipathy he expresses for the sensory expression of morality comes from a profound admiration for the power of human thought and its ability to elevate humanity to a level of pure concept. One need not rely on the "childish devices" because the moral law—or the sacred, for the purposes of this paper—operates neither as a picture nor as a word but rather as an idea that surpasses both in potential of expression.

The notion that the idea is greater than both word and image underscores a crucial scene in Sfar's *The Rabbi's Cat*. The novel chronicles the tale of a feline protagonist who surprises himself by acquiring the power of speech. His astonished rabbi decries the manner in which his cat comes to language—he ate a talking parrot that annoyed him—but nevertheless helps his pet explore the possibilities, limitations, and responsibilities within it. In an effort to legitimate his new ability, the cat declares his desire to activate his own sense of religiosity, affirm his Jewishness, and become bar mitzvah. The rabbi brings his cat to his own rabbi to determine whether such an act is possible; the rabbi defers to his teacher's authority to determine whether the cat is Jewish.

Drawn in rich, bold, warm colors and exploding with nonverbal cues, Sfar's novel unfolds in roughly drawn square panels that run six to a page. Text accompanies image in two ways. In the first, the cat's narration appears at the top of each panel. His monologue directs the attention of the reader toward the activity in the frame, and he accepts fully his role as the reader's interlocutor by intentionally offering context and commentary. In the second, his conversation with other characters appears in word bubbles within each frame. The two neither intersect with nor impose on each other. Conversation occurs simultaneously on three levels, each of which references its own series of associated ideas: the reader must process the image within the frame, the narration at the top of the frame, and the dialogue inside the frame simultaneously. The story explores the terrain between the sacred and the profane by presenting word and image not in dialogue but in competition with each other. Though the action in the novel is propelled by the cat's acquisition of speech, the novel's narration remains independent of it. The cat's thoughts drive the story. His devotion to his master allows the cat to explore Judaism through an ostensibly strange gaze serving as a proxy for the reader, for the cat articulates questions and arguments against the traditional Judaism his rabbi practices. As characters debate Jewish practice and mysticism, historicism and myth, the novel displays multiple, unconnected narratives (image, dialogue, narration) that appear on the page simultaneously. Here, heteroglossia operates differently: the author forces the reader to navigate the cat's theological concerns through pictorial representation

Figure 3.2. The rabbi's cat and the rabbi's rabbi face off about the Divine, "The Bar Mitzvah," *The Rabbi's Cat*, page 11, by Joann Sfar. Copyright © 2005 Pantheon Books

(a highly untypical form of Jewish theological debate) while following a storyline that explores personal identity and political tension. The reader must navigate between the cat's (seeming) disdain for the sacred, the rabbi's ability to integrate contradictory expressions of that sacred, and the political reality of a Jew in Algeria in the beginning of the twentieth century. Toggling between visual idea and written word, *The Rabbi's Cat* forces the reader to reconcile multiple story arcs that, ironically, coalesce in illustrations of divine providence.

The deep theological conversation between the cat and the rabbi's rabbi begins poorly: the rabbi's rabbi rejects the cat's request to embrace Judaism based on the idea of *b'tzelem elohim*, the creation of humanity in God's image. Emboldened by his ability to communicate all the Jewish textual knowledge he has passively acquired while listening to his own rabbi study over the years, the cat challenges the rabbi's rabbi to show him a picture of God. The rabbi's rabbi is taken aback: "He tells me that God is a word," the cat narrates (Sfar 11). The rabbi's teacher's silhouette appears against a yellow background; Sfar draws only the outline of his features. The panel appears directly opposite an equally close-up image of the cat, whose eager face appears against an all-black backdrop. The two face each other in a standoff: the cat stares across from one panel at the rabbi's rabbi, who points his finger directly at his mouth.

Sfar eschews dialogue in these two frames, and the reader is privy to their conversation only through the cat's recollection. The artistic rejection of a divine image allows the idea of God to fill the physical absence of form. And in this rabbinic rejection of a divine image—locating God not in the visual but in the aural and linguistic—the rabbi's rabbi falls head first into the cat's rhetorical trap: if God is language and the cat has language, surely the cat can participate in the divine, too. The ensuing conversation twists and turns; the debate itself illustrates the power and dangers inherent in language. The cat's thoughts operate as a supratext: his words make the reader juggle multiple visual stimuli simultaneously. Yet one is not entirely sure whom to follow. The cat himself reminds the reader that "with speech, you can say what you want, even things that aren't true . . . it's an amazing power" (Sfar 12). Sfar sets that revelation against a play of graphic illustrations involving light, shadows, and the interior decorations of the rabbi's teacher's sitting room. Physical space interacts with visual space just as word and image jump toward and repel each other. The effect is an illustrated, verbal, visual volleying for meaning.

When the conversation returns to the nature of the divine, specific visual references fall away to be replaced by geometric designs. As the cat narrates the theology of his opponent, each frame depicts the rabbi's deep and ranging emotions:

> He explains to me that to become Jewish, you have to fear God and put yourself under his protection and cherish him. He says that a Jew must see in all things the presence of God. He says that thinking of God fills even the grayest days with sunlight. He says that the love of God must be almost carnal. He tells me that it is an intellectual love but you should always feel as though you were cradled in the arms of a master who is invincible, benevolent, and just. (Sfar 17)

Finally they come to a moment of potential recognition. But when the cat admits that he loves the rabbi's daughter exactly as the rabbi's rabbi loves God, he is thrown out of the house.

Sfar's choice to represent Jewish theology as a series of repeating shapes against a monochromatic background has the advantage of expressing the conceptual. Both the colors of the background and the shapes themselves illustrate the teacher's heightened emotional connection to his own argument. The patterns are repetitive within each panel but differ from panel to panel. Attuned to a reluctance to depict the divine directly, Sfar substitutes conversation for divine image; silhouettes describe forms without any identifying details.

Later in the novel the cat returns to theology in his attempt to help his rabbi pass a language proficiency examination required in order to keep his

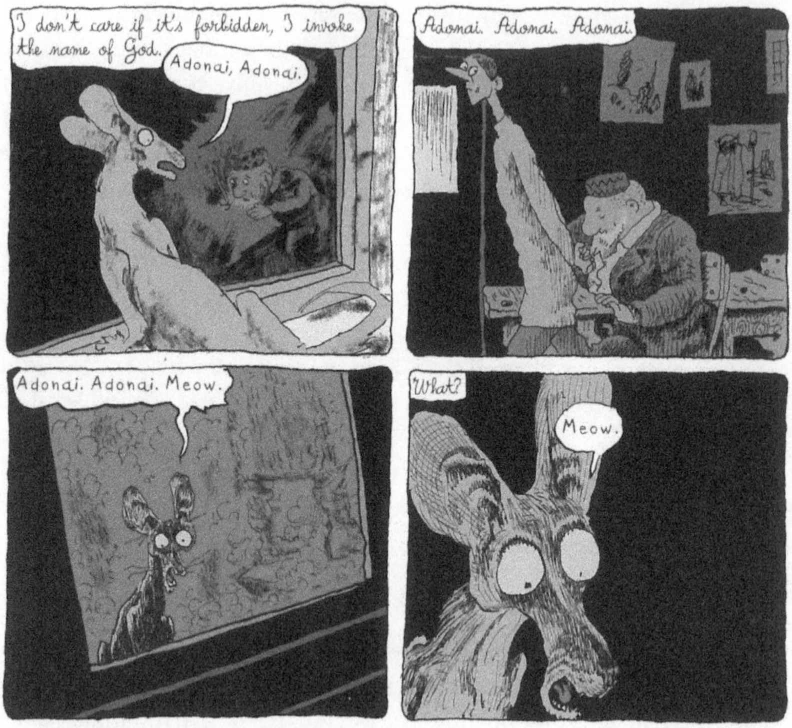

Figure 3.3. The cat's invocation of God's holy name, "Malka of the Lions," *The Rabbi's Cat*, page 66, by Joann Sfar. Copyright © 2005 Pantheon Books

community rabbinical position. As Sfar utilizes a full six panels to break the fourth wall and explain to readers why observant Jews revere the holiness associated and invoked by the name of God, the cat constructs a narrative definition of the sacred. His narration serves to set up his ambivalent feelings toward that very holiness: on the one hand, he knows how much power that ineffable name holds, but on the other, he despises the superstition that endows it with that power. Watching his rabbi from outside through a window, the cat sees his master struggling—he knows they need "a miracle" (Sfar 65). "'Thou shalt not invoke the Lord's name in vain,'" he intones to the reader. And then he speaks directly to himself: "It's not in vain. I'm going to perform an act of sacrilegious magic. I don't care if it's forbidden, I invoke the name of God" (65–66). The cat's repeated intonation of the *tetragrammaton* is placed physically over the narration at the top of the frame; the pictorial viewpoint tightens closer and closer on the cat's body until the panel is filled entirely by his face against a black background. After the seventh repetition of God's Hebrew name, the cat loses his language ability; the dialogue bubble reads "meow."

Without the ability to speak to the rabbi, the cat can explain neither what he has done nor what has occurred as a result of it; the rabbi assumes the cat has made a conscious choice not to speak. As the novel's narrator, the cat continues to communicate his thoughts and commentary to the reader, though he is depicted as communicating feelings and opinions to other characters only through his actions and reactions. Much later, the cat and the rabbi (and the reader) are surprised to discover they have passed the test.

. . .

The sacred receives very different treatment in Kashyap's novel. Though the reader is implicitly invited through the form of the diary to engage with Tina's musings and assume her viewpoint, the text also makes clear that her journey of discovery includes her own misperceptions about her family's traditions and religious leanings. She struggles to accept what Hinduism means and how to integrate its different elements with her understanding of herself as occupying multiple identities.

Several interlocutors help. After a painful breakup with her best friend, Tina has a brief but influential visit with her beloved senior Auntie who asks her about her life. Tina tells her about her philosophy class. Reflecting on the trappings of young love, the fecklessness of friends, and the limits of existentialism, the slightly intoxicated Urvashi Auntie offers some advice: "Always remember what lies in here"—the page shows the two women in profile looking pointedly but not directly at each other. As the finger of Tina's aunt reaches across the page to point directly at her, the teenager looks just below her aunt's sightline, directly at her mouth, and watches the decorated and adorned prose that comes out of it. "This heavenly and mysterious expanse. Be true to yourself," she begins. The conversation ends abruptly with Tina's aunt tipping over onto the floor (Kashyap 83).

In an apologetic note left for Tina the next day, Urvashi Auntie explains her advice and its intention through a liberally interpreted story involving Krishna's (step)mother. Tina herself appears on the page holding her aunt's letter, staring out directly at the reader impassively. Her form is superimposed onto a large, slightly open mouth (whose interior is dark and unexplored), adorned with decorative elements that reference the illustrations that accompanied the encounter between the two women the previous day. The letter itself is enlarged and shown in full:

> When Krishna was a small baby, he used to do naughty things. One day, his mother found him lolling about in the forest and he was dirty as hell. She bent down to wipe his mouth. But as she did so, something very strange happened. She peered inside his mouth and before her lay THE ENTIRE UNIVERSE. She saw herself in there, in her little village in Gujarat, cleaning the mouth of her son and then MANY MORE UNIVERSES inside his mouth and so on so forth.
>
> This story illustrates what I meant yesterday, though mostly it is interpreted by total idiots. My interpretation goes as follows and it is the best one.
>
> 1. People will tell you all sorts of things.
> 2. Don't listen to them.
> 3. Do as you please but on one condition.
> 4. Know that there is a universe inside yourself.
> 5. And examine it.
>
> (Kashyap 84; *Śrīmad Bhāgavata Mahā Purāṇa* 10.8.37–39)

The possibility of discovering the sacred and, perhaps, mimicking it is represented here by an open mouth and a pointed finger. Urvashi Auntie's retelling of this canonical story of Krishna's revelation to his stepmother Yashoda takes many liberties; it displaces the primary focus—the revelation of Krishna's infinite, unending, and all-encompassing divine existence, which is at once so vast and so mind-boggling that his stepmother cannot process it—onto the human exploration of oneself. Her moral—know thyself—replaces divine knowledge with human knowledge. The original story of Krishna's mother finding his mouth soiled, her attempt to clean it, and his subsequent revelation to her, makes it clear that human beings cannot grasp the divine, and any attempt to process that sacrality will render one, at best, speechless (see *Śrīmad Bhāgavata Mahā Purāṇa* 10.8.37–39). Urvashi Auntie's twenty-first-century diasporic reinterpretation not only shifts Tina toward what is knowable but also empowers her to discover her own interior holiness. Her letter—processed by the reader as visual content rather than through oral dialogue—does for Tina what the conversation with the rabbi's teacher did for the cat: it provides a rubric for assessing what does and does not suit Tina's growing awareness of her own agency.

This encounter with her aunt also frames Tina's dawning understanding of the ways in which her Hindu heritage provides an infrastructure for that exploration. Though Urvashi Auntie's letter provides the reader the same opportunity for self-reflection, the gesture toward religious truth can be interpolated both as a form of intimate, interior knowledge and as a method for self-empowerment. That duality underscores the interplay between the graphics and the narrative throughout the novel itself. In asking how one excavates one's many interior mysteries and suggesting ways one can examine the universe(s) inside oneself, Tina's aunt forces the reader to question the multiple ways of expressing and experiencing truth. The relationship between word as image and image as text helps navigate that multiplicity.

The invocation of Krishna forces mouths—both the divine and the human—into a metaphorical relationship with knowledge. And Tina's mouth becomes a literal portal for self-knowledge. As she allows herself to enjoy the company of her heretofore unrequited crush, she experiences a type of conscious joy that strikes her as utterly unfamiliar. On a date biking along a beach path on a sunny Southern California day, Tina and her crush, Neil, discuss existentialism, Neil Young, and the weather. At a scenic overlook, he turns the conversation toward the sacred: "I had a question for you. Since you're a Buddhist. Can you tell me what you know about **nirvana**? Like what it is . . . ?" (Kashyap 128). Tina is stumped:

> There he went again. With all the religious stuff. I had some vague idea that nirvana had something to do with love and the universe and some kind of New Age nonsense that [the philosophy teacher] Mr. Moosewood would love. Or that it was something like that mysterious expanse Urvashi Auntie was talking about. I didn't know.
>
> What I **did** know was that all of his **talk** was getting us **nowhere** as far as **kissing** was concerned. (128)

Tina's narration—unframed and stretching across the full page—is interrupted by Neil's dialogue. He asks her why she seems to be staring at his mouth. And in her confusion she answers him: "Because that's what it is. Nirvana" (Kashyap 129). Employing frames to slow down the action of the page, Kashyap depicts Tina and Neil moving incrementally close to one another; she blushes and they lock eyes.

And then she experiences her first (real) kiss. The novel depicts that kiss first purely metaphorically: in a splash page, an open mouth anchors shooting stars and shooting hearts, rosebuds with butterflies, a rocket shooting straight up adorned with the onomatopoeic expression for Tina's emotional thrill "Zoom" (Kashyap 130–31). While the next page shows their kiss literally—a physical joining of two mouths—its connection to the spirituality of the preceding page illustrates that kiss as a pictorial nirvana. Here we see the sacred

Figure 3.4. Tina kisses Neil, *Tina's Mouth: An Existential Comic Diary*, page 129, by Keshni Kashyap, illustrations by Mari Araki. Copyright © 2011 Keshni Kashyap

as dis/embodied bliss, and infinite wisdom characterized by an illustration of suprasensory experience. Tina's mouth serves as the representation of emotional and physical desire fulfilled, knowledge obtained, and multiple universes revealed.

. . .

These two depictions—God as a word, the kiss as revelation—unveil the fundamental aniconism of graphic representations of the sacred. The divine lies somewhere embedded in the dynamic between image and text; depictions of sacrality express an ongoing relationship between visual expectation, intellectual projection, and literal description. As both the rabbi's cat and Tina realize, albeit in different ways, one can hear and read about the idea of the sacred, but one must come to know it oneself. At the heart of both of these novels and their protagonists' respective explorations of truth is the understanding that such truth can and should be described in multiple, overlapping ways that allow for flexible interpretations. In giving expression to the deep ambivalence within Jewish tradition toward literal representations of the sacred, Sfar's cat shares with the reader the textual context for that reticence. Yet depicting the consequence of testing that boundary—the loss of his ability to engage in words, sacred or profane—actually illustrates that theology. Similarly, Kashyap's Tina invites the reader to join her in exploring the multiple forms of divine representation within Hinduism. The explosion of the knowledge unleashed by her kiss with Neil—her own realization of the sanctity of connection—leads her also to know that such delight is temporary. Nirvana is more than a momentary fulfillment of desire; over the course of the novel, she comes to understand that she deserves someone who respects her for who she is and who can distinguish Hinduism from Buddhism (among other things). Those two very different approaches—Judaic ambivalence and Hindu enthusiasm—provide very rich examples of the ways in which graphic novels employ multilayered representations of the sacred. And, in their unique ability to bring the textual into conversation with the visual, they also protect the integrity of how the sacred can and should look—the sacred word sealed with a kiss.

BIBLIOGRAPHY

Bakhtin, M. M. "Discourse in the Novel." In *The Dialogic Imagination: Four Essays*, edited by Michael Holquist. Austin: University of Texas Press, 1981.

Kant, Immanuel. *Critique of the Power of Judgment*. Translated by Paul Guyer and Allen Wood. New York: Cambridge University Press, 2000.

Kashyap, Keshni. *Tina's Mouth: An Existential Comic Diary*. New York: Houghton Mifflin, 2011.

Sfar, Joann. *The Rabbi's Cat*. Translated by Alexis Siegel and Anjali Singh. New York: Pantheon Books, 2005.

Chapter Four

THE SEVEN TRAITS OF FICTOSCRIPTURE AND THE WORMHOLE SACRED

A. DAVID LEWIS

GARY LADERMAN, PROFESSOR OF AMERICAN RELIGIOUS HISTORY AND CULture at Emory University, is being somewhat irreverent when he reports, "Religion has been compromised." His comment has less to do with faith and spirituality than it does formal religious institutions and rigid definitions of what religion *is* and *is not*. Ritual and belief can now surround the popular and secular as easily—perhaps even more easily—than it can modern religious institutions. "Surfing the waves and online communities; combinative beliefs drawing from multiple religious streams and celebrity culture; gothic themes and hell, even God—these are sources for sacred expression and ritual activity in American cultures today for more and more people dissatisfied with Religion" (Laderman). Comic books and graphic novels are proving to be no exception, of course. Numerous scholarly publications have been permeating the weakening barrier between the real-world spirituality and the popular medium. In all of these, however, an odd subset of phenomena has gone unmentioned: when, as Laderman puts it, "the Man of Steel has greater theological resonance in American society than the man of peace," what is to be done with, for instance, the religions of Krypton, Superman's home planet? To put it another way, if fiction informs our religion, how might fiction's religion likewise influence us? The concern is not with Superman or any one character in particular but with the potential for readers' own spiritual patency irrupting from an engagement with the fictional. In examining the fictitious scriptures of several comics works, I arrive at a theory suggesting that these imagined sacred texts, these "fictoscriptures," may allow us a new path for contact with our own sacred.

A number of comics series or storylines were considered for this analysis, but only a few significant ones will be highlighted to clarify the details of the theory, to test its use, and to suggest how it might be taken even further. The breadth of consulted works represents a span of years, publishers, and genres, and there is no reason to believe that omitted works would not fit into the analyses that emerged from the given sample.[1] In reviewing this corpus, seven traits frequently arose, communicating to audiences that a fictional writing within the narratives was held as sacred by populations of the characters—an intradiegetic sacred text, or, for the sake of brevity, what I'm calling fictoscripture. These fictoscriptures resembled, often in superficial ways, real-world scripture recognizable to the reader, yet were clearly inventions (and not adaptations) for the narrative. For *Cerebus*, Dave Sim, with assistance from Gerhard, fashioned the Booke of Ricke and, later, the Booke of Cerebus in the self-published collected volumes *Rick's Story* and *Latter Days*. Jonathan Hickman and his art team of Nick Dragotta, Frank Martin, and Rus Wooton centered their series *East of West* on the Message, a tripartite prediction of the end of the world for an alternate-history Earth. And the eponymous Crime Bible, a sacred text of villainy, was featured across several comics series in the DC Comics superhero universe involving author Greg Rucka. I will begin by utilizing these three in-story sacred texts to demonstrate the seven observed traits of most fictoscriptures.

(1) *Archaic diction.* Few of the fictoscriptures are written in an informal vernacular. Moreover, they often employ archaic word spellings, forms, and grammar to convey a sense of historicity and authority. This style of diction usually invokes the language of the King James Bible, employing frequent sentences beginning with *and*, as well as rhetorical devices such as syndenton and polysyndeton. Sims's *Cerebus* seems to take particularly unrestrained glee at these archaisms, giving the sincere Booke of Ricke a tinge of satire: "And that first morning was Cerebvs with mee in the sanctvarie and hee spake vnto mee" (*Book 12* 108). The Crime Bible, utilized across DC Comics 2006–2009 storylines in *52*, *The Crime Bible: The Five Lessons of Blood*, and *Final Crisis: Revelations*, utilizes a mix of the antiquated "ye" and interjection "yea" along with a tellingly informal "ain't" and modern "handcuffs" to suggest the writing's utilization by the undereducated criminal element: "'For choice is the domain only of the strong, the way of true freedom. / Trapped within the law, weak ye are revealed, and thus choice ain't for ye.' And saying thus, the handcuffs snapped closed, the beatings did begin. For forty days and nights, yea, they did torture the detective . . . / Until his mind became as broken as his body" (Johns, Morrison, et al., "Week Twenty-Three" 8).

(2) *Kephalaiac paratext.* When the service leader reads the Crime Bible passage aloud, she concludes by citing it as "from the Epic of Moriarty, Book of Crime, Chapter twenty-seven, verses seven through twelve" (Johns, Morrison, et al., "Week Twenty-Three" 8). Frequently, when the Crime Bible is recited, the passage is identified as being part of a contingent book, such as "The Book of Blood," "The Book of Kürten," or "The Book of Lilith," with an assigned chapter and verse. The overall effect is one of cohesion: though only snippets are given, the reader is left to understand that they are part of a larger whole text. This technique can be found throughout the fictoscriptures, though not always in the biblical chapter-and-verse form of the Crime Bible, the Booke of Ricke, or the Booke of Cerebus. So, rather than situate this trait in purely Judeo-Christian terms, I like to qualify this form of paratext as kephalaiac (Aland and Aland 247), namely, the system predating the canonization of the New Testament and applicable to other sacred texts (e.g., the surat and ayat of the Qur'an).

(3) *Prophetic revelation.* While the scheming Cerebus's "revelations" for the Booke of Cerebus were likely guileful constructions, the words in the Book of Ricke from his erstwhile apostle come from a sincerely inspired, if also delusional, place. In Image Comics' *East of West* series, the Message is constructed of not one but three separate prophecies: Prophet Elijah Longstreet's "The Second Book of Revelation," Chief Red Cloud's waking vision, and preceding exiled Chinese leader Chairman Mao Zedong's deathbed addendum to "The Little Red Book." Individually, each of the three texts makes little sense; only together do they become an "interlocking apocrypha, collectively called by believers *The Message*" (Hickman et al., Vol. 1, 11). Moreover, Ezra Orion, the Keeper of the Message, must take desperate measures and physically ingest the pages of the Message. Thereby he "devoured the three-fold Message at the fall of Armistice and became the Living Word. Apocrypha made flesh," guided by an external or, rather, internalized transcendent source (Hickman et al., Vol. 5, 116–17).

(4) *Rarity.* None of these fictoscriptures are the product of commercial or mass production. Quite the opposite, they are usually extremely rare artifacts, lending to the aura of their supposed power. The Crime Bible is not only made of stone physically, but, in fact, "Cain used that stone to commit the first murder, when he battled his brother Abel to the death" (Johns, Morrison, et al., "Week 25" 1). The Message, too, resides primarily at Armistice, the landing site of a colossal meteor, later made a pilgrimage site for the faithful; it could be said to be all the rarer still when it becomes physically and spiritually embodied in Ezra Orion as the Living Word.

Figure 4.1. A page from the Crime Bible, demonstrating a stylized font and kephalaiac form, *Final Crisis: Revelations*, page 1, by Greg Rucka, Philip Tan, Jonathan Glapion, and Jeff de los Santos. Copyright © 2008 DC Comics

(5) *Stylized font*. When the fictoscriptures are shown directly to the reader, the letterer or designer necessarily employs a manner of font distinct from that of any other caption or dialogue. Each issue of Crime Bible begins with an excerpt from the Book of Blood specially designed by Steve Liber and Eric Trautmann. In addition to its kephalaiac paratext, the page also features an illustration in the style of Gustav Doré, dark red italicized type, and an almost-rune-like title across the top. Rucka continues with this motif in the collected *Final Crisis: Revelations* with a similar selection from the Crime Bible's "Words of Lilith" (aka "The Book of Lilith") as its first page.

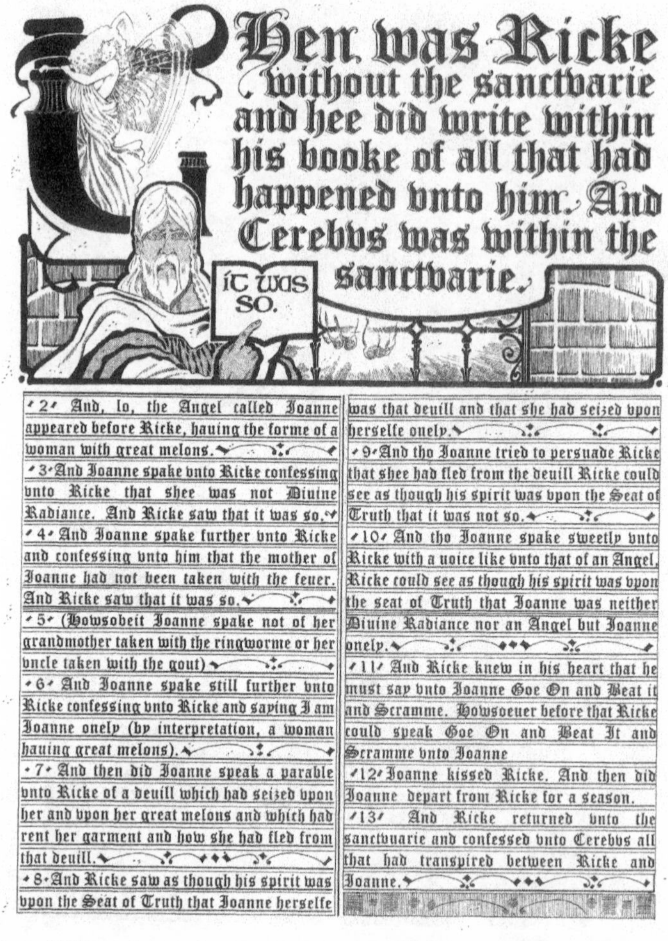

Figure 4.2. A page from the Booke of Ricke, with archaic diction accompanying kephalaiac form and heavily stylized font, *Cerebus, Book 15: Latter Days*, page 64, Dave Sim, Gerhard. Copyright © 2001 Aardvark-Vanaheim

When Sim first relates the Booke of Ricke in his *Cerebus* comic, it takes on the form of a traditional Christian Bible with historiated drop caps and pilcrows (e.g., Sim, *Rick's Story* 108); when he revisits more of the text later in the series, it is highly illuminated, set in multiple columns, and calligraphic (e.g., Sim, *Latter Days* 64).The overall effect in each of these cases is the imbuing of the objectively mundane words with special significance, a kind of typographic elevation.

(6) *Coded gnosis.* As noted, the Message from *East of West* becomes somewhat choate only once Longstreet's, Red Cloud's, and Mao's words are

combined. Even then, when the words are grammatical and syntactical, they operate at an abstracted level of metaphor and symbol, only through exegetic interpretation arriving at concrete meaning. For example, it is only upon the revelation that anthropomorphized Death and Mao's descendent have had a child that a passage of the Message makes literal sense: "Of the third, but not of the three. A lotus, the death and resurrection of love" (Hickman et al., Vol. 1, 45)—where Premier Mao Xiaolian is the "lotus," Death is no longer "of the three" with the other apocalyptic Horsemen, and, with their child, they together are "of the third." Their offspring, the boy dubbed Babylon, is the prophesied bringer of the end, the Beast, made possible only by the attempts of Death and Xiaolian's adversaries to destroy them: "To rise up against the Beast will be to bring him forth, all weep at the coming of last days" (Hickman et al., Vol. 3, 96). The Crime Bible engages in similar coding, never outright naming characters in its fictoscripture but plainly referring to Renee Montoya (in her garb as the featureless Question) as the "Faceless" or to centuries-old antagonist Vandal Savage as the mythic Cain. Cerebus himself is captured and indoctrinated into the cult that worships him only once he can correctly interpret passages from the Booke of Ricke. This coded gnosis in each case not only lends a mystique to each fictoscripture but also creates a space for those like Eliza Orion to serve as pious experts and powerful exegetes of the words. One must have a gift—or a blessing—in order to properly comprehend what is being communicated, in effect.

(7) *Actualization.* The corollary to the coded gnosis is the realization of the fictoscriptures' prophetic messages of what is to come. That is, what they predict, in fact, occurs. "The Crime Bible foretells Cain's return, and the vengeance he wreaks upon the world, upon God's creation for the punishment he has endured. Cain's return heralds the end of the world, the death of the old God. In the Book of Adumbrations, we are told, Cain ushers in the age of Apokolips on Earth" (Rucka et al., 106). All this proves true: Cain indeed returns, and his opponent, the Spectre, is made his thrall to overwrite the Earth in evil's likeness, but only temporarily (126–28). A last-minute sacrifice by the Question allows the Spectre to reassert control and undo Cain's actions. Additionally, the Booke of Ricke and the Booke of Cerebus are similarly fulfilled, even if it is accomplished by Cerebus's own executive fiat. Even the supernatural beings in *East of West*, the Four Horsemen, are beholden to the Message's actualization. Death explains, "The Message dictates all of what the Chosen do. It's what guides the Horsemen. None of them will step outside the path that word has laid before them" (Hickman et al., Vol. 1, 134); even those who attempt to do so end up, as in the case of

the Beast, bringing about that which they seek to prevent. Whatever actions they take adhere to the "structure" of "the Message," "that order that rules this world. There's a place where all mankind is headed, and the Message shows the way" (Hickman et al., vol. 2, 48). Ultimately, explains the shaman Cheveyo, while "there's always a choice, son . . . one either follows the winding way, or wanders in the wilderness. One path is The Message. The other . . . is not" (Hickman et al., Vol. 2, 130).

One can reverse the process and ask whether a comic includes what I have termed fictoscripture by testing it with these seven traits. Take the case of "The Book of Black," the chronicles of the supervillain Black Hand during DC Comics' "Blackest Night" storyline. While much of the fictoscripture is written in casual, modern language, its final installment is a blend of both the coded gnosis and archaic diction traits, transcribed almost entirely in an alien language (Johns 104). Its sections are distinctly marked as chapters and verses (kephalaiac paratext), and it is lettered in a jagged, black script suggesting its connection to death and rot (stylized font). Its rarity (along with the "gnosis" aspect of the coded gnosis trait) is difficult to ascertain, since the reader does not know who possesses this "Book of Black" during the "Blackest Night" storyline or what allusions would have been taken as either figurative or symbolic. Yet, as with the Crime Bible, its predictions of the dead returning prove true (actualization), if temporary (95).

Do the Black Hand's words qualify as prophetic revelation? That is, can readers ascribe the source of his thoughts to a power or divinity outside of himself? In the story, William Hand becomes empowered by a Black Lantern ring, similar to the heroic Green Lantern's power source, upon committing suicide (Johns, Mahnke, et al. 20). His reanimation as the Black Hand heralds the coming of Nekron, Lord of the Unliving, who is later defeated by Green Lantern and his allies. Therefore, in some sense, one could shoehorn the prophetic revelation trait into his "Book of Black" if it is viewed as being inspired by either Nekron or the Black Lantern energy itself. At the same time, neither one is properly divine or transcendent, so, unless the reader wishes to grant the Green Lantern a similarly spiritual status, the Black Hand might fail as prophetic, and, in turn, his "Book of Black" may be only the rantings of a madman penned in semi-biblical form.

Of course, probing the "properly divine" status of any of these fictoscriptures produces dubious results. Above it was suggested that Cerebus could be deemed a prophet if his words originate from without, from a transcendent source. Strictly speaking, *all* words, either in fictoscriptures specifically or in comics in general, come from an outside source: the author. To borrow from

Foucault, the author function here could refer to the comic's writer alone, its writer and artist(s) as visual storytellers, the entire creative team in addition to the editorial staff, or even all the comics professionals involved in a shared property (e.g., Green Lantern over the decades).

Asking what does and does not qualify as "prophetic" in the case of fictoscripture opens the discussion to a broader question: before considering the fictional, how do we judge what is to be regarded as prophetic in real-life scripture? Some degree of authority, implicit or explicit, lies behind the assignment of genuine prophecy in a text. And, even as "religion has been compromised" (to invoke Laderman again), recognition of core scriptures remains relatively unchallenged. Therefore, another way of asking the question of judging prophetic value would be, What makes a sacred text sacred?

Mircea Eliade's model for the sacred has some specific applications to fictoscripture—and, in return, fictoscripture may have its own insights into the Eliadic sacred. In Eliade's system, a hierophany is where the godly, the transcendent, or the divine (what Eliade calls in toto "the sacred") emerges into mortal, physical, worldly space ("the profane"); moreover, this "irruption of sacred space" is not only a functioning paradox—somehow, the unlimited and godlike existing in finite and concrete material—but allows access to what Eliade considers the truly Real (Eliade qtd in Wagner 172). "While the profane is vanishing and fragile, full of shadows, the sacred is eternal, full of substance and reality" (Pals qtd in Wagner 172). A hierophany can occur anywhere if only because everywhere is lacking in its connection to the Real.

As a general concept hierophany has its problems. In her book *Godwired: Religion, Ritual, and Virtual Reality*, Rachel Wagner confronts weaknesses in Eliade's system. Though the concepts of sacred and profane are alluringly useful in theological and religious studies, she admits, they may present a "too easy dualism" (78). Additionally, Eliade had to gloss over much in the way of any culture-specific history and envision an ahistorical space in which to anchor his model. Bryan S. Rennie, Westminster College Professor of Religion, compiles a list of indictments against Eliade's ahistoricity:

> J. Z. Smith accuses Eliade of ignoring the categories of space and time and excluding historical data. Ninian Smart also makes this accusation of ahistoricism and the devaluation of historical consciousness. Robert Baird criticizes the ahistorical nature of Eliade's search for structures. Guilford Dudley considered Eliade's interpretation of archetypes to be so insulated from history as to be closed to empirical verification. (229)

Such problems with hierophany, however, are not insurmountable, especially given the proper environment in which to apply them. Perhaps it cannot be used in all times and in all places, as Eliade may have imagined. Moreover, it may come with a Christian bias or an ahistorical skew; left unaddressed and uncorrected, these issues largely hobble the concept. However, when applied to circumstances that frustrate such incarnation and operate outside of traditional history and temporality, hierophany can be recovered as an immensely powerful theological tool. In a sense, hierophany can be redeemed. What would such a circumstance be?

Fictoscripture is the ideal environment for invoking hierophany. Indeed, Rennie's examination of hierophany points to a hypothetical scenario in which Eliade's ideas would function more stably: "It is not so much that Eliade depreciates history, rather that he insists on the *appreciation* of the non-historical, the imaginative" (228). While modern society may put great value on what appears as the solid footing of history, closer inspection might reveal historicizing as its own, specialized version of mythologizing (231). Like Laderman, "Eliade is not particularly explicit about the survival of 'religion' in secular thought by that name. He is more forthcoming about the survival of myth. In Eliade's thought the two categories are inseparable. Where there is religion, there is myth; where there is myth, there is religion" (225). But rather than engage in a battle over whether history is myth, whether myth is religion, and which of either is the most "real," the more promising approach may be to sidestep the debate entirely and enter into a consciously non-real arena. Rennie almost suggests this as he repositions Eliade as "insist[ing] that the sacred (and therefore the real) is present and active *in the imaginary universes of contemporary humanity*" (233, my emphasis). Wagner, channeling J. Z. Smith, points to the same maneuver: "Reverse the polarities of the maxim 'as above, so below,' yielding the formula 'as below, so above' thereby suggesting some theory of projection in the service of legitimating human institutions and practices" (Smith qtd in Wagner 173). Both Rennie and Smith-cum-Wagner are hunting for a diegetic space for which they do not have a name: Comics.

Eliade, too, could practically have been discussing comics when detailing where hierophany today occurs. He considered the sacred to exist, but hidden in modern human culture (i.e., for Eliade, the West): "Even the non-religious Western man still dreams, reads novels and poetry, listens to music, goes to the theatre, loved 'Nature,' and so forth. And this means that *unconsciously* he communicates with the sacred" (Eliade, "Sacred Tradition," cited in Rennie 227). As such, the sacred is quietly mixed into the culture, knowingly or otherwise. His non-religious man still seeks, unwittingly, to recapture the space of the religious man, one with "interruptions, breaks in it; some parts of space are qualitatively different from others" (Eliade 20). On one level, this reads as a description of the panels and gutters of the comics medium; the white of the page and the border of a panel as "the experience of an opposition between space that is sacred—the only *real* and *real-ly* existing space—and all other space, the formless expanse surrounding it" (20), except the formlessness here is reversed. Sacred space is the surrounding, formless expanse around the unreal panels. The medium could, arguably, be the unconscious expression of non-religious man's search for the sacred, recreating a model of sacred and profane space with every layout.

However, one need not accept an idea of unconscious intent or a clean divide between religious man and non-religious man in order to witness fictoscripture embodying Eliade's planar concepts more generally. Eliade claims, "Where the break-through from plane to plane has been effected by a hierophany, there too an opening has been made, either upward (the divine world) or downward (the underworld, the world of the dead). The three cosmic levels—earth, heaven, underworld—have been put in communication" (26). Elsewhere, he qualifies the "cosmic levels" as "individual, social, and cosmic" (170), but the overall trajectory remains the same. Downward moves thicker into the profane, while upward moves toward the sacred. These are not to be taken literally but as expressions of what theologian Jeffery Burton Russell calls "metaphorical ontology":

> Traditional Jewish and Christian thinkers recognized that metaphor expresses a deeper reality than can be attained through the overt sense. . . . Because the vastness and richness of reality cannot be expressed by the overt sense of a statement alone, metaphorical ontology is necessary. It is also necessary because a sense of contemplation and wonder are at least as important for understanding the world as efforts to determine facts. (8–9)

Metaphor, according to Russell, has a closer, deeper relationship to Eliade's Real than the literal and profane. Therefore, the metaphorical relationship here between up and down, between traversing planes, echoes and enforces the divine-like role of authors creating these fictoscriptures. To the characters of their stories, authors occupy a sacred space similar to that of real-world prophecy's divinities. Comics creators are the godhead of fictoscriptures.

Not only do comics and their inclusion of fictoscripture bypass many of hierophany's problems conceptually but, perhaps surprisingly, they also invite its practice. Is our relationship to the sacred or the divine also like that of comics characters to an author? Are we trapped by the profane in our own panels, only experiencing the divine when/if we witness the formless, invisible divide between all things? Is our universe flat and static compared to the flow of a surrounding sacred space? Quite possibly, perhaps. "Eliade predicted, a 'new literature of the fantastic' is destined to evolve," reminds Professor of Bible Eric J. Ziolkowski, and comics may be that literature. "Far from being escapist or 'unconnected with reality and history,' this fantastic literature of the future will be 'like a window onto meaning,' and will thus enable us to 'rediscover the epic quality . . . We will finally rediscover the mythical element, the symbolical element, the rites which have nourished all civilizations. Certainly, they will not be recognized as such under their camouflage. It will be a *new* mythology'" (510). Possibly, fictoscripture is that "new mythology." But, whereas it may be helpful for us to envision imperfectly Eliade's sacred planes, fictoscripture more compellingly provides a method by which to experience hierophany.

Since hierophany can be taken as a compressed point between up and down that is more accurately communicated metaphorically than envisaged literally—as sacred both within and around and through the profane—fictoscriptures may direct an audience's attention "downward," toward the dead tree of paper and dyes of ink, even as they simultaneously redirect focus upward, toward not only the authors and authorities of the would-be prophecies but also beyond to the sacred. The best example, the truest metaphor, may be the wormhole, described by Brian Greene, author of *The Elegant Universe*, "as a bridge or tunnel that provides a shortcut from one region of the universe to another" (264). Such a tunnel occurs only when there has been a puncture in the fabric of space, a downward thrust that meets with a matching point at another, faraway point in space. "If the fabric of space can tear, developing punctures as in 11.1(b), and if these punctures can 'grow' tentacles that merge together as in 11.1(c), a spatial bridge would connect the previously remote regions. This is a wormhole" (265). Drive one's attention downward toward the fictoscripture, toward the profane and material comic book, and enough of a focus could, theoretically, connect one to the sacred, inverted on the other side of the same plane.

This model of a "wormhole sacred" is necessarily imperfect, for either hierophany or wormholes, since, as Greene explains, "Regions lying off of the membrane merely reflect the inadequacy of the illustration which depicts

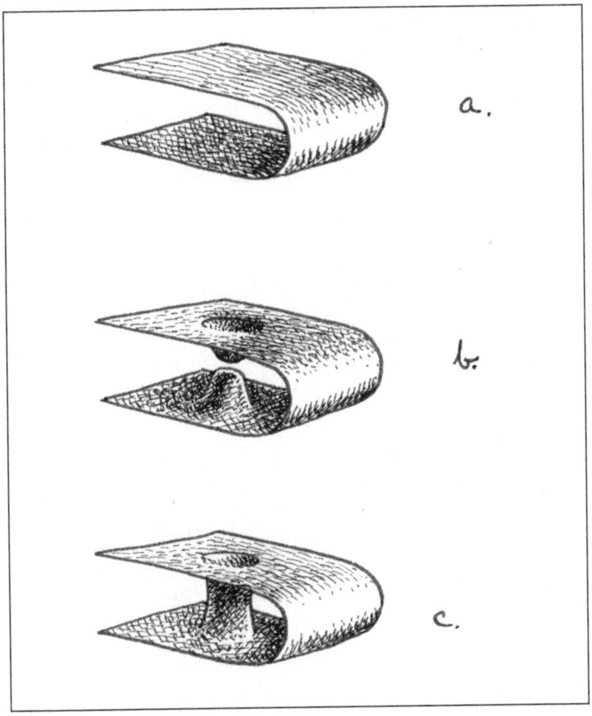

Figure 4.3. A u-diagram of theoretical wormholes in quantum physics, a model for this sacred "shortcut." Original rendering by Carla Speed McNeil.

the U-shaped universe as if it were an object within our higher-dimensional universe" (265). In short, the limitation is not that of the model but of our imaginations. In fact, Russell himself foresaw these shared limits when discussing metaphorical ontology: "The intellect can conceive of these options [eternity, timelessness, transcending time] but the imagination balks—as it does *in quantum physics*" (Greene 9, my emphasis). The idea is more important than the map: plunging from the profane of fictoscriptures into them could transport us through to a distant sacred that we might never reach traditionally.

To serve as an example of this potential experience—of this driving down into the profane of the fictoscripture in order to access what I term a wormhole sacred on the other side—I offer a reading of *Animal Man* #5, "The Coyote Gospel." The 1988 issue by writer Grant Morrison and the art team of Chas Truog, Doug Hazelwood, John Costanza, and Tatjana Wood tells of the title character encountering in the desert a strange, coyote-like humanoid creature whom the narrator identifies as Crafty. Readers are informed that

Crafty comes from another reality, one of endless cartoon violence between all manner of anthropomorphized animals, all unable to suffer permanent, mortal injury. Crafty was banished from that reality after he confronted its God, but his life of condemnation in "the hell above" (also called "the second reality") would grant peace to the warring beasts of his world (Morrison et al. 20). This whole backstory is told via "The Gospel according to Crafty,"[2] easily discernable as a piece of fictoscripture, given the criterion listed above: it features verse-like diction—"He took himself into the desert. And rose up. And went into the presence of God. And God spoke unto Crafty" (19)—that exists solely as a scroll in a cylinder around Crafty's neck, is written in an indecipherable language embellished with flourishes of nonsense type, and tells of an ersatz *Looney Tunes* reality coded behind copyright-safe alternatives (e.g., "Crafty" for "Wile E. Coyote," "AJAX" for "ACME"). However, the "Gospel" offers a hesitant prophecy for Crafty, namely, that "while he lived, there still remained the hope that one day he might **return**. And on that day **overthrow** the tyrant God. And build a **better** world" (21).

Initially, the prophecy of Crafty's "Gospel" does not appear to be actualized, since Crafty is finally slain at the issue's end. In fact, an unnamed trucker who, a year prior, had accidentally run down Crafty with his vehicle is bent on destroying Crafty, believing him to be a diabolical creature, "the devil" (Morrison et al. 10). The trucker's life had coincidentally unraveled after his encounter with Crafty, as did life for the would-be starlet hitchhiking with him: she became a prostitute and died in a drug raid, while he lost his partner Billy to a similar truck run-down. Now the trucker has found Crafty and shoots him off a cliff, then drops a massive boulder on him, all to no avail. The man also has set bombs that prematurely detonate, still failing to kill Crafty but accidentally wounding the trucker himself. Only a "magic bullet," smelted from the silver cross Billy had given him, terminates Crafty, just moments after conveying his unreadable "Gospel" to Animal Man. The trucker dies, thinking he has saved the world, while Crafty, too, bleeds out in the crossroads. He was unable to return to his world and stage a revolution or to maintain the peace that his expulsion guaranteed. Most tragically, Crafty dies both from the trucker's own religious dedication and also without anyone, save perhaps the reader, knowing his story in full—"The Coyote Gospel."

However, Crafty may have been more successful than he knew. Morrison's story underscores the hierophantic nature that informs all fictoscriptures. Crafty's cartoon-world, perhaps hyperbolically, is considered "heaven and earth," while Animal Man's superhero universe is labeled "the hell above." Regardless of how they are described, heavenly or hellishly, one or the other

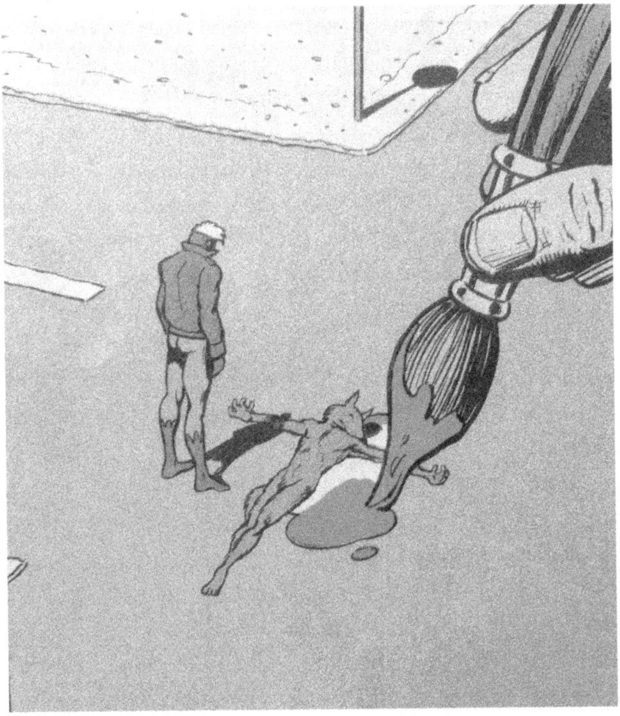

Figure 4.4. The final panel from *Animal Man* #5, wherein Crafty's God is seen to exist in an elevated state above the titular character's reality, as well, *Animal Man* #5, by Grant Morrison, Chas Truog, and Doug Hazlewood. Copyright © 1988 DC Comics

is a move closer to or further from the Real. If Crafty was looking to "overthrow the tyrant God," then he was looking to overthrow the power that controls Animal Man's world too, namely, the comics creators themselves. *Animal Man* hints at the rule of the author(s) over the diegetic landscape in its final panel of "The Coyote Gospel": the same paintbrush and hand of God that governed Crafty's cartoon-world also controls Animal Man's own (Morrison et al. 24). To a character like Animal Man, the comics authors exist on a transcendent plane,[3] and Crafty has already demonstrated, albeit fictionally, that one cannot only ascend to confront sacred beings but can be personally transported to a higher plane. If readers invest any emotion or sympathy in Crafty's plight, it is because they acknowledge something true about his story—that there is something sacred beyond our profane world that we might access hierophantically. In such a way, his prophecy remains active: each time we read *Animal Man* #5, Crafty is resurrected to convey his message and to prod readers toward engaging the forces above us.

Of course, we readers cannot take a cartoon elevator, as Crafty does, up to a sacred space, but we could utilize the fictoscripture to move down, further into the profane, and effect a wormhole to such a sacred. If reversed, "The Gospel of Crafty" offers a fictoscriptural path down several layers of reality, from our experienced real-world to that of Animal Man's superhero reality, and further to the godhead of Crafty existence and, even deeper, into his native cartoonish world. The tendency here might be to see the *Looney Tunes*–like plane as extraordinarily profane, at a *greater* distance from the Real than the reality in which *Animal Man* #5 can be purchased. However, its exaggerated images and ridiculous proportions lie just atop pure metaphor and abstraction. If we were to invert our orientation, pass through the modeled wormhole, Crafty's cartoonish land may exist just slightly below a plane consisting entirely of ideas and concepts, divorced from profane material and matter. Here, we once again find Russell's metaphorical ontology, where the less tangible is the more real. Regardless of his fictionality, sympathy for Crafty and for his undying brethren is the first step in connecting with a Real that lies through the wormhole. Allowing ourselves into the profane and considering a power behind it may chart us closer to an inverted sacred.

In Laderman's landscape, the wormhole sacred could look something like this chapter—according sincere consideration to fictional relics from popular commodities. The brilliance of a lightsaber, the global echo of a retweet, the guerilla artistry of graffiti: any of these could be a focus point for a sacred we locate less in them than through them. "We are consumers and manufacturers of the sacred," says Wagner (93), and we can also be its surfers, riding a wave of fictoscriptures' sacred on through to the experience of a genuine source. "The sacred and profane are at root simply a means of considering reflections, of making sense of signs and signifieds" (97), and we must not discard fictional signifiers simply because of their fictionality.

Religion *has* been compromised; but we've found another access point. Perhaps we have hacked the religious system with a comics code.

NOTES

1. In earlier drafts of this chapter, I included analyses of the following additional works that I would welcome interested readers to consider for themselves. See Bill Mantlo (w), Mike Mignola (p), Al Gordon (i), Christie Scheele (c), and Ken Bruzenak (l), "Rocket Raccoon," in *Annihilation Classic*; and Alan Moore (w), Gabriel Andrade (a), Digikore Studios (c), and Jaymes Reed (l), *Crossed Plus One Hundred*, vol. 1.

2. Interestingly, the narrative voice translates the scroll's title as "The Gospel of Crafty"; the title of the actual issue is "The Coyote Gospel." This slippage suggests that the story's

title might not be referring directly to the text Crafty is carrying but, instead, to the overall narrative—the cruel trick of fate played on Crafty, leading to his permanent demise.

3. Notably, Morrison concludes his run on *Animal Man* by visiting the character on the page and revealing himself to be the comics writer penning the superhero's adventures.

BIBLIOGRAPHY

Aland, Kurt, and Barbara Aland. *The Text of the New Testament*. Translated by Erroll F. Rhodes. Grand Rapids, MI: Eerdmans, 1987.

Eliade, Mircea. *The Sacred and the Profane: The Nature of Religion*. New York: Harcourt, 1987.

Greene, Brian. *The Elegant Universe: Superstrings, Hidden Dimensions, and the Quest for the Ultimate Theory*. New York: W. W. Norton, 1999.

Hickman, Jonathan, Nick Dragotta, Frank Martin, and Rus Wooton. *East of West, Volume 1*. Berkeley: Image Comics, 2013.

Hickman, Jonathan, Nick Dragotta, Frank Martin, and Rus Wooton. *East of West, Volume 2*. Berkeley: Image Comics, 2014.

Hickman, Jonathan, Nick Dragotta, Frank Martin, and Rus Wooton. *East of West, Volume 3*. Berkeley: Image Comics, 2014.

Hickman, Jonathan, Nick Dragotta, Frank Martin, and Rus Wooton. *East of West, Volume 5*. Berkeley: Image Comics, 2016.

Johns, Geoff. "The Book of Black." *Blackest Night: Tales of the Corps*. New York: DC Comics, 2010, 100–12.

Johns, Geoff, Doug Mahnke, Christian Alamy, Nei Ruffino, and Rob Leigh. "Tales of the Black Lantern." *Green Lantern* #43. New York: DC Comics, 2009.

Johns, Geoff, Grant Morrison, Greg Rucka, Mark Waid, Keith Giffen, Drew Johnson, Ray Snyder, and JG Jones. "Week Twenty-Three." 52. New York: DC Comics, 2006.

Johns, Geoff, Grant Morrison, Greg Rucka, Mark Waid, Keith Giffen, Drew Johnson, Ray Snyder, and JG Jones. "Week Twenty-Five." 52. New York: DC Comics, 2006.

Laderman, Gary. "Religion Is Dead; Long Live . . . the Sacred." *Sacred Matters: Religious Currents in Culture*. Emory University, April 18, 2014. Web. Accessed July 28, 2016.

Morrison, Grant (w), Chas Truog and Doug Hazlewood (a), and John Costanza (l). "The Coyote Gospel." *Animal Man* #5. New York: DC Comics, 1988.

Rennie, B. S. "The Religious Creativity of Modern Humanity: Some Observations on Eliade's Unfinished Thought." *Religious Studies* 31, no. 2 (June 1995): 221–35.

Rucka, Greg, Philip Tan, Jonathan Glapion, and Jeff de los Santos. *Final Crisis: Revelations*. New York: DC Comics, 2008.

Russell, Jeffrey Burton. *A History of Heaven: The Singing Silence*. Princeton: Princeton University Press, 1997.

Sim, Dave, and Gerhard. *Cerebus, Book 12: Rick's Story*. Windsor, ON: Aardvark-Vanaheim, 1998.

Sim, Dave, and Gerhard. *Cerebus, Book 15: Latter Days*. Windsor, ON: Aardvark-Vanaheim, 2001.

Wagner, Rachel. *Godwired: Religion, Ritual and Virtual Reality*. New York: Routledge, 2012.

Ziolkowski, Eric J. "Religion and Literature: Mircea Eliade and Northrup Frye." *Journal of Religion* 71, no. 4 (October 1991): 498–522.

Part II

REIMAGINING SACRED TEXTS THROUGH COMICS

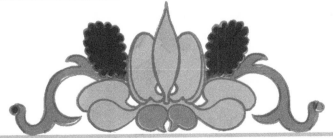

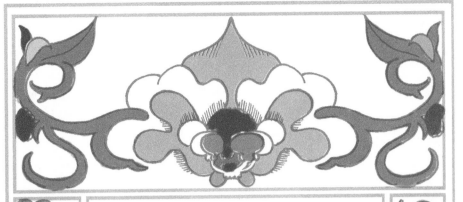

There are now Christian, Jewish, Hindu, Buddhist, and Muslim comic adaptations of sacred texts in English. For some children, this is their first (and perhaps only) encounter with the traditional stories and characters that have shaped their religious traditions. Yet, even as these graphic texts present themselves as faithful translations, they are instead critical reappropriations of sacred literature; they reimagine the sacred in the text/image form of the comic. These reimaginings can be as subtle, nuanced, and provocative as any Jewish midrash or Muslim hadith. But these graphic narratives do something these other, more traditional literatures do not: comics move us to *revision* the sacred within those traditional texts. This should be read both as a reimagining and a revisioning. In other words, the biblical text looks different to us now that we *see* how it appears in comic form. This visual appropriation of the sacred is really a thoughtful reworking of sacred literature. Where a painting might present a pictorial representation of sacred moments or religious characters, a comic weds image to text in order to rework the narrative itself. So if the comic is successful, a reader will not only see the text differently but also read the text anew. The scripted text itself, and not merely its representation in image, has changed for the comic reader. This is the radical pedagogical challenge of reimagining sacred texts through comics.

Chapter Five

MANY COMIC BOOK RAMAYANAS

Idealizing and Opposing Rama as the Righteous God-King

KARLINE McLAIN

THE RAMAYANA IS ONE OF INDIA'S TWO GREAT EPICS (THE OTHER BEING the Mahabharata), and its influence in the history of Hindu religious tradition and South Asian civilization cannot be overstated. Indeed, the acclaimed Indian author R. K. Narayan famously stated in the introduction to his shortened English translation of the epic that every individual living in India is aware of the story of the Ramayana in some measure or other (xxiii). The Ramayana is the story of Rama, who is frequently—though by no means universally—described as an ideal man and as a god incarnate in human form. In his roles as a son, husband, prince, and then king, Rama is often said to perfectly uphold *dharma*—a Sanskrit word that refers to righteous action in accordance with moral law—or, to uphold dharma as close to perfectly as anyone embodied in human form can be expected to. And yet certain episodes within the Ramayana are especially thorny—and therefore are of great interest to storytellers—for they raise important ethical questions about Rama's purported idealism in particular and about the human condition more generally.

Within Hinduism the two overarching categories of scripture are *shruti*, primary or direct revelation, comprising Vedic Sanskrit hymns believed to have been received by Hindu sages long ago directly from on high; and *smriti*, secondary or indirect revelation comprising texts composed by human beings. Whereas *shruti* scripture must be preserved precisely in its original language and metrical form, there is greater flexibility with *smriti* scripture, which can be retold in different languages and forms. The Sanskrit epics, including the Ramayana, are a subset of *smriti* known as *itihasa* ("history").

The earliest literary telling of the Ramayana was composed in Sanskrit by the poet Valmiki sometime during the first millennium BCE, and since its composition the story of Rama has been retold and re-created by many authors and performers utilizing numerous venues and media. In his oft-cited essay "Three Hundred Ramayanas," scholar A. K. Ramanujan has argued that these many Ramayana tellings may have very different relations to predecessors, and he reminds us that the Valmiki version should not be regarded as an Ur or original scripture, for the story was oral before it was written down: "In this sense, no text is original, yet no telling is a mere retelling—and the story has no closure, although it may be enclosed in a text. In India and Southeast Asia, no one ever reads the *Ramayana* or the *Mahabharata* for the first time. The stories are there, 'always already'" (46). In the past several decades, scholars have examined this multivocal nature of the Ramayana story over time, highlighting its variations according to historical period, political context, regional literary tradition, religious affiliation, intended audience, and genre.[1]

This chapter focuses on the multivocal nature of the Ramayana epic in Indian graphic narratives from the 1970s to the present. There is now a wealth of comic book and graphic novel retellings of the Ramayana that have been created either in India or by Indians living throughout the global Indian diaspora, including: "Rama" and "Valmiki's Ramayana" in the *Amar Chitra Katha* comic book series; the multi-issue "The Ramayana" line in the *Dreamland Publications* comic book series; the *Godavari Tales* issue in the *Vivalok Comics* series; the "Ramayan 3392 A.D." line in the *Liquid Comics* (formerly *Virgin Comics*) series; the "Sita" and "Ravana" comics in the *Campfire Mythology* comic book series; the graphic novel *Sita's Ramayana* by Samhita Arni and Moyna Chitrakar; and the graphic novel *Ramayana: Divine Loophole* by Sanjay Patel. Scholars have critically examined the Ramayana in a variety of popular media, from television to film to street theater, but no one has yet done an in-depth examination of the Ramayana in graphic narratives.

While Indian comics collectively present a spectrum of opinions about the god-king Rama and his moral idealism, there are two dominant narrative trends that arise in these graphic retellings of his story. The first trend is to uphold Rama as the ideal god-king by presenting Rama as the clear hero of the epic story both textually and visually, and by providing an apologetic defense of any of his deeds that could potentially be perceived as morally questionable. The second trend is to critique Rama as the ideal god-king by focusing the textual and visual narrative on other protagonists within the epic storyline, and thereby engage in a critical examination of Rama through feminist and/or subaltern perspectives. To limit the scope of analysis in this essay, given the elongated and meandering nature of epic Indian storytelling, I will focus on three episodes in the Ramayana, engaging in a comparative analysis of how these episodes are told, both textually and visually, first in a subset of comics that idealize Rama and next in a subset of comics that call his idealism into question. The three episodes are: 1) the slaying of Vali; 2) Sita's trial by fire; and 3) the epic conclusion.

Through this exploration of comic book Ramayanas, this essay sheds light on the continuing influence of the Ramayana epic among the current generation of Indians, and the contested interpretation of the god Rama within contemporary Hinduism and South Asian culture more broadly. Whereas the comic book medium is especially noteworthy for its hero-making capacities, the comics that critique Rama demonstrate how the interplay of text and image in comics can also be put to work to raise critical questions about religious and cultural definitions of the heroic. As I will discuss in the concluding paragraphs of this chapter, these comics that idealize Rama and those that question his idealism, when taken together, are valuable for their ongoing contributions to the multivocal nature of the Ramayana story—and this is especially important now, when such multivocalism is often threatened by forces that would prefer to reduce this scripture to a single, hegemonic interpretation centered on Rama's idealism.

. . .

The earliest Indian comic book retelling of the Ramayana appeared in the *Amar Chitra Katha* series in 1970. *Amar Chitra Katha* (or *ACK*) is the dominant Indian comic book series. Loved by millions of fans in India and throughout the global Indian diaspora, it has sold over 100 million issues and has dominated the Indian comic book market since it was founded by Anant Pai in 1967. *Amar Chitra Katha* means "Immortal Picture Stories," and these comics immortalize India's own mythological and historical heroes as their protagonists. They are created for the English-speaking middle classes: those that Anant Pai feared were not learning Hindu mythology or Indian history in their English-medium schools and were therefore losing touch with what it meant to be Hindu and Indian.[2]

Anant Pai has repeatedly stressed the importance of accuracy in retelling classical Hindu scripture in the comic book medium. For instance, in 1975 there was a big Ramayana festival in Mumbai, with performances, scholars discussing the epic, and other activities that drew a large audience. At one of the academic panels, a question arose about the parentage of Ravana, the lead villain of the Ramayana, and in response a man pulled out his copy of

"The Lord of Lanka" comic book to answer the question. Anant Pai recalled the impact this made on him: "This made me realize that I must be accurate, that people think the *ACKs* are a legitimate source of these sacred stories" (McLain, *India's Immortal Comic Books* 35).

In creating the "Rama" comic book, Anant Pai set out to retell, accurately, the epic based on its earliest literary telling—the Ramayana composed in Sanskrit by the poet Valmiki—but rendered in a visual medium that would be appealing to the generation of children growing up in India in the 1970s. In his telling, Rama is a martial hero who valiantly defeats the ten-headed demon-king Ravana in an epic battle, thereby ending a period of great chaos and immorality and initiating an era of peace, justice, and prosperity. The introduction to the "Rama" issue proclaims Rama as an ideal god-king: "The idea that God fulfills Himself in the best of men is conveyed by the life of Rama and that is the story of Ramayana." Yet all claims of accuracy aside, Anant Pai made noteworthy editorial decisions in retelling the Ramayana epic that served to highlight Rama as an ideal king and as a god incarnate. Indeed, Rama is so perfectly heroic that there is no room for moral ambiguity in this telling of the epic, as can be seen when we analyze how this comic approaches each of the three episodes noted above: the slaying of Vali, Sita's trial by fire, and the conclusion.

Rama's encounter with Vali takes place after Rama's wife, Sita, has been abducted by Ravana. As Rama is roaming about, seeking clues to figure out who has captured his wife and where he has taken her, Rama encounters Sugreeva in the jungle. Sugreeva is a monkey-king-in-exile, who offers to help Rama form an army to reclaim his wife, if only Rama would first help Sugreeva to reclaim his own throne and his wife, Tara, from his brother, Vali. Rama agrees, and a battle ensues between Vali and Sugreeva, while Rama watches from behind a tree, with his bow and arrow at the ready. When he gets a clear shot, Rama shoots Vali. As Vali lies dying, he questions Rama's act on several grounds—including the justice of shooting Vali while in hiding, for the warrior's code of honor requires face-to-face combat; the justice of immediately taking Sugreeva's side in their brotherly dispute, without ever speaking with Vali; and the justice of convicting Vali for improper behavior with Tara, for the social mores of monkeys and humans are different. Rama defends his action against each of these charges, providing a counterargument for why his action is dharmic. Ultimately, Vali is persuaded and, through this exchange, comes to have faith in Rama during his final moments of life.

This episode is one that can provoke debate about who is in the right and who is in the wrong, and it is not always apparent that Rama is in the right. For instance, in his prose retelling of the Ramayana epic, author R. K. Narayan expresses his own discomfort about the moral ambiguity of the slaying of Vali by including these editorial comments at the outset of his "Vali" chapter:

> The perfect man takes a false step, apparently commits a moral slip, and we ordinary mortals stand puzzled before the incident. It may be less an actual error of commission on his part than a lack of understanding on ours; measured in Eternity, such an event might stand out differently. But until we attain that breadth of view, we are likely to feel disturbed and question the action. Rama was an ideal man, all his faculties in control in any circumstance, one possessed of an unwavering sense of justice and fair play. Yet he once acted, as it seemed, out of partiality, half-knowledge, and haste, and shot and destroyed, from hiding, a creature who had done him no harm, not even seen him. This is one of the most controversial chapters in the Ramayana. (90)

In the "Rama" comic, Anant Pai chose to eliminate Vali's lengthy death scene, and thereby avoid any moral ambiguity over Rama's decision to kill Vali. The entire encounter at the monkey kingdom is presented in just two panels in the comic. In the first, Sugreeva requests that Rama help him to overthrow Vali and regain his wife, in exchange for his help in finding Sita. In the second, we see a coronation scene, and the text informs us, "Rama killed Vali and set Sugreeva on the throne. Vali's son, Angada, was crowned prince" (18). Vali therefore does not charge Rama with cowardice in this telling, nor does he question the morality of Rama's action in taking sides, perhaps for selfish reasons, in the dispute between Vali and Sugreeva.

Through omitting other episodes with the potential to be morally discomforting, Pai unquestioningly presents Rama's idealism throughout the "Rama" comic. A second example is found in the omission of the trial by fire episode in this comic book. This incident takes place after Rama has defeated Ravana in battle, and he then sends for Sita. Sita, who has been imprisoned by Ravana for months, looks forward to rejoining her husband. When she arrives, however, Rama does not welcome her with open arms but instead coldly declares that he has completed his duty, and she is free to go. Here I quote Rama in Narayan's prose retelling:

> My task here is done. I have now freed you. I have fulfilled my mission. All this effort has been not to attain personal satisfaction for

> you or me. It was to vindicate the honour of the Ikshvahu race and to honour our ancestors' codes and values. After all this, I must tell you that it is not customary to admit back to the normal married fold a woman who has resided all alone in a stranger's house. There can be no question of us living together again. I leave you free to go where you please and to choose any place to live in. I do not restrict you in any manner. (148)

Sita is deeply troubled by the implication that she has not remained faithful to her husband during her period of imprisonment. She commands that a fire be built, swears to the god of fire, Agni, that she has been loyal to Rama, and steps into the pyre as Rama watches. But Agni refuses to consume Sita and instead returns her to Rama, assuring him and the assembled crowd of Sita's faithfulness. As Linda Hess points out, this test of Sita's chastity is one episode in the Ramayana tradition that has remained controversial over the centuries; another is her later abandonment by Rama (to be discussed shortly). Examining these episodes in medieval vernacular retellings and in modern mediated tellings, she writes, "These episodes have disturbed Indian poets and audiences for many centuries. . . . Creative alterations of the fire ordeal in textual traditions reflect anxious discomfort with the scene. I have often heard people suggest that the abandonment episode is inauthentic, a later addition to the text" (3). Hess also points out that R. K. Narayan's prose version, the one cited above, titles the markedly short chapter "'Interlude,' suggesting that it is not integral to the story," and then "gives a very mild one-page summary of the Valmiki version (compared to seven pages in the Shastri translation)" (fn. 10).

In the "Rama" comic book retelling, the trial by fire episode is elided entirely. In this version, after Rama defeats Ravana on the battlefield, then crowns Ravana's brother Vibheeshana (and Rama's ally) the new king of Lanka, Rama and Sita are shown seated together in the miraculous flying chariot that speeds them back to the kingdom of Ayodhya. Within, the victorious Rama proclaims, "Sita, my dear, your days of unhappiness are now over!" (32).

A third example of this strategy of narrative omission to preserve Rama's idealism occurs in the story's conclusion. In the *Uttarakanda*, the final book of Valmiki's *Ramayana*, Rama banishes his wife Sita—now pregnant—based upon unfounded rumors that have again surfaced of her infidelity during her time as Ravana's prisoner. Exiled to the forest, Sita gives birth to twin sons and raises them at the forest hermitage of Sage Valmiki. When the twins are young men, Rama encounters them, recognizes they are his sons, and invites the twins and their mother to return to the kingdom with him—on the condition that Sita go through one more fire ordeal to prove her loyalty. Sita instead swears to the Earth goddess, asking the Earth goddess to receive her if she has always been faithful to Rama. Testifying to her fidelity, the Earth goddess swallows Sita up.

The "Rama" comic, on the other hand, ends on a happily-ever-after note in the final panel: Rama and Sita are depicted seated side by side on the throne of Ayodhya for their coronation ceremony. The text proclaims, "Rama was crowned king in Ayodhya and he ruled for many years" (32). The *Uttarakanda* is eliminated entirely, and through this act of narrative omission and closure, Rama remains unquestionably the hero. The comic book here draws on a long tradition of eliminating the *Uttarakanda* and ending with the coronation. Again, I quote Linda Hess: "Many devotional *Ramayanas* from the twelfth century on eliminate the episode of Sita's abandonment. Kamban and Tulsidas, for example, end the story with *ramrajya*, the golden age of Rama's reign, iconized in the image of Rama and Sita sitting together on the throne with gods, family, and loving devotees all around" (3). Like these medieval vernacular tellings by the poets Kamban and Tulsidas, the modern author R. K. Narayan also chose to end with the coronation in his prose retelling of the *Ramayana*. His final chapter is titled "Coronation," and in it he writes,

> I am omitting a sequel which describes a second parting between Rama and Sita, with the latter delivering twins in a forest. . . . But this part of the story is not popular, nor is it considered to be authentic, but a latter-day addition to Valimiki's version. Kamban does not take note of this sequel but concludes his tale on the happy note of Rama's return to Ayodhya, followed by a long reign of peace and happiness on this earth. And there I prefer to end my own narration. (157)

In spite of founding editor Anant Pai's professed concern for accuracy in retelling classical Hindu scripture in the comic book medium, an even greater priority for him was the preservation of Rama's heroic idealism.

Following the lead of the *Amar Chitra Katha* series, many other comic book tellings of the Ramayana were produced in the 1980s and 1990s. These similarly upheld Rama as the ideal god-king by presenting him as the clear hero of the epic both textually and visually, and by either omitting entirely or providing an apologetic defense for any of his deeds that could be perceived as morally questionable. Examples include the multi-issue line "The

Figure 5.1. Final panel of the *Rama* comic, ending happily with the coronation of Rama and Sita as king and queen of Ayodhya. *Rama*, page 32, by Amar Chitra Katha. Editor: Anant Pai. Artwork: Pratap Mulick. © India Book House Pvt. Ltd., 1970

Ramayana" in the *Dreamland Publications* comic book series and the graphic novel *Ramayana: Divine Loophole* by Sanjay Patel.

. . .

The twenty-first century has given rise to a new crop of comic book Ramayanas, created by a new generation of comics artists. While some of these continue to follow in the footsteps of *Amar Chitra Katha* in upholding Rama as the ideal god-king, others raise questions about Rama's purported idealism and, as a result, also rethink the overall meaning of the Ramayana as scripture. I turn now to three examples of comics that critically question Rama's heroic idealism: *Sita: Daughter of the Earth*, in the *Campfire Mythology* series (2011); *Godavari Tales*, in the *Vivalok Comics* series (2003); and the *Sita's Ramayana* graphic novel by Samhita Arni and Moyna Chitrakar (2011). All three of these comics focus the textual and visual narrative on Sita as the protagonist, rather than Rama, and thereby engage in a critical examination of Rama through feminist and/or subaltern perspectives. My discussion of these three comics is organized along a spectrum of critique of Rama, moving from the mildest to the staunchest.

The *Campfire Mythology* series is produced by Kalyani Navyug Media in New Delhi, India. *Campfire Mythology*'s mission is to "entertain and educate young minds by creating unique illustrated books to recount stories of human values, arouse curiosity in the world around us, and inspire with tales of great deeds and unforgettable people."[3] Campfire has four lines in their catalogue of graphic novels: classics, mythology, biographies, and history. The mythology line focuses on stories from ancient India and Greece, seeking to bring the messages of these stories to a twenty-first-century audience. *Sita: Daughter of the Earth* is one of several Ramayana-themed comics in the mythology line (others include *Sundarkaand: Triumph of Hanuman* and *Ravana: Roar of the Demon King*). This issue focuses its narrative on Sita, Rama's wife, rather than on Rama himself, and through this narrative shift Sita is presented as the hero of the epic.

Sita: Daughter of the Earth highlights Sita's innocent childhood as a princess, her joyous marriage to Rama, her brave decision to accompany Rama to the jungle when he is exiled from Ayodhya for fourteen years, and her long-suffering faith in Rama while she is held prisoner by Ravana in Lanka. Due to this narrative shift in focus from Rama to Sita, some key events that occur in most Rama-centric Ramayana tellings are overlooked if they occurred when Sita was not present. Thus, the slaying of Vali does not enter into this storyline. Instead, Sita learns of Rama's alliance with Sugreeva through the monkey Hanuman, when he arrives in Lanka as Rama's messenger. From a tree branch, Hanuman sings to Sita of Rama's efforts to locate Sita after her kidnapping, and Sugreeva's role in this process: "Further south the brothers [Rama and Lakshmana] sped / To Kishkindha, their journey led / There, with Sugriva, the vaanara [monkey] lord / A firm friendship the brothers forged. / To Rama, Sugriva's vaanaras [monkeys] brought / Glowing ornaments in orange cloth. / Rama, recognizing these / Wept in misery. / 'I swear to set my Sita free!'" (60–61). Here, the slaying of Vali is eliminated, and with it the moral ambiguity surrounding Vali's death, in favor of a narrative focus on Sita's long imprisonment while Rama undertakes the quest to locate his wife and then fight for her freedom from her captor. This then sets up the startling climax of Sita's reunion with Rama after he is victorious in battle against Ravana.

When Sita and Rama finally meet again after the war, Rama states that he cannot take Sita back according to the laws of the kingdom of Ayodhya, for she has spent nearly a year in another man's palace, and her chastity will therefore be viewed with suspicion—and as a prince his first duty is toward the citizens of Ayodhya (72). Sita, humiliated and angry, decides to kill herself. She orders that a fire be built and then enters into it, calling to the Earth goddess, "Bhudevi! You know I am innocent. You know I have suffered. Give me the strength to do this" (73). When she doesn't burn, the fire god Agni arises and tells Rama and the assembled crowd, "Rama, I cannot burn this pure, innocent, and loyal lady. She has passed the *agni pariksha* [trial by fire]. No one should mistrust her now" (74). Rama thanks Agni, stating, "I never doubted her, but as a prince who upholds the law, I needed her to prove that she is pure" (74). Sita and Rama are next shown embracing one another lovingly.

Here, by shifting the focus from Rama to Sita, we as readers are asked to empathize with her humiliation and anger at having her faithfulness publicly questioned by her own husband, when we know that she has remained completely loyal to Rama. We also witness Sita's strength in her dramatic decision to prove her innocence. In the end of this episode, two kinds of redemption have taken place: Sita is bodily redeemed by the fire god, who refuses to allow his flames to burn her; and Rama is morally redeemed, for his proclamation proves both his commitment to dharma—his willingness to uphold the law that punishes wives who are not faithful—and his utmost faith in his wife, for he knew all along that she would emerge unscathed from the fire ordeal, due to her fidelity.

In concluding its retelling of the Ramayana, *Sita: Daughter of the Earth* does not end on the happily-ever-after note of the coronation of Rama and Sita. Instead, it relates some of the events of the *Uttarakanda*, the final book of Valmiki's Ramayana. Following the coronation, a heavily pregnant Sita realizes that her husband is deeply worried about something. He won't tell her what is wrong, so she sends her maidservant Malvika to mingle among the citizens and then report back. Malvika hesitantly reports the gossip that Sita's pregnancy is a result of her time as Ravana's prisoner, and that Rama has forgotten the law out of his love for her. Sita sobs, realizing that because of her Rama is being called an *adharmic*, or lawless, king. She proclaims, "A queen's first duty is to her citizens. My relationship with Rama comes second. Therefore, I must do what is necessary to uphold the law and keep the citizens' faith in their king" (79). She first prays to the Earth goddess, then dresses herself in a hermit's garb, and then tells Rama she is leaving. Here Rama is not shown banishing his wife; rather, Sita is the agent who takes the initiative to leave and thereby uphold her own dharma as queen and also enable the people of Ayodhya to regain faith in their king's adherence to dharma.

At Valmiki's ashram, Sita is still portrayed as an ideal wife, though she is now far from Rama's side, for she teaches her sons about Rama and his greatness. Ultimately, when Rama discovers the whereabouts of Sita and his sons, he invites them to return with him to Ayodhya, where Sita can again rule by his side as his queen—if she will only take a public oath to proclaim that she has remained loyal to Rama. Saddened, Sita states that "mortal memories are fickle. People forgot the *agni pariksha* in Lanka. And in a few years, people will again forget my oath today, and again accuse us of violating the law. . . . I will not remain here any longer, where people will always doubt me and my love for you. . . . If I have always loved only my husband and if I am pure in thought, word, and deed, then may my true mother take me back in her embrace" (88–89).

Following this proclamation, Sita is shown in a full-page final panel descending into the bowels of the earth, with the blessing of the Earth goddess. Here, Sita is cast as the tragic hero of the Ramayana epic. She is a faithful wife, but more than that, she is a queen who upholds her duty to the kingdom above all other commitments. And though Rama's treatment of his wife seems cruel at times, he is also portrayed as a king who upholds his duty to the kingdom above all other commitments. Sita and Rama are star-crossed lovers in this comic book telling, destined not for a happily-ever-after ending together, but for a tragic separation at her choosing so that the moral order may once again prevail.

In 2001 the Viveka Foundation began a new comic book series called *Vivalok Comics*. Viveka is a Delhi-based alternative publisher whose mission is to provide a counterbalance to dominant publishers by upholding "democratic values, pluralistic traditions, gender equality and cultural, ecological and spiritual heritage" (McLain, *Vivalok Comics* 26–27). To date, they have produced a handful of comics that retell Indian myths, legends, and folktales. Rukmini Sekhar, the editor of *Vivalok Comics*, states that her series stands apart from other Indian comics in its depiction of the "smallest geographical unit, societal unit, and community" in an effort to celebrate "the smallest suggestion of diversity showing that only a pluralistic society is sustainable" (McLain, *Vivalok Comics* 27).

Vivalok Comics' telling of the Ramayana is one among several stories told in their issue *Godavari Tales* (2003). The title of its story is "Sita Banished," and the introduction reads: "The pan-Indian epic of *Ramayana* lends itself to many local versions. Here is the well-known episode of Sita's expulsion to the forest. This version is particularly popular among the women of the Godavari region" (37).[4] "Sita Banished" begins with a frame story, featuring women from the Godavari region of the Indian state of Andhra Pradesh, who ask an old woman to tell them a story while they take a break from working in the rice fields. As they speak, another woman walks by, and they gossip about how they heard her husband beating her last night and accusing her of infidelity. This provokes the old woman to tell the story of Sita's expulsion.

Figure 5.2. Final panel of the *Sita: Daughter of the Earth* comic, ending tragically with Sita's descent into the bowels of the earth. *Sita: Daughter of the Earth*, page 91. Author: Saraswati Nagpal. Artwork: Manikandan. © Kalyani Navyug Media Pvt. Ltd., 2011

This story then begins where the *Amar Chitra Katha* version ended: with Rama and Sita in the palace at Ayodhya, after Rama has been crowned king. But here there is no happily-ever-after ending, for the demoness Surpanakha (Ravana's sister) schemes to eliminate Sita, so that she may have Rama to herself. Surpanakha first tries to trick Sita into drawing a picture of Ravana, but Sita protests: "What are you saying? . . . I never set eyes on Ravana. I only saw his toes" (39). Here she stresses her loyalty to her husband by explaining that the whole time Ravana held her captive, she did not even look at him, keeping her eyes constantly downcast. Intent upon her purpose, Surpanakha creates her own drawing of Ravana, which follows Sita everywhere, despite Sita's attempts to be rid of the image by burning and drowning it.

Here, as Rama and Sita sit together, the drawing reappears. In the bottom left panel, we see Rama's anger and jealousy as he looks at the image, assuming that Sita drew it out of longing for Ravana. In the bottom middle panel, we return to the frame story, as the women ask the old woman what Rama did next. She replies, "Rama's response has disturbed generations of women!!" (41). In the final panel, a full-bellied Sita wanders alone in the forest, as the old woman concludes, "Since he was king, he banished Sita to the forest. That too when she was carrying her first child! So . . . what do you make of Rama's decision?" (41).

Whereas the *Amar Chitra Katha* comic and others that idealize Rama end with a happily-ever-after scenario, the *Vivalok Comics* telling ends with this image of innocent Sita's banishment and the didactic insert asking us to evaluate Rama's action. This is a very different approach to storytelling in the comic medium, in keeping with Rukmini Sekhar's desire to "draw out the undercurrents and subtleties of mythology, to use comic books for rigorous inquiry" (McLain, *Gods, Kings, and Local Telugu Guys* 163). This telling of the Ramayana dwells upon the moral ambiguities in this epic, calling into question not only the justness of Rama's behavior toward Sita, but also the dominant version of the Ramayana comic by *Amar Chitra Katha*, which presents Rama as a flawless god-king and the "best of men."

It is noteworthy that this dominant version of the Ramayana is also called into question visually in *Vivalok*'s depiction of Rama and Sita. This is not the blue-skinned Rama of *Amar Chitra Katha*, a color indicative of his divinity in human form.[5] In my interview with her, Rukmini Sekhar stated:

> We try to consciously deconstruct physiognomy in all our stories. Here, look at Rama—he is a local Telugu [south Indian] guy. Look at his hair, his skin tone. He does not wear a sacred thread. He has a subaltern appearance. You see, image is very important in representing diversity—I can't stress this enough. (McLain, *Gods, Kings, and Local Telugu Guys* 163)

Whereas the *Amar Chitra Katha* creators sought to reduce the diversity of the many *Ramayanas* to the single and accessible theme of Rama's idealism,

Figure 5.3. Concluding panels of "Sita Banished," asking readers to critically evaluate Rama's decision to banish Sita. *Godavari Tales*, page 41. Authors: Syamala Kallury and KVSL Narasamamba. Artwork: Jayanto Banerjee. © Viveka Foundation, 2003

the *Vivalok* creators sought to preserve not only localized versions of mythology that call into question patriarchal norms, but also the local context and imagery—for this richness, this narrative and cultural diversity, is key to their interpretation of the epic scripture.

...

Sita's Ramayana is a graphic novel that was written by Samhita Arni and illustrated by Moyna Chitrakar. Like the previous two examples, this comic also tells the epic story from Sita's perspective, but of the three it stands out as presenting the strongest critique of Rama's purported idealism. In this retelling Rama is a warrior to his core, eagerly and single-mindedly pursuing war with Ravana. Through this pursuit, multiple characters come to question Rama's leadership as they witness the great cost to life of such a war. Sita narrates the story of this epic war in her voice, describing the suffering that she personally endured during her long imprisonment in Ravana's island abode, as well as that of her female captors as a result of the widespread death and devastation caused by the war.

During her imprisonment, Sita befriends one of her captors, Ravana's niece Trijatha, who is gifted with the miraculous ability to see events happening near and far. Trijatha gives Sita consolation, telling her that Rama is building an army to reclaim her, and narrates key events happening far from Lanka—such as the slaying of Vali. The slaying of Vali (here called Valin) is the first episode in this telling wherein Rama's much-lauded epithet as the upholder of *dharma* is questioned. Here we see Rama crouching behind a bush, waiting for the perfect moment to strike as the two brothers, Vali and Sugreeva, are locked in combat with each other. When that moment arrives, Rama lets loose his arrow and shoots "Valin from behind as he wrestle[s] with Sugriva" (45). The focus then shifts to Tara, who is shown mourning at Vali's side. In this telling, Tara loved her second husband, Vali, with all of her heart. When the victorious Sugreeva demands that Tara return with him to his home and resume her role as his wife (for he was her first husband), she is aghast. Tara confronts Rama and asks him, "I have just been made a widow and now I am to be a bride! All this in the course of a single day! Is this right or just, Rama?" (47).

The most outspoken critic of Rama's idealism in this graphic novel is Sita herself, who grows increasingly critical of her husband as the story progresses. This criticism begins with subtle phrases at the outset of the graphic novel but grows overt in the trial by fire episode, which spans multiple pages. At the end of the battle, when Sita's tormenter is dead and Lanka is in ruins, we are presented with an image of Ravana's three grieving wives, while the text gives us insight into Sita's thoughts:

> I should have been happy, overjoyed. But I was not. I heard the women of the palace, shrieking. I saw Ravana's queens running to the battlefield, tears streaming down their faces. Their screams rent the air. Even I, enclosed in this garden, could hear their grief. They would be queens no more, and their people had met death on the battle-

> field—for what? For one man's unlawful desire. Men had been killed, wives widowed and children orphaned. It was such a high price to pay. But I couldn't help feeling nervous and frightened. Where was Rama? (112–13)

On the following pages Rama is described as "aloof and distant" at their reunion, and he is depicted with a stony face proclaiming to Sita, "I have freed you. You can do whatever you want. Go wherever you want" (115). When Rama explains that he cannot take Sita back because Ravana must have touched her, Sita firmly avers her purity and then grows angry. Sita embarks upon a monologue, and as it progresses we dwell upon successive close-ups of her face. With a righteous indignation, she counts the bloody price of Rama's war:

> Then why did you fight this war? If you had told Hanuman to tell me that you weren't coming, I would have killed myself. Valin and Indrajit dead, both killed by deceit. Tara and Mandodari are widows, and so are the women of Lanka. Their children and the children of Lanka are orphans. The battlefield is drenched with blood and corpses. (116–17)

Falling silent, Sita turns within, and the next two-page spread reveals to us her inner thought process as she decides to undergo a trial by fire. We see her, head in hand and tears streaming from her eyes, questioning whether Rama had ever truly known her—she who had suffered the taunts of her jailers while firmly adhering to the belief that Rama loved her and would rescue her. In the lower right corner of this spread, she commands Lakshmana (Rama's brother) to build a pyre (118–19). The next two-page spread is dominated by a large image of Sita in the midst of flames. Her narrative on the injustice of war continues, as she meditates upon its impact on both men and women: "War, in some ways, is merciful to men. It makes them heroes if they are the victors. If they are the vanquished—they do not live to see their homes taken, their wives widowed. But if you are a woman—you must live through defeat . . . you become the mother of dead sons, a widow, or an orphan; or worse, a prisoner" (120). But as she stands in the midst of the pyre, its flames lapping at her skin, she does not burn. Agni, the fire god, lifts her out and pronounces to Rama that Sita is pure: "Take her and do not doubt her!" (122).

And so, we are told, Rama and Sita returned to Ayodhya together. And yet, as we have already seen, when told from Sita's perspective, the story does

Figure 5.4. Conclusion of the graphic novel *Sita's Ramayana*, focusing on Sita's suffering and fortitude. *Sita's Ramayana*, page 148. Author: Samhita Arni. Artwork: Moyna Chitrakar. © House of Anansi Press/Groundwood Books, 2011

not end on the happily-ever-after note of their coronation. Rumors begin to circulate about Sita's alleged infidelity, and Rama decides to abandon Sita in the forest. In this telling when Sita—now pregnant—learns of this, the page goes entirely blank with the exception of a small circle highlighting her tear-laden eyes, and words expressing her despair and fear:

> The same accusation. The same doubts. I wish I had died in Lanka. Now I am pregnant, and alone. My belly is huge, and I cannot see the ground under my feet. How will I avoid the poisonous snakes that slither across the earth? How will I, with my heavy belly and swollen ankles, outrun beasts of prey? And when my hour draws close,

> when my child is to be born, who will calm my fears and assist me in my labour? How will I, alone, raise a child, born to be kind, in this forest? (127)

Sita gives birth, as we know, to twin sons, and raises them at Sage Valmiki's forest hermitage, where they are taught the story of Rama. In time, Rama learns that he is a father, and in this telling he recalls his sons to the royal palace, along with Sita. From his seat on the throne, Rama tells Sita, "the princes need their mother, and the palace waits for its queen." Sita, shown bowing before her husband and king, replies, "I do not wish to be queen. I have been doubted once, twice, and I do not care to be doubted again" (145). On the next page, the earth cracks open and Agni arises from within, grasping Sita in a protective embrace. Rama reaches for her, but Sita says to him, "Let me go. Take care of our children. Having gained a father, they now lose a mother. You must be both to them!" (147).

The final page of the graphic novel shows Sita disappearing into the earth, hands folded in prayer, tears falling from her eyes. The final line of text concludes the story, "She disappeared, and was never seen again" (149). Like the creators of *Vivalok Comics* in their retelling of the Ramayana in comic form, so too were the creators of *Sita's Ramayana* inspired by earlier regional storytelling traditions in creating both the images and text for their graphic novel. The images, which were created first by artist Moyna Chitrakar, were painted in the tradition of the *patua* scroll painters of Bengal, in eastern India. They feature a subaltern Sita, dark in skin tone and painted in a regional folk style. The text was then written by Samhita Arni to complement the artwork in its focus on Sita's travails. Like the images, the text also draws upon Bengali regional tellings of the epic and was particularly inspired by the sixteenth-century Bengali Ramayana composed by the female poet Chandrabati, which focused on Sita's suffering and fortitude (150–51).[6]

...

In his essay "Three Hundred Ramayanas," A. K. Ramanujan asks how the many different Ramayana tellings relate to one another and sets forth three primary translation relationships (while recognizing that any telling may fall into more than one category). First is an "iconic" relationship, where "Text 1 and Text 2 have a geometrical resemblance to each other, as one triangle to another" (44). Second is an "indexical" relationship, where "although Text 2 stands in an iconic relationship to Text 1 in terms of basic elements such as plot, it is filled with local detail, folklore, poetic traditions, imagery, and so forth" (45). Third is a "symbolic" relationship, where "Text 2 uses the plot and characters and names of Text 1 minimally and uses them to say entirely new things, often in an effort to subvert the predecessor by producing a countertext" (45).

The three comics discussed herein that focus their textual and visual narratives on Sita, rather than Rama, as the protagonist function in a symbolic relationship with the version of the Ramayana told by *Amar Chitra Katha* in their "Rama" comic. Rather than highlight Rama as a righteous god-king, *Sita: Daughter of the Earth*, "Sita Banished," and *Sita's Ramayana* instead present countertexts that raise critical questions about Rama's purported idealism—and, in so doing, raise critical questions about the meaning of the Ramayana as scripture. The moral of the Ramayana epic as stated in the beginning of *Amar Chitra Katha*'s "Rama" is clear: "The idea that God fulfills Himself in the best of men is conveyed by the life of Rama and that is the story of Ramayana." The overall intent of this comic book is to cultivate *bhakti*, or devotion, to Rama as the ideal god-king and upholder of dharma. In these countertellings, on the other hand, the intent is not to praise Rama and cultivate a devotional mind-set toward him as an ideal god-man, but to raise critical questions about the dharmic morality of Rama's deeds and their impact upon others, especially his wife, Sita.

Linda Hess describes well this form of symbolic countertext: "Today more than ever before, Sita is a site of contestation. The Sita who clung to the *dharma* of worshipping her husband and bowing to his will, even when he repeatedly and cruelly rejected her, is still embraced as the ideal woman by many Hindus of both sexes. But others, increasingly, are describing that ideal as concocted by and serving the interests of dominant males from ancient times to the present" (27–28). That the Ramayana scripture is a site of hermeneutic contestation can be seen in the controversy over Ramanujan's essay, which has been widely praised in scholarly circles but was loudly protested by right-wing Hindus after it began to be included on the syllabus for the course "Culture in India: A Historical Perspective" at Delhi University in 2006. Those opposed to the teaching of Ramanujan's essay argued that it was an offense to Hinduism because it presented Rama in a derogatory manner through the inclusion of countertexts or "symbolic" translations. However, many others rallied around the teaching of the essay in the interest of academic freedom.[7] The debate over Ramanujan's essay was ongoing in public media and the law courts in India from 2008 through 2011, and the publication of both *Sita: Daughter of the Earth* and *Sita's Ramayana* in 2011 at the height of this debate indicates that these comics creators sought to ensure that the Ramayana tradition remained a multivocal one within the comics medium.

It is in this larger context of both a long and multivocal tradition of telling and retelling the Ramayana scripture in South Asia, and an impetus among some politically vocal right-wing Hindus to homogenize the Ramayana story to one that unquestioningly idealizes Rama as a heroic god-king, that a new generation of comics creators has arisen in India. With its combination of sequential images and narrative text, the comic book medium is especially noteworthy for its hero-making capacities. While some among these new Indian comics creators have put this graphic medium to work to continue to uphold Rama as an ideal god-king, others—including many female authors and illustrators—have instead used this medium to challenge Rama's purported idealism. In their retellings of the Ramayana epic, the creators of *Sita: Daughter of the Earth*, "Sita Banished," and *Sita's Ramayana* rework this sacred scripture, using text and image not to cultivate devotion (*bhakti*) toward Rama, but to raise critical questions about religious and cultural definitions of the sacred.

NOTES

1. See especially the edited volumes Richman 1991 and Richman 2001.

2. For further information on the *Amar Chitra Katha* comic book series, see Pritchett, Hawley, and McLain *India's Immortal Comic Books*.

3. "About Us," *Campfire*, http://www.campfire.co.in/about-us. Accessed April 30, 2016.

4. There has been a significant amount of scholarship on women's retellings of the *Ramayana*. For a sampling, see Kishwar, Nilsson, and Rao.

5. For an overview on the changing depiction of Rama in the modern period and in Hindu nationalist imagery in particular, see Kapur.

6. For more on Chandrabati's Ramayana, see Sen.

7. On protests over Ramanujan's essay, see Gohain.

BIBLIOGRAPHY

Arni, Samhita, and Moyna Chitrakar. *Sita's Ramayana*. Toronto: House of Anansi Press/Groundwood Books, 2011.

Gohain, Manash Pratim. "Ramanujan Essay: Debate Turns Political." *Times of India*, Oct. 25, 2011. http://timesofindia.indiatimes.com/city/delhi/Ramanujan-essay-Debate-turns-political/articleshow/10480716.cms?referral=PM. Accessed July 11, 2016.

Hawley, John Stratton. "The Saints Subdued: Domestic Virtue and National Integration in Amar Chitra Katha." In *Media and the Transformation of Religion in South Asia*, edited by Lawrence Babb and Susan Wadley, 107–34. Philadelphia: University of Pennsylvania Press, 1995.

Hess, Linda. "Rejecting Sita: Indian Responses to the Ideal Man's Cruel Treatment of His Ideal Wife." *Journal of the American Academy of Religion* 67, no. 1 (1999): 1–32.

Kallury, Syamala, KVSL Narasamamba, and Jayanto Banerjee. "Godavari Tales." *Vivalok Comics*. New Delhi: Viveka Foundation, 2003.

Kapur, Anuradha. "Deity to Crusader: The Changing Iconography of Ram." In *Hindus and Others: The Question of Identity in India Today*, edited by Gyanendra Pandey, 74–109. New York: Viking, 1993.

Kishwar, Madhu. "Yes to Sita, No to Ram: The Continuing Hold of Sita on Popular Imagination in India." In *Questioning Ramayanas: A South Asian Tradition*, edited by Paula Richman, 285–308. Berkeley: University of California Press, 2001.

McLain, Karline. "Gods, Kings, and Local Telugu Guys: Competing Visions of the Heroic in Indian Comic Books." In *Popular Culture in a Globalised India*, edited by K. Moti Gokulsing and Wimal Dissanayake, 157–73. New York: Routledge, 2009.

McLain, Karline. *India's Immortal Comic Books: Gods, Kings, and Other Heroes*. Bloomington: Indiana University Press, 2009.

McLain, Karline. "*Vivalok Comics*: Celebrating All That Is Small in India." *International Journal of Comic Art* 11, no. 2 (2009): 26–43.

Nagpal, Saraswati, and Manikandan. *Sita: Daughter of the Earth*. Campfire Mythology. New Delhi: Kalyani Navyug Media, 2011.

Narayan, R. K. *The Ramayana: A Shortened Modern Prose Version of the Indian Epic*. New York: Penguin Books, 2006.

Nilsson, Usha. "Grinding Millet but Singing of Sita: Power and Domination in Awadhi and Bhojpuri Women's Songs." In *Questioning Ramayanas: A South Asian Tradition*, edited by Paula Richman, 137–58. Berkeley: University of California Press, 2001.

Pai, Anant (ed.). *Amar Chitra Katha*. "Rama." Artwork by Pratap Mulick. Mumbai: India Book House, 1970.

Pritchett, Frances W. "The World of Amar Chitra Katha." In *Media and the Transformation of Religion in South Asia*, edited by Lawrence Babb and Susan Wadley, 76–106. Philadelphia: University of Pennsylvania Press, 1995.

Ramanujan, A. K. "Three Hundred Ramayanas: Five Examples and Three Thoughts on Translation." In *Many Ramayanas: The Diversity of a Narrative Tradition in South Asia*, edited by Paula Richman, 22–49. Berkeley: University of California Press, 1991.

Rao, Velcheru Narayana. "A *Ramayana* of Their Own: Women's Oral Tradition in Telugu." In *Many Ramayanas: The Diversity of a Narrative Tradition in South Asia*, edited by Paula Richman, 114–36. Berkeley: University of California Press, 1991.

Richman, Paula (ed.). *Many Ramayanas: The Diversity of a Narrative Tradition in South Asia*. Berkeley: University of California Press, 1991.

Richman, Paula (ed.). *Questioning Ramayanas: A South Asian Tradition*. Berkeley: University of California Press, 2001.

Sen, Nabaneeta Dev. "Rewriting the Ramayana: Chandrabati and Molla." *India International Centre Quarterly* 24.2, no. 3 (1997): 163–77.

Chapter Six

THE ENDING OF MARK AS A PAGE-TURN REVEAL

ELIZABETH RAE COODY

GOSPEL MESSAGES CAN BE "SUCCESSFUL" IN THEIR TIME ONLY IF AN AUDIence receives the "good news" they report and then acts upon it. In order to read these stories well, interpreters must be aware of this need to electrify their intended audience. Comics share this need to excite.

At the bottom of a right-hand page, print comics creators have one of their best opportunities to thrill their readers. Comics almost always save important reveals for this sort of cut. With skilled design, each page-image *recto folio* ("on the right side of the page") anticipates the image *verso folio* ("on the turned side of the page"). The panel that falls at the end of the reading track on the recto offers the creator the best chance to build anticipation for the verso. The recto anticipates the verso in innumerable ways: a character will react to something off-panel that the reader does not see until after she has turned over the page, a bit of narrative will dangle a sentence unfinished, a noise will occur in-panel that comes from an action off-panel, or one or several of many other possible tantalizing hints will lead the reader on. The technique is common in what Neil Cohn calls the American Visual Language (AVL) and its dialects, which is the visual language used by the North American subjects of this study (139–46).[1] These comics tools engage the human emotional desire to understand what happens next.

As interpreters of an emotionally entangled and meaning-laden text, biblical scholars have much to learn from what comics can reveal about the act of reading texts with emotions engaged. This particular branch of scholarship is often guilty of an Enlightenment-inspired exaggerated distance from the emotional language of confessional uses of the text. A flat affect makes it difficult to understand the emotionality of texts like the moving ending of Mark. Instead of a glory-filled revelation or comforting reassurance that Christianity might suggest by reputation, the original ending of Mark has women who have come to Jesus's tomb fleeing in terror at the suggestion that Jesus might have been raised from the dead. So stunned are the women that they tell no one what they have seen, because, as the text says, they are terrified. As David Rhoads and Don Michie argue in their analysis of this narrative ending:

> This abrupt ending, which aborts the hope that someone will proclaim the good news, cries out for the reader to provide the resolution to the story. The reader alone has remained faithful to the last and is now left with a decision, whether to flee in silence like the women or to proclaim boldly in spite of fear and death. The implied reader will choose to proclaim. (140)

The ending of the text calls for the reader to provide something, to act. I will demonstrate how scholarly readers of the Christian Testament might find *The Action Bible* (2010), *Marked* (2005), and the "Gospel of Mark" story in the *Yummy Fur* series (1987–1989) useful for identifying characteristics of the peculiar ending of Mark. In particular, I argue here that the ending of Mark, which has long puzzled scholars, can be more fully understood when compared to the technique of the page-turn reveal commonly used by comics creators. That is, the shorter ending of Mark is a "page-turn" teaser. It is not a deficient ending, but rather invites the reader or listener to create the verso. Reading Mark through comics makes visible how the author of Mark accomplished with language what the comics form is uniquely able to display visually. Comics interpreters of the Gospel do better or worse jobs of interpreting that "page-turn" ending successfully.[2]

While I use comics that treat the Gospel of Mark in comics form, the major lesson I draw here is from a technique common to the form of comics itself, the page-turn reveal, rather than these specific examples. These particular comics creators act as interpreters of the text and as "designers" of particular reading experiences with Mark. The characteristics I identify for the "page-turn reveal" are the designed pre-turn anticipation, a reader-directed pace, the promise of a payoff, and an (at least attempted) emotional impact.

. . .

Mark is a plot-driven narrative that lends itself to visual storytelling; it works well with imagining comics as a form and method of exegesis. It is fashionable and popular to use Mark as this sort of methodological proving ground in Christian Testament biblical studies in the last several decades, especially for new theoretical approaches such as narrative and reader-response (Anderson and Moore 2008). The unusual feature of Mark in this exploration of the page-turn reveal is its contested series of endings: the "original" ending (at 16:8), the shorter ending (16:8 plus a contested, usually unnumbered, single verse), and the longer ending (which includes 16:9–20). Although standard English translations of the New Testament end the book at 16:20, most scholars conclude that the oldest extant version of the gospel ended at 16:8, hence what biblical scholars call—perhaps misleadingly—the "original" ending.[3] Of course, as with all the Gospels, there is no true "original" copy. Scholars have done some fruitful work in this area, colored by various theologies and cutting-edge theories (Gaventa and Miller; Juel).

While manuscript evidence makes this "original" ending clear, many interpreters resist ending the Gospel there because of the unsettling way this ending cuts the story. Chapter 16 tells of women mourning Jesus's crucifixion and coming to his tomb to anoint his body. They find the stone that covered the entrance rolled away and the body gone. A mysterious "young man" in a white robe tells them that Jesus has been raised from the dead and instructs them to tell Peter and the other disciples to meet Jesus in Galilee. The women flee from this sight in terror and amazement. Verse 8 concludes without a word to anyone, because the women are afraid. The phrase ends with the Greek word "γαρ" (roughly translated "for") in an unusual, though not unprecedented, ending for a whole work (Lincoln 300).[4] Ending a sentence and a whole work with this word has the effect of leaving the reader hanging, waiting for another word. This hasty ending leaves the implied reader with the task of interpretation. The reader remains at the bottom of a metaphorical recto, set up for the verso. But in the original ending there is no verso page. The writer has set them up to expect a payoff, thereby forcing readers to provide their own resolution. This pull seems to be strong enough to inspire some later readers to include their versions of further endings in the text itself. Yet my concern here is not a question of "authorial intent" but of reading design. The difference is clearer if we turn to comics to see the mechanics of this sort of "page-turn" moment.

. . .

Creators often use a "page-turn reveal" to put the unique design elements of comics to their best advantage. In a book that follows a left-to-right, top-to-bottom reading track or convention, the panel at the bottom right-hand corner of a recto shows some hint of what is to come, and so offers some element of suspense or builds anticipation. Will Eisner offers a discussion on this "reading track" in his classic *Comics and Sequential Art* (40–41). Because this relies on comics-style visual and narrative tactics, like specific pagination and individual control over turns, this technique is unique to comics. It gives readers rare control over their reading that places them in the action.

Serialized stories in other media can offer similar cliffhangers but none offer the combination of control and immediacy of comics. In a novel, authors with some control over the design of their books can make sure that chapters end on a suspenseful note or that readers still have burning questions at the end of one page that the next page answers. Comics have the advantage of offering their answers in the form of images. As Ann Marie Seward Barry claims in her work on the neurological dynamics of visual communication:

> The image is . . . capable of reaching the emotions before it is cognitively understood. The logic of the image is also associative and holistic rather than linear, so that not only does the image present itself as reality, but it also may speak directly to the emotions, bypassing logic, and works according to alogical principles of reasoning. (78)

More than illustrating text, "artwork dominates the reader's initial attention" (Blackmore 122–23). In a text-heavy work like a novel, the reader is in control of the page turn as in a comic, but this "initial attention" in image-centric comics makes the power of the verso far more immediate.

In film, the viewer might see an image that anticipates the next, such as a reaction shot of an actor before the camera reveals the stimulus of the reaction. The film image and the comics image offer similar immediacy. However, in film, the editor controls the speed at which the reveal happens. In comics reading, the control is in the hands of the reader. As "juxtaposed pictorial images" rather than images in sequence, comics give the reader options (McCloud 9). A reader might follow the discipline of the reading track the creator expected, or she may go off course—reading the last panel first, turning a page to see a verso before reading a recto, flipping to the end, turning a page too quickly or too slowly, or perhaps refusing to turn a page at all! Readers often make unexpected use and even seemingly contradictory reappropriations of texts. Comics help reveal this productive tendency in readers in general. If we turn this tendency back to Mark, it helps to connect readers to textual "design" and the ways they use it.

The "frame" is a primary tool of comics design. The frame both limits what the reader sees and suggests more beyond the frame. Umberto Eco talks about these complementary yet opposing functions as "form" and "infinity." When the artist shows us a complete form in each panel with images and words, she "tells us about this scene and not about another" (Eco 12). In each panel, there is a complete and limited *form*. Simultaneously, the gutter surrounding the panel selects one moment in time or image out of what the gutter suggests is the possibility of the infinity of time or an infinite number of possible moments outside the frame. The frame limits the picture and so "conveys an 'etcetera,' i.e. one that suggests it may continue beyond its own physical limits" (37). Comics convey the interplay of form and infinity as a sort of series of frames that concern space and time, a version of Eco's poetic visual list.

In the world of comics, characters are acting on a stage that the reader can assume continues past the point where the gutter interrupts the view. Often, comics are one of those works that "make us think that what we see within the frame is not all, but only an example of a totality whose number is hard to calculate" (Eco 38). The reader joins a "silent dance of the seen and the unseen, the visible and the invisible" (McCloud 92). Nowhere is the frame's tendency to inspire what moves beyond it more conspicuous than in the page-turn reveal. The frame device of the page sets another kind of limit that suggests infinity when it comes in the languages of comics. The ending of Mark suggests this infinity, too, if we are able to see it with eyes trained by these visual languages.

The scandal of the ending of the Gospel of Mark is its supposed lack of resolution; each of the comics I engage in this essay addresses the interpretive challenge differently, acting as both interpreter and designer. *The Action Bible* achieves a heroic sensibility with a gospel harmony and a reliance on more action tropes than biblical ones. In *Marked*, the startling conclusion remains open with wordless images. Even more daring is the decision in the strict retelling of the Gospel in independent comic *Yummy Fur* to allow it to hang open, off the edge of the page. While each uses the same visual language, attitudes toward the story strongly influence how the comic creators design the resolution.

. . .

Perhaps the most common way for interpreters to deal with the disturbing ending of Mark is to simply treat Mark as a supplement to other accounts of the Jesus story, rather than as a complete story on its own. Among these comics, *The Action Bible* shows the least disruptive (or innovative) interpretation of Mark for an American Christian audience, for which it is designed (Cariello and Mauss). The book is an interpretation/illustration, at least in part, of every book of the Bible from Genesis to Revelation. The New Testament portion is a harmony—that is, a telling of the Jesus story that uses elements of all four Gospels simultaneously. Like many other harmonies, this telling rounds off sharp edges or disagreements among accounts. Luke, Matthew, and even John outstrip the material that Mark alone includes. Because Matthew and Luke both include Markan material, there is still plenty of material in this comic that is in Mark. But this material is included only when it agrees with the other Synoptic Gospels (Matthew and Luke). Where Mark differs, editor Doug Mauss chooses to follow another source, usually Luke.

What's remarkable about this version is how little the page-turn reveal or any surprising comics design technique appears in the retelling of the otherwise startling moment at the tomb. The artist Sergio Cariello is certainly familiar with the technique. His art here is what Neil Cohn calls the "Action" or "Kirbyan AVL," a dialect of the American Visual Language named after classic US action comics creator Jack Kirby (Cohn 139).[5] Examples of Kirby's tendency to offer an awe-inspiring alien world or startling plot development on a page turn are too many to name; he uses majestic splash pages to startle his reader whenever possible. Cariello does not engage the page-turn reveal here because the emotional impact of the piece is not in disruption, but in confirmation, of the superiority of Jesus. What's anticipated here is that Jesus will return as he had said, but there is no doubt presented. The pre-turn anticipation, the reader-directed pace, the promise of a payoff, and emotional impact center on the heroic resurrection of Jesus, not on the actions of the women. This reassures the reader that the activity of the disciples and the formation of the church are not in doubt. The design ignores even the possibility of terror or uncertainty in the Gospel of Mark. This is, after all, an action comic. The values are hypermasculine; Jesus's superior manly physical prowess and ability to influence his followers are not called into question, even in death.

The harmony of the Gospels presented in the chapter "Crucified!" notes that it is "based on Luke 23:26–52; John 19:23–28; Matthew 27:32–58; Mark 15:21–45." It depicts a muscular Jesus dying on a cross stoically with his traditional physical beauty unblemished. "Crucified!" ends on a verso with Pilate agreeing to give Jesus's body to Joseph of Arimathea for burial. The line "Yes. I'll give the order to the officer in charge" transitions into "The Sealed Tomb," which begins on a recto. Although Mark contains a story of the sealed tomb, editor Mauss does not use it. Rather than draw upon Mark's abrupt and uneasy ending, this comic does not make the women's report from the tomb a moment of doubt. Instead, the page breaks on the moment Mary asks a man she thinks is a gardener, "If you have taken Jesus' body, please tell me where you have put it" (John 20:14–17).

The pre-turn anticipation here is severely undercut by the fact that the reader can see the full front-facing figure of Jesus as the "gardener." The text indicates that Mary does not recognize him, but the reader should. The anticipation is built around whether or not Mary will recognize Jesus, but even that is undercut by her baffled expression. There are few surprises here; the story reassures the reader that Jesus is indeed powerful, despite his recent death. The reader does not have the option to delay the women's message or anticipate their answer. The comic is not interested in following the women characters or their point of view; instead, every page has a least one man to follow. To ensure this, Peter and John discover the empty tomb in an inset, while a glimpse of the "devious" plan of the priests moves the plot.[6] The women come to the tomb, but they do not run away in fear. Neither fear nor the women's perspective is appropriate to this story.

The promise at the end of the recto is not about the women, except that Mary will eventually recognize Jesus. The pace, even if directed by a suspicious reader, cannot build drama in this story by delaying page turns. The design of the page turns, together with the certainty with which the story views its hypermasculine hero, only weakens the emotional impact. In tone and design, there is no fear that the verso will hold anything but a conquering, victorious Jesus. The potential for emotional tension is muted by the provided and expected closure.

. . .

Whereas *The Action Bible* avoids the complicated ending of Mark, Steve Ross's *Marked* dares to treat Mark's ambiguity through a dystopian aesthetic. While an unusual work, *Marked* still forms part of a church-sanctioned interpretive tradition; Seabury, the Episcopal Church publishing house, marketed and published *Marked* to its constituents. This book needs an "in-group" audience to connect the dots of the story. That is, some knowledge of the narrative of Mark will help a reader follow the plot. Although even a careful reader would be hard-pressed to line up *Marked* to the Gospel panel by panel or verse by verse, a reader who knows the plot of Mark will be able to see the contours. Without that knowledge, *Marked* can be a confusing read. Ross uses page turns that repeatedly engage his readers in pre-turn anticipation and payoff with unpredictable emotional impact. These require the reader to interpret the meaning.

Marked is in Cohn's Cartoony AVL or Barksian dialect (Cohn 141–43).[7] Ross uses heavy, cross-hatched lines, exaggerated people of irregular sizes,

Seuss-style machines, and worlds riddled with bulbous, surreal creatures that infest bodies and move between panels, "somewhere between 'Doonesbury' and *Mad* magazine" (Tintera). Ross scatters clues to the Markan source material throughout in background illustrations and in the framework of the events, although there are no precise verses noted on the pages.

Ross saves his most startling reveal for the moment at the tomb. He builds the pre-turn anticipation for several pages. The journey of the women to the tomb, which the text does in half a verse, Ross builds over several silent panels and page turns. Once the climax of Jesus's death is over, Joseph of Arimathea wordlessly takes Jesus's corpse down a dank stairwell to a storage vault tomb, which he locks with a key (cf. 15:45–46). He slips the key under Jesus's mother's door. She reads his instructions with a flat affect and simply does what is necessary, task by task. Ross features every step in its own silent panel: going up her stairs, packing Jesus's burial suit, pacing slowly through the streets. The number of panels and their growing size (two featuring her walking down the street are each half of a page) slow the action to a crawl, building anticipation. She finds the door to the tomb unlocked and slowly works her way down dark stairs, finally speaking to ask if anyone is there. Over a second two-page spread, she finally discovers the rubble of the blasted door to the tomb. Then, at the page turn, there is a voice from off-panel near the blasted door: "Sob! It wasn't us. I swear." Now the pre-turn anticipation builds to its height, dangling over the edge of the recto. Even a reader who knows the story intimately cannot be quite sure what she will see next.

An experienced biblical reader might *assume* that it is the women who are speaking off-panel, but even she would be startled by the reveal at the turn. What is made most striking here in the layout is not the figures of the women on the verso (although their huddled, wide-eyed forms are remarkable), but the figure of the tragic clown peering from the blasted hole in the wall on the opposite page. In this case, the freedom of pace in reading comics allows, and nearly dictates, that all but the most unreasonably disciplined comics reader will observe this clown before heading back to the verso to pick up the conversation between Mary and the women. The clown arrests attention from across the page. The single figure dominates the page alone, staring out of a smashed hole in a wall with unnerving blank eyes; spare Auguste-style clown paint encircling the muzzle of the mouth, with a single dark dot on his nose; and a costume drawn from the *Pagliacci* tradition. His face, obscured by make-up but clear in line, is expressionless. This flatness recalls the wretched clowns of French Expressionist painter Georges Rouault (1871–1958). Rouault painted the tension he saw between the joyful

Figure 6.1. The clown dominates the page, *Marked*, no pagination, by Steve Ross. Copyright © 2005 Steve Ross

amusements of the clown's craft and the impoverished condition of these performers as transient laborers. As Rouault said, "I saw quite clearly that the 'Clown' was me, was us, nearly all of us. . . . This rich and glittering costume, it is given to us by life itself, we are all more or less clowns, we all wear a glittering costume" (Mormado). There is for Rouault a jarring disconnect between appearance and reality.

Ross's page turn reveals a payoff that by design shocks by its attention to this disconnect. It returns to what Rouault called *Sunt Lacrymae Rerum*—"There are tears at the very heart of things" (Mormado). There is a death at the heart of this story that cries out—the clown image shouts without words—hoping to disturb even the most complacent reader. As Ross himself has said, "I fear that two thousand years of 20/20 hindsight have sucked the surprise, awe and sheer weirdness out of the Gospels" (Wilson). There is an emotional impact that hangs in the air. The final image in the book, just a few pages later, is another splash page on the recto—a sunflower growing through the skeletal remains of an ominous black bird. The meaning is perhaps vaguely triumphant, it may even be positive, but it is certainly unsettling. It resists closure.

The women leave slowly on the penultimate pages, their feelings ambiguous. *Marked* leaves the door open to infinite possibilities by shying away from words at the end of the comic, leaving the reader a punctuated, but not final, ending in symbolically laden images. Ross removes the flight and terror from the postures of the women and leaves the reader with an uneasy image. It pays off emotionally, but it does not overdetermine what happens at the end of Mark.

. . .

Chester Brown's multi-issue "Gospel of Mark" title interweaves Mark's story of Jesus through his *Yummy Fur* series (1983–1994) in issues #4 through #14. The curiously named *Yummy Fur* is an often-crass independent comic in the vein of other underground comix that flourished in the 1980s in the Independent AVL (Cohn 143). The Mark story ran as a second story alongside the surrealist farce "Ed the Happy Clown" from April 1987 to January 1989. Brown strove to work against expectations in his Gospel interpretation:

> People were expecting me to do something weird with Mark. . . . I know that readers, when they started reading *Yummy Fur* #4, didn't know I was planning on doing all four, but I knew I was going to. And so starting from a traditional view seemed like a good place to start. And I can get weirder as I go along, but. . . . (Brown 2013, 64)

Brown did not complete this trailing thought, but then, neither did he complete his planned four Gospels. His interest in the Bible has grown into other avenues, such as his deep musings on the will of God and sex work in his 2016 book (Brown 2016). His adaptation begins with a very traditional reading, one verse per panel, six square panels per page, of an English translation of Mark.[8] He creates each square panel on a larger page separately and then combines them with an even number of panels per page. In the case of *Yummy Fur* issue #15, which contains the climax and denouement of the Gospel, Brown regiments each page on the grid. This process does not lend itself to the traditional page-turn reveal; the frames are not shown to connect in a way that suggests a cliffhanger, but the restraint of this telling packs an emotional impact and suggests infinite possibilities at the edge of the frame.

Though he has published *Ed the Happy Clown* as a complete graphic novel, Brown has never collected or republished "Mark." Brown has explicitly said that he has no interest in republishing them or completing the "Gospel of Matthew" adaptation that ran in *Yummy Fur* #15–#32.[9] As he baldly admits, "I am reluctant to release it because it was poorly done" (Everson 124). Brown is unduly hard on his work; what he finds poor, as an interpreter of the Bible, I find rich. The extremely close attention he pays to each verse gives a tight focus on the structure of Mark. He shows an interest in the possibilities offered by contemporary alternative versions of the Gospel.

The ending, however, sticks to the material he finds in his printing of the Bible, including the longer ending that includes verse 16:20. However, by stopping the action-oriented illustration at the events of 16:8 when the women run from the tomb, he is able to suggest a sort of liminal place for everything after that point. This material is in the text, but it is spoken by a wizened unnamed character, centered on a black background, and so utterly different from the panels that have come before. The story ends on a recto. The last action panel is the second of six even panels on top of this recto. It has a slightly aerial, middle-distance view of the stone rolled from the round mouth of the cave tomb with three women fleeing out of the panel at the bottom of the frame. Their faces are too distant to read, but they are fleeing with speed, their cloaks wide behind them, one's hair loosed from her veil in flight, the last with her face turned over her shoulder toward the door. She is reminiscent perhaps of Lot's wife, fleeing, straining to take one last backward look. At the bottom of a page, this would be a set-up to a page-turn reveal. There is anticipation in the very framing.

Brown subverts the expectation of a reveal at this pivotal moment. First, in the frame, the women flee toward the middle of the page, rather than off the page. They go back toward the story. And, in the next panel, which the reader can hardly help but notice when she opens the page, the action ends, and there is only the wizened and distant figure, floating in inky black over the last four panels. The promise here is not of payoff, but of something off-center. Brown has not given his readers the "something weird" they might have expected; he has pulled the story from its traditional axis. The emotional impact comes from this lurch that a reader might feel. If they are familiar with the traditional story, the lurch might come from the change in tone, suggesting the final verses are simply not part of the action. If readers are unfamiliar with the story, the lurch might come from the way the story fails

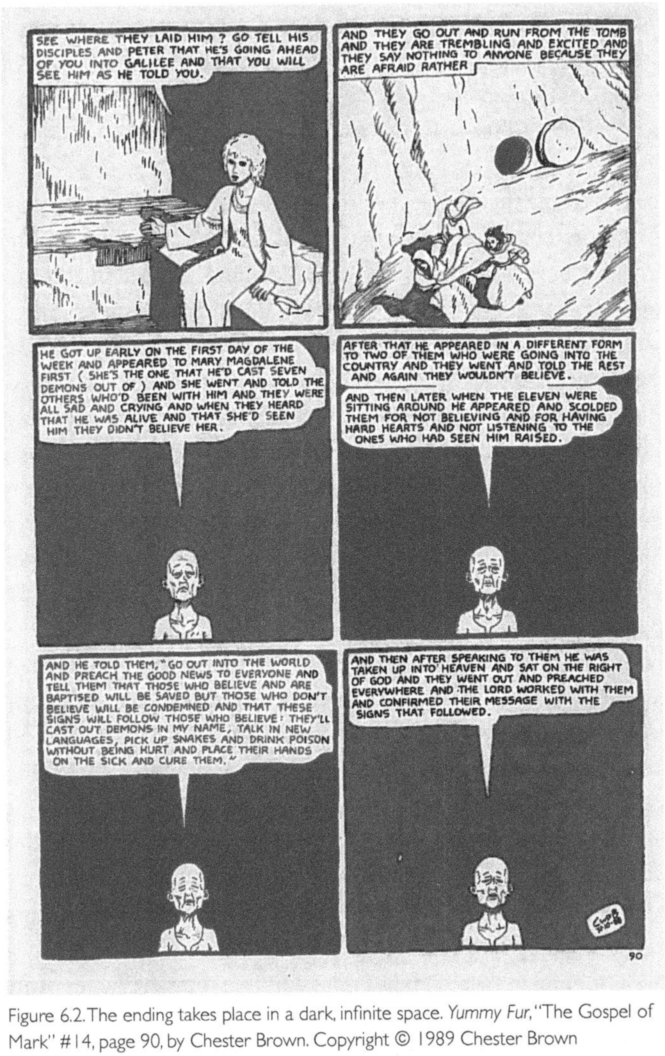

Figure 6.2. The ending takes place in a dark, infinite space. *Yummy Fur*, "The Gospel of Mark" #14, page 90, by Chester Brown. Copyright © 1989 Chester Brown

as a modern story. There is no internal character work here. Everything is at a middle distance. When the story ends, it must be with a lurch, as there is nothing anchoring it other than the reader. There is only the place where the author chooses to end the story—that is, to place the frame—that interrupts a long view of infinite possibilities, even as it suggests the presence of infinite possibilities.

Brown's rigidly square frames consistently suggest an infinite number of possible tellings. By the stark background signal at the end of the book,

Brown's *Yummy Fur* "Mark" allows the reader to separate the "longer" ending verses (16:9–20) from the "original" ending (at 16:8). The action stops with the women running away, perhaps in terror. But the story is set in a world that has concerns other than the story.

. . .

Perhaps it is tragic that at the very moment when digital comics experience explosive growth, a biblical scholar would find that her long-ignored print counterparts have something to teach her field. Even with the new possibilities that digital comics offer, there is much that print comics—struggling to thrill and capture the reader's imaginations—can teach religious studies scholars. Comics and sacred texts is a wide-open field of possibility. The poor communication between the intellectual biblical scholar and the practicing confessional congregant calls for resources. Here is an emotional problem begging to be understood by the scholar: the original ending of Mark was perhaps too unsettling; some early scribes refused to leave that "γαρ" dangling there with the women fleeing in terror. Instead, they gave it a closed form that has become canonical. They simply could not leave the anticipation unsatisfied.

This urge to proclaim a closed, triumphant ending is characteristic of narrative design. By leaving the reader to anticipate a page turn and promised payoff, the author of Mark has allowed the reader to become a biblical interpreter with emotional complexity. In comics, though, there is a common practice to cut a reader off at a page turn, leaving him with something out of frame to run toward. But in a work of daring uncertainty, the reader leaves the story at the edge of the page, before the reveal. The revelation is not on the verso, but in the gutter. What revelation there is lives only in the reader. This is a daring step into the ineffable, into infinity.

For interpreters of sacred texts, understanding their ineffable natures takes delicacy. Comics can help with this complex process through reimagining. Whether or how comics authors intend to move their readers emotionally is immaterial. The design of comics means that images are presented in a sequence that drives a reader to seek out the next image. Gospels, like comics, aim to move an embodied reader and do not appeal strictly to the *logos* of an ahistorical and imperturbable subject. The clinical Enlightenment-style study is an important part of critical analysis, but it is not the sum total of that practice or even necessarily its core. Readers who cut emotion from the ending of Mark will not be able to imagine its full meaning but can find assistance in the thrill of the page turn.

NOTES

1. Idiomatic versions of the page-turn reveal appear in Cohn's Japanese and European Visual Languages as well. I will define these dialects of the AVL as they appear.

2. In what follows, I use "page-turn" as the adjective and "page turn" as the noun. That is, the "page-turn reveal" happens after the "page turn."

3. Ending the Gospel at 16:8 is a common practice; the reliable and popular Codex Vaticanus and Codex Sinaiticus both stop at 16:8. Shorter and longer endings are noted in many manuscripts. The point is sometimes contested, but I do not see the need to argue it further here when it is so well established in the field (cf. Aland 435–70; Lightfoot 106–16; Metzger 122–26). The multiple endings are indeed fertile sources of interpretation. Bridget Upton uses speech-act theory to discuss the possibilities of reactions to these other endings. The audience listening to 16:8 has to deal with the disobedience and failure of the women. The audience of 16:20 loses the momentum of the story muted in extraneous detail. And the 'shorter ending' audience is left with the security and excitement of a completed story, which is, at the same time, undeniably supernatural and personally demanding (Upton 195, passim).

4. For Lincoln, this ending at 16:8 can be appreciated only if both 16:7 and 16:8 are given full weight and their juxtaposition is appreciated.

5. Steve Ditko, Neal Adams, John Byrne, Jim Lee, and many others significantly influenced this style as well.

6. Along with other Jewish characters, these priests are part of an anti-Semitic current that runs through this interpretation. This particular point can be accounted for in the anti-Semitism often attributed to the Gospel of John, but other biases are present that are not in the text, for example, "bad" characters have darker skin, while "good" characters are white.

7. "Barksian" refers to the comics style of Carl Barks of Scrooge McDuck fame.

8. Some off-book weirdness comes in where Brown inserts events from Morton Smith's controversial and probably not authentic *Secret Gospel of Mark*. While certainly not in mainstream Christian tradition, the *Secret Gospel* is widely available. The flow of the narrative is not interrupted in Brown; rather, Smith's work counts on equal footing with the traditional text (Smith).

9. Brown skipped Matthew in issues 18, 23, 28, and 30. Several other autobiographical or surrealist stories ran in these issues.

BIBLIOGRAPHY

Aland, Kurt. "Der Schluss der Markusevangeliums." In *L'evangile selon Marc*, edited by M. Sabbe. Louvain, Belgium: Leuven University Press, 1974.

Anderson, Janice Capel, and Stephen D. Moore (eds.). *Mark and Method: New Approaches in Biblical Studies*. Minneapolis: Fortress, 2008.

Barry, Ann Marie Seward. *Visual Intelligence: Perception, Image, and Manipulation in Visual Communication*. Albany: State of New York Press, 1997.

Blackmore, Colin. "The Baffled Brain." In *Illusion in Nature and Art*, edited by R. L. Gregory and E. H. Gombrich, 120–30. London: Gerald Duckworth, 1973.

Brown, Chester. "The Chester Brown Interview with Steve Grammel, 1990." In *Chester Brown: Conversations*, edited by Dominick Grace and Eric Hoffman, annotated by Chester Brown, 24–72. Jackson: University Press of Mississippi, 2013.

Brown, Chester (w, a). "Mark 14:53–16:20." *Yummy Fur* #14 (January 1989). Toronto: Vortex Comics, 1989.

Brown, Chester. *Mary Wept over the Feet of Jesus*. Montreal: Drawn and Quarterly, 2016.

Cariello, Sergio, and Doug Mauss. *The Action Bible: God's Redemptive Story*. Colorado Springs: David C. Cook, 2010.

Cohn, Neil. *The Visual Language of Comics: Introduction to the Structure and Cognition of Sequential Images*. New York: Bloomsbury, 2013.

Eco, Umberto. *The Infinity of Lists*. Translated by Alastair McEwen. New York: Rizzoli, 2009.

Eisner, Will. *Comics and Sequential Art*. Tamarac, FL: Poorhouse Press, 1985.

Everson, Brian. *Ed vs. Yummy Fur: Or, What Happens When a Serial Comic Becomes a Graphic Novel*. Minneapolis: Uncivilized Books, 2014.

Gaventa, Beverly Roberts, and Patrick D. Miller (eds.). *The Ending of Mark and the Ends of God: Essays in Memory of Donald Harrisville Juel*. Louisville: Westminster John Knox, 2005.

Juel, Donald. *A Master of Surprise: Mark Interpreted*. Minneapolis: Augsburg Fortress, 1994.

Khouri, Andy. "Mark Waid Demos 'Truly Digital Comics.'" *Comics Alliance*, February 12, 2012. http://comicsalliance.com/mark-waid-digital-comics-demo-video/. Accessed August 1, 2015.

Lightfoot, R. H. *The Gospel Message of Mark*. Oxford: Clarendon, 1950.

Lincoln, Andrew. "The Promise and the Failure—Mark 16:7–8." *Journal of Biblical Literature* 108 (1989): 283–300.

McCloud, Scott (w, a). *Understanding Comics: The Invisible Art*. New York: Kitchen Sink/ Harper Perennial, 1994.

Metzger, Bruce M. *A Textual Commentary on the Greek New Testament*. London: United Bible Societies, 1971.

Mormado, Franco. "Of Clowns and Christian Conscience." *America Magazine*, November 24, 2008. http://americamagazine.org/node/149039. Accessed October 2, 2014.

Rhoads, David, and Donald Michie. *Mark as Story: An Introduction to the Narrative of a Gospel*. Philadelphia: Fortress, 1982.

Ross, Steve (w, a). *Marked*. New York: Seabury Church Publishing, 2005.

Smith, Morton. *The Secret Gospel: The Discovery and Interpretation of the Secret Gospel According to Mark*. London: Victor Gollancz, 1974.

Tintera, John. "Review of *Marked* by Steve Ross." *Bookshelf*, 2006. http://www.explorefaith .org. Accessed October 5, 2011.

Upton, Bridget Gilfillan. *Hearing Mark's Endings: Listening to Ancient Popular Texts through Speech Act Theory*. Boston: Brill, 2006.

Wilson, Rebecca. "The Angel Is a Clown: First Graphic Novel Based on a Gospel Captures Vivid Power of Mark." *New Testament Gateway*. Posted November 10, 2005. http:// ntweblog.blogspot.com/2005/11/graphic-novel-based-on-marks-gospel.html. Accessed October 5, 2011.

Chapter Seven

SLAYING A BIBLICAL ARCHETYPE

I Samuel, Gauld's *Goliath*, and the New Midrash

RANEN OMER-SHERMAN

> And David put his hand in his bag, and took thence a stone, and slang it, and smote the Philistine in his forehead. . . . David ran, and stood upon the Philistine, and took his sword . . . and slew him.
>
> —I SAMUEL 17:49

ACCLAIMED SCOTTISH CARTOONIST AND ILLUSTRATOR TOM GAULD'S PROfound and gently subversive reading of 1 Samuel, chapter 17 provides the kind of modern literary midrash that makes the original text appear just as fresh and strange as it rightly should, suggesting that traditional Jewish, Christian, and Muslim understandings of what is arguably humanity's most noble "underdog story" too often overlooks its darker currents and contradictions.

In a commentary altogether representative of how the David story has been glorified, biblical scholar Joel Baden assesses the crux of why, though David wages war throughout his lifetime, in and out of power, it is *this* battle that is endowed with sacred resonance: "If David playing the lyre is an image of faith expressed in words, David defeating Goliath is an image of faith expressed in action. Taken together, they present a complete picture of the authentic man of God, one as emotionally insightful as he is physically courageous, all parts of his character testifying to his devotion. David stands as a model for all who pray and act in God's name" (21). Obstinately contrapuntal to the corpus of interpretation in synch with Baden's scriptural logic as well as the hollowed legacy of visual iconography by artists supporting that traditional view (Bernini, Donatello, Michelangelo, and Verrocchio, among others), Gauld's mischievous reading against traditional interpretation's grain

Figure 7.1. Front cover, *Goliath*, by Tom Gauld / Drawn and Quarterly. Copyright © 2012 Tom Gauld

addresses readers in a century that seems increasingly under siege by those who "pray and act in God's name."

This timeless resonance of Gauld's *Goliath* is signaled by the stark brutality of the opening salvo of its first page in large black lettering: Now THE PHILISTINES GATHERED THEIR ARMIES ON A MOUNTAIN AND THE ARMIES OF ISRAEL STOOD ON A MOUNTAIN ON THE OTHER SIDE: AND THERE WAS A VALLEY BETWEEN THEM. Yet since Gauld is not the first to challenge this sanctified tradition, it is useful to consider a few creative antecedents by way of comparison to more fully grasp what he is about. Not unlike in the reversals that inform the poetic exemplars discussed in this comparative essay, in Gauld's *Goliath* readers enter the story from the *other* side of the Valley of Elah than that presented in the optics of the biblical story, to face the Israelite camp. Though its sparse visual style is surely intended as an

Figure 7.2. Gustave Doré, *David and Goliath*, 1866.

analogue to the sacred text's unadorned language, scripture is otherwise turned upside down through Gauld's relaxed tonal register (varying from dry humor to melancholy) and spare geometric imagery, a visual style occasionally reminiscent of Gustave Doré (1832–1883). However, as we will see shortly, when it comes to the latter's famous engraving, Gauld tweaks its glorious triumphalism considerably.

Gauld's graphic art regularly appears in venues such as the *New York Times Magazine*, the *New Yorker*, and the *Guardian*, but familiarity with his previous work does not really prepare one for the ambition of his *Goliath*. When I first came across the serious whimsicality of his biblical retelling, I was immediately put in mind of the Jewish American poet Charles Reznikoff's (1894–1976) kindred sensibility, his spare decompression of vaunted biblical heroics in this short lyric:

> I do not believe that David killed Goliath.
> It must have been—
> you will find the name in the list of David's captains.
> But, whoever it was, he was no fool. (29)

The poet goes on to speak of a warrior removing the conventional implements of war and finding his own way, abruptly turning back to align the poetic speaker, perhaps Reznikoff himself, writing lines in his own humble way under the shadow of genocide and totalitarianism. Here in his poetic midrash of 1941 (writing at a time when the poet was acutely mindful of the brutal persecution of the Jews as the Nazi army rapidly occupied Poland and Soviet lands), Reznikoff deflects our interest from the usual highlights conjured up by this scene—martial victory, a fallen giant, a jubilant mob and the ascendancy to power—and points instead to images of resiliency and adaptation, the peculiar triumphs of smallness. As is characteristic of his entire oeuvre, the poet's gaze is focused upon the "little" people of history, Jewish and otherwise. Furthermore, by authorizing a gap of mystery and indeterminacy ("It must have been—") over a cherished self-righteous narrative of a recovered heroic past, this poet advocates a history that is not compelled to serve ideological formations. Always an obdurate skeptic of master narratives, aware of their co-opting power, Reznikoff is blithely indifferent here to the myth of an ancient dynasty; instead, he shifts the story's focus to valorize individualist idiosyncrasy and unconventional strategies born of the contingency individuals always face. Instead of presenting a divinely anointed figure, he makes do with a schlemiel, a long-forgotten quick thinker of indeterminate origin who just happened to be at the scene.[1]

By way of comparison, the reader of *Goliath*, which expresses similar minimalist values and aesthetics, is placed in the position of a hapless Philistine in a visually and textually poetic rendering that ultimately challenges the mythic portentousness of all messianic/nationalist narratives. Though not a Jewish artist, Gauld may be profitably compared to Reznikoff in the affirmation that both "sacred" and secular texts are part of the same continuum, an intertextuality in which the sacred and profane are placed in conversation. In their recent book *Jews and Words*, novelist Amos Oz and his daughter historian Fania Oz-Salzberger argue that to participate in secular Jewish intertextuality "you don't have to be an observant Jew. You don't even have to be a Jew. Or for that matter, an anti-Semite. All you have to be is a reader" (2). In a mode not dissimilar to the spirit of Reznikoff's lyric, *Goliath*'s two-color panels counter the traditional ways that the story has been construed in

Gauld's appealing portrait of a gentle giant who is entirely content to spend his days poring over official paperwork (in Gauld's affecting affirmation of Goliath's humanity, we don't even glimpse him in military accoutrement or accompanied by weaponry for many pages). Whereas the Goliath of scripture is, as Robert Alter has it, "a man of material military impedimenta . . . everything given gargantuan size or weight" (101–102), accompanied to the battlefield by a servant bearing his master's shield of similarly outsize proportions, Gauld's exploited protagonist ("the fifth worst swordsman in his platoon"), while drawn on a scale that preserves his startling stature, is consistently unthreatening, more of a hapless freak than the monster bellowing at the Israelite lines (his shield-bearer is an affectionate nine-year-old boy).

When revisiting 1 Samuel, it is not difficult to grasp the strong temptation for a cartoonist of Gauld's postmodern sensibility. In the Bible, Goliath is little more than a cipher, the last obstacle to expelling the "alien" Philistines from the territory of Judah, which happens to be David's homeland (convenient as a milestone in the divinely sanctioned process of consolidating David's royal personality). Moreover, as Gauld once wryly observed to a young fan: "He's hardly a character at all in the bible, he's more of a list of measurements" (Miller). Indeed, he is little more than a motionless, implacable figure, placed entirely in thrall to his adversary's ascendancy, both martial and rhetorical. Of the latter's faith-based riposte to Goliath in 1 Sam. 17:45 ("You come against me with sword and spear and javelin, but I come against you in the name of the Lord of Hosts, the God of the ranks of Israel"), Baden appraises it "as one of the great declarations of faith in the face of adversity, worthy of any Sophoclean or Shakespearean hero. . . . A thrilling statement that reshapes the entire story, changing it from one of combat to one of belief" (21). And yet of course that "sacred" manifesto of faith culminates in a death, not so very unlike any martial tale of heroism in the semimythical annals of ancient epic. Hence, the legend itself inevitably looms like a Goliath before the cartoonist's subversive inclinations.

As it turns out it is not only artists who are overturning the pivotal terms of the myth. Most intriguingly, Gauld's "disruptive" text may be usefully considered alongside new scholarly interventions that assess the inconvenient material and historical realities that may be lurking just beneath the biblical insistence on the cherished category of the "underdog." Let us reconsider the epigraph to this chapter. Most recently, Malcolm Gladwell's *David and Goliath: Underdogs, Misfits, and the Art of Battling Giants* boldly reexamines our underlying assumptions in approaching the text. Basing his inquiry closely on the work of recent Israeli scholarship, Gladwell begins by grappling with the hidden nature of David's weapon; so often imagined as a child's toy, its true effectiveness has been vastly misconstrued over the centuries:

> It's in fact an incredibly devastating weapon. When David rolls it around like this, he's turning the sling around probably at six or seven revolutions per second, and that means that when the rock is released, it's going forward really fast, probably 35 meters per second. That's substantially faster than a baseball thrown by even the finest of baseball pitchers. More than that, the stones in the Valley of Elah were not normal rocks. They were barium sulfate . . . rocks twice the density of normal stones. If you do the calculations on the ballistics . . . it's roughly equal to the stopping power of a [.45 caliber] handgun. This is an incredibly devastating weapon. Accuracy, we know from historical records that slingers—experienced slingers could hit and maim or even kill a target at distances of up to 200 yards. From medieval tapestries, we know that slingers were capable of hitting birds in flight. They were incredibly accurate. When David lines up—and he's not 200 yards away from Goliath, he's quite close to Goliath—when he lines up and fires that thing at Goliath, he has every intention and every expectation of being able to hit Goliath at his most vulnerable spot between his eyes. If you go back over the history of ancient warfare, you will find time and time again that slingers were the decisive factor against infantry in one kind of battle or another. (May)

For Gladwell, David's decision to employ this "incredibly devastating weapon" immediately reverses the true nature of the battle, and it emerges that "he's not the underdog anymore." Moreover, Goliath, already burdened with heavy armor, is not only little more than a "sitting duck" but quite possibly further impaired by a severely compromising medical condition that has only begun to be fully understood in recent scientific history.[2] Weighing such tantalizing revelations against centuries of traditional hermeneutics, 1 Samuel reads now like a superb con job. Yet it should also be noted that the Davidic myth strains or competes against another, equally formidable biblical ethos, the much earlier Mosaic tradition where some might find a more radical, or at least universal resonance.

In this regard, it is worth heeding Walter Brueggemann's insightful analysis of how the Mosaic tradition born in the desert experience "tends to be a movement of protest . . . situated among the disinherited and which articulates its theological vision in terms of a God who decisively intrudes, even against seemingly impenetrable institutions." In contrast, the royal "Davidic tradition tends to be a movement of consolidation . . . situated among the established and secure, and which articulates its theological vision in terms of a God who faithfully abides and sustains on behalf of the present order" (Brueggemann 202). In Gauld's secular imagination the ancient tension between these clashing paradigms still reverberates meaningfully.

Then, too, Gauld knows that due to the story's pervasive nationalistic overtones we cannot easily forget the contemporary resonance of this fable in the festering Israeli–Palestinian conflict that has been embedded in each side's self-understanding since 1948. As Amos Oz famously argues:

> The Europeans were guilty of anti-Semitism and the Holocaust, and the Europeans were guilty of colonialism in the Middle East and of the exploitation of the Arabs. In Brecht's poems, the oppressed join hands and march together. But the two children of the same oppressive parent can often be the worst of enemies. The Palestinians look at me, the Israeli, as an extension of white, sophisticated, colonizing Europe, which returned to the Middle East to do the same old thing: dominate, humiliate, like European crusaders. The other side, the Israelis, see the Palestinians not as fellow-victims but as pogrom-makers, Cossacks, Nazis, oppressors in kaffiyehs and mustaches playing the same ancient game of cutting Jewish throats for the fun of it. You will hear this in many synagogues: They are pharaohs, the goyim, and we are lambs surrounded by seventy wolves. *Neither party will ever give up this sense of victimhood and will forever dispute who was David and who was Goliath.* (Remnick; italics mine)

Hebrew literary scholars attuned to biblical resonances in modern Hebrew literature, from Nurith Gertz to David Jacobson, have noted how in the pre-state period, the Yishuv understood its "relatively small size as a community to be analogous to the young, seemingly defenseless David taking on the more powerful Arab enemy, analogous to the giant Goliath," thus empowering the community well beyond the demarcation of statehood "that they need not see themselves as vulnerable, despite the relatively small size of their state in comparison with the Arab world." Jacobson further notes the strategic uses of the Davidic myth in Zionist utopianism:

> The story of David and Goliath provided a reassuring myth of survival, not only because it told of the victory of the weak against the

> strong but also because the youthful victor of the battle with Goliath eventually emerged as the great ruler of ancient Israel, King David. By identifying with David, the Jews of both the pre-State and State periods could allow themselves to believe that they too would eventually achieve a high degree of political sovereignty, analogous to that of David in ancient times. (83–84)

...

Obviously, this adopted tradition was brimming with dormant messianism.[3] How, then, might Gauld's resolutely antimythic *Goliath* be read against the grain of this troubled ancient/modern paradigm?

To begin with, Gauld's gentle giant is revealed as an unredeemed *outsider*, more at home in the wilderness (whose serene bare lines seem to intentionally evoke the spiritual mysteries of Saint-Exupéry's landscape sketches for *The Little Prince*) than in the society of the army camp. Throughout, the artist's laconic Goliath is a sorrowful figure but never less than amiable, reluctant from the very beginning to play the role he is assigned. He seems as utterly at odds with his own body as he is with the violent warring camps that engulf him. Most notably, when we first meet him, he isn't even yet a warrior, just a clerk assigned to "admin." While Gauld faithfully preserves Goliath's famous speeches and insulting declarations, these are portrayed as a script delivered to him by a Philistine child; we see him poring over those portentous lines day and night, bewildered and bemused, without any apparent connection to their meaning (Gauld strategically employs two different typefaces: serif for biblical texts, and sans serif for his own). Visually this arrangement suggests the dialogic nature of midrash itself, the tradition in which Gauld proves a bold interlocutor. However, textually it also contributes an indelible note of almost perversely deadpan humor, contrasting what one early critic called Goliath's "beautifully pitched normality" (Alderson), against the grandeur of the King James Bible.[4]

The relative lack of dialogue keeps readers focused on the visual, and his uncluttered images are clean and sharp, which is the way one typically perceives objects and beings in the desert. Gauld's desert renderings seem to slow down time itself, the visual equivalents of Ursula K. Le Guin's poem "A Meditation in the Desert," which conceives of a stone "full / of slower, longer thoughts than mind can have" (Phillips 38). And always in Gauld's drawings, we glimpse the stark distances between Goliath (it's a solitude that looks like freedom even when he goes to meet his lonely fate) and all the other warriors. Yet, in striking contrast to these crystalline qualities, Gauld avoids highly detailed facial images; aside from their grizzled faces, these are simple, iconic images, indistinct stick figures rather than realistic and complex ones, which all lends itself well to Gauld's universalizing sensibility.[5] Though there is a relatively short gap of time between frames in which dialogue is represented, much of the narrative consists of a much longer span of time between frames, creating moods that traverse relaxed, meditative, pensive, perhaps even eternal states. Thus, the visual architecture of *Goliath* bridges the conventionally chronological and fragments of timelessness, providing space for the reader's own reflections even as it hints at the protagonist's detached consciousness. As can be seen in each of the images included in this essay, Gauld's lines consistently express serenity, contemplative reason, and slow introspection, a poignant and witty counterpoint to *Goliath*'s ostensible context of martial conflict. Ultimately, these concrete and economic illustrations open up a wide-reaching philosophical terrain that transcends the narrative's immediate context.

When it comes to filling in the lacunae scripture leaves us, Gauld seems most interested in reimagining the giant as stubbornly resistant to being co-opted by the violent scripts of others, whether the God of the Hebrews or his own camp. After they encounter a wandering shepherd who trespasses the Philistine lines speaking an alien tongue, Goliath disappoints his child servant, who chides him for refusing to kill the rustic; it is a characteristically prosaic exchange that is humorous yet also tugs at the heart ("We are soldiers you know." "Ok. Next time I'll kill somebody." "Really?" "No."). Yet more often than not, the giant's perspective is subtly signaled by wry visual elements rather than language. And cumulatively that visual language constitutes a panoply of quiet, small and seemingly inconsequential movements. Yet together they add up to everything. For example, surprised when he is peremptorily summoned, in order to be fitted out with a full set of ceremonial armor, shield, sword, and spear, Goliath passes a chained, fly-tormented bear. Waiting in bewilderment outside the armory, he casts a rueful glance back toward the beast, and in that decisive instant, which comes and goes in a twinkling, the reader cannot fail to recognize the insinuated doppelganger and thus make the poignant connection between Goliath's hapless position and that of the trapped animal.

It is a moment representative of the narrative's entire thrust, which novelist Chris Adrian (quoted on the book jacket) aptly remarks "describes a world and a life where just showing up is half the misery, and you don't actually have to do anything wrong to merit the wrath of an angry God." In fact, this takes us to the very essence of Gauld's midrashic intervention. Some

Figure 7.3. Goliath refuses to fight the bear, *Goliath*, unpaginated, by Tom Gauld / Drawn and Quarterly. Copyright © 2012 Tom Gauld

panels later, a warrior asks Goliath, seated at his scribe's desk, if he has seen the army's new bear and relates that the night before, it was forced to fight three dogs and a leopard, killing them all. Looking down at his parchment, he tersely mutters, "It's not really my thing," a wry utterance that speaks volumes of his benign nature. Dismissively acknowledging that his passivity is well known, the warrior nonetheless presses Goliath to fight the bear for his own profit, but the appalled giant refuses.

When at last the famous challenge he is commanded to utter to the Israelite camp is first placed in his hands (I AM GOLIATH OF GATH, CHAMPION OF THE PHILISTINES. I CHALLENGE YOU: CHOOSE A MAN, LET HIM COME

TO ME THAT WE MAY FIGHT. IF HE BE ABLE TO KILL ME THEN WE SHALL BE YOUR SERVANTS. BUT IF I KILL HIM THEN YOU SHALL BE OUR SERVANTS), the giant faints dead away, and Gauld represents that loss of sentience with an entire page rendered in black, a rendering that also communicates the abyss between his pacific nature and the nationalistic bloodlust surrounding him. And at this juncture Gauld forces readers to pause and question just where we have been and where we are going.

Another pivotal strategy by which Gauld gently reduces the lofty layers of divinely sanctioned military triumph is by elevating something in its place that will be appreciated by any former soldier: the monotony of waiting, downtime, the sheer ennui of routine. For Gauld, these are far more compelling than the dramatic action of the original. Numerous panels are devoted to desultory exchanges between Goliath and his shield-bearer as they are forced to while away the time waiting for a response from the Israelites or to receive further orders. As for the intriguing choice to provide his protagonist with a child companion, Gauld has often indicated that while he sought to put as much focus as possible on Goliath of Gath's isolation and hapless servitude, he was also committed to including all the elements of the original story (in which a servant does appear). Since giving his character an adult companion threatened to undermine the tone and mood of his retelling, he settled on a little boy whose naïveté further underscores the giant's plight.

Goliath is a work exquisitely aware of the space between word and image, brimming with fraught silences. Humorous images are juxtaposed with urgently somber ones. Abandoned in his cherished solitude, sitting under the cold stars in a lonely outcrop of boulders (Gauld's sparsely rendered desert expanse underscores the story's deliberate pacing and Goliath's loneliness), Goliath contemplates simply fleeing the entire morass, a despondent reverie that for some may evoke Jesus's sorrowful doubt in the Garden of Gethsemane. When at last he meets David, a heavy fog descends (a wonderful metaphor for the twisty miasma of scripture itself), so that he neither sees his adversary nor hears the famous divinely sanctioned utterances clearly before he is slain. However, it is crucial to stress that Gauld's reader *does*, and this demonstrates the author's reverential insistence that we encounter his work in conjunction with the passages of the Bible that inspired the new meanings he gleans. One of the most visually demonstrative ways that Gauld achieves this aim is through the dual-font format mentioned earlier:

> I use the serif lettering whenever the text is quoted from the bible. It's intended to be a bit of an ominous reminder of where he's inevi-

tably headed. When Goliath speaks his declaration for the first time it's in that style to suggest that it's not natural to him, that he's being manipulated into the role by what he's been forced to read out, as time goes on and he settles into the role he starts just saying it like anything else. At the end when David appears talking in King James Bible quotes in serif I wanted it to feel like he's not there just as a person, he's an unstoppable force of nature, or God. Or as if he's part of a bigger story, which has overpowered Goliath's story. (Spurgeon)

The implication behind this visual strategy would seem to clearly underscore that virtually all readers of sacred texts, to quote Jonathan Kirsch, writing in a related context, should be "willing to penetrate the veil of piety" (16). Thus, the grandiose strands of the spiritual and politico-military episode that launches David's rise and eventual reign are recast as the inevitable product of the bloated mythology of national origin. In the tradition of the boldest midrashic writers, ancient and modern, Gauld opens up the spaces between the sacred text's divine advocacies, implementations, and choices. In other words, as much as the profane artistic imagination subverts or challenges the sacred text, it is unwilling to disregard it altogether. In his spare yet vibrant imagery, Gauld's melancholy retelling is as memorable a commentary on the futility of war and nationalist excess as some of the strongest responses to militarism in the graphic canon.[6] As such, *Goliath* participates in an artistic tradition that understands war as "a condition of existence so murderous and absurd that a romantic or heroic attitude became impossible" (Packer).

Asked by an interviewer just why he was initially attracted to the Goliath story (at roughly ninety pages this is his most elaborate narrative to date, consuming his artistic life intermittently over a period of seven years), Gauld explains that even before considering the biblical story,

> I wanted to make a story about a giant. . . . I started a story about a giant being hidden away by his family to avoid being called up by the army then abandoned it. . . . When I read the Goliath story in the Bible I realized how little it said about him: basically just a description of his height, weapons and armor, his challenge and a short dialogue with David. So there was space for me to make my story in. I liked the idea that David's triumph is Goliath's tragedy. (Spurgeon)[7]

From the perspective of anyone confronted by the daily headlines, in its insistence on making that inversion, Gauld's version of the tale cannot avoid

Figure 7.4. Goliath shoos away a crow and sits down to eat, *Goliath*, unpaginated, by Tom Gauld / Drawn and Quarterly. Copyright © 2012 Tom Gauld

winking at the present, with Palestinians and Israelis each in thrall to a script in which each side can imagine itself only as the underdog David of the story.[8]

In the charged context of modern militarism, Gauld's poetic fable about a hapless individual compelled to perform before army and state can also be usefully compared to yet another Jewish poem of a midrashic inclination, this one by the young Yehuda Amichai (1924–2000). In "Young David" (*David Hatsa'ir*), a famous poem of the 1950s, Amichai takes a similarly elliptical approach to political realities in suggesting the inadequacy of the David-and-Goliath archetype for coming to terms with Arab–Israeli hostilities, writing

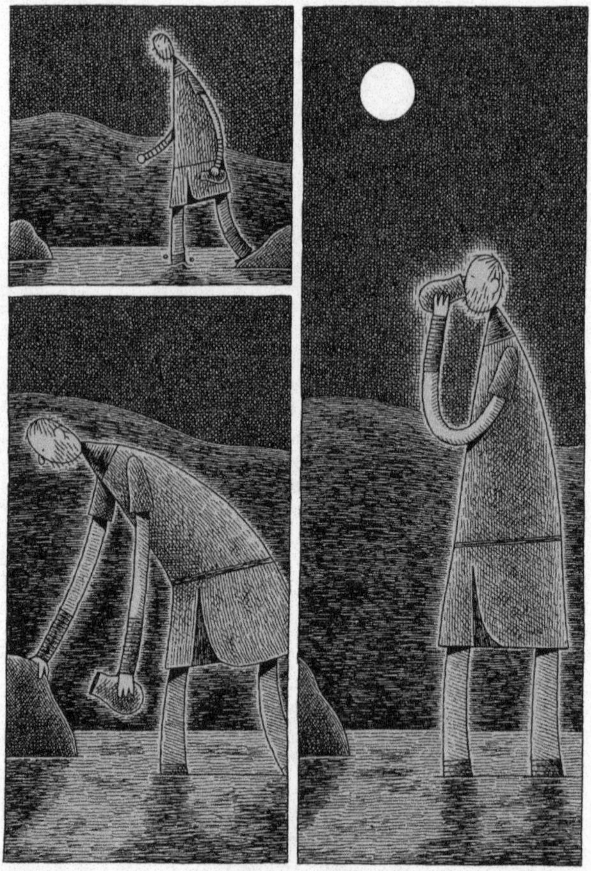

Figure 7.5. Goliath sips water from a stream at night, *Goliath*, unpaginated, by Tom Gauld / Drawn and Quarterly. Copyright © 2012 Tom Gauld

in the distinctive sonnet form he then championed: "After the first cheers / David returned to all the youths / and already the armored revelers / were so grown up" (119).[9] The speaker describes the warrior's raucous reception by the other youths and then the moment of alienation when he discovers how remote he feels from the rites and rituals of machismo, the unbearable weight of the gory head of his defeated adversary. Here in the aftermath of war, Amichai, hailed throughout his lifetime and beyond as one of Israel's leading poets, questions the nationalistic euphoria that sweeps through society, expressing unease over the dangerous linkage of ancient myth with contemporary contexts. As Chana Kronfeld elegantly asserts, "the image of 'bread and circuses' as the epitome of distracting entertainment—or of war as distraction—provided by institutional religion and the state recurs throughout Amichai's poetry" (348). In this regard, the poet stands apart from his association with the legendary pre-state Palmach generation, those who celebrated their own hypermasculinity and the righteousness of their national cause around campfires.

Read against that context, "Young David" embodies a thrilling lyrical paean to alienated skepticism, for this David is rendered with the same sense of unhappy isolation with which Gauld portrays Goliath; both share a palpable exhaustion with their cohorts' bloodlust and adolescent fervor. Moreover, Amichai's David is "lonely / and felt for the first time there were no more Davids" (the gory trophy of the war, Goliath's severed head, reduced to an irrelevance), forcibly marking the irreparable abyss between those who have lost their innocence on the battlefield and the rest of humanity. Moreover, if tradition usually conceives of David as a rustic shepherd barely out of childhood, in contrast to Saul's seasoned warriors, Amichai's imagery reverses that expectation. In his resonant analysis of Amichai's lyric, David Jacobson considers David's return to

> his fellow youthful soldiers, whose noisy revelry is nothing more than the haughty attempts of insecure adolescents to play at being adult by imitating the actions and speech that to them are so adult-like: slapping the hero on the shoulder, laughing hoarsely, cursing, and spitting. The speaker's negative evaluation of these young soldiers vicariously celebrating with the only true warrior among them, comes through clearly when the speaker sarcastically describes them as "already . . . / . . . so grown up." (97)[10]

Similarly, both visually and textually, Gauld's unsettling graphic treatment abounds with a strident critique of infantilized or otherwise uncritical responses to the futility of military conflict, sacred and otherwise.

As such it forcibly challenges the dominant modes of both history and the sacred that fatally confuse one with the other. In their prefatory remarks, coeditors Assaf Gamzou and Ken Koltun-Fromm perceptively argue that "if the comic is successful, a reader will not only see the text differently but also read the text anew." In that regard, Gauld's conscientious attunement to the tragic ways that ancient scripts of violence are encoded in the mythic conflicts of a tiny homeland should be appreciated as an expression of a growing artistic movement impatient with the dominance of conventional alliances between political hegemony and the sacred.[11]

NOTES

1. Though the lyric can read like a wry joke, it actually reveals the poet's deep biblical knowledge, for the story of David's defeat of Goliath presents us with one of scripture's innumerable and fascinating contradictions. For later, in 2 Samuel 21:19, we find that "[a] gain there was a battle with the Philistines at Gob; and Elhanan son of Yaare-Oregim the Bethlehemite killed Goliath the Gittite." Nor is this likely a case of mistaken identity; as Baden observes, not only is the later Goliath identified as a Philistine of Gath, he wields the same magnificent spear (38). It would seem that Goliath was hard to kill. Accordingly, Reznikoff apparently aspires to restore the honor to the resourceful common man (Elhanan in scripture) from whom it was stripped. As Baden argues, both Chronicles and 1 Samuel are filled with tantalizing evidence that "David's legend could have been embellished by appropriating the glory of a relative nobody. This sort of transferal from the unknown to the known is a well-attested feature of heroic tales." And: "The Goliath of 1 Samuel 17 is a secondhand creation, and the entire narrative is a literary exercise in Davidic glorification" (40–41). Baden cites exemplars such as the historical but unknown outlaws whose exploits were later attributed to Robin Hood as well as the Arthurian epic.

2. It is impossible to resist recounting a few of the insights Gladwell gleans from medical literature, as so many of his sources, beginning in the mid-twentieth century, have determined that there is something fundamentally wrong with Goliath:

> The first one was in 1960 in the *Indiana Medical Journal*, and it started a chain of speculation that starts with an explanation for Goliath's height. . . . Goliath is head and shoulders above all of his peers in that era, and usually when someone is that far out of the norm, there's an explanation for it. So the most common form of gigantism is a condition called acromegaly, and acromegaly is caused by a benign tumor on your pituitary gland that causes an overproduction of human growth hormone. And throughout history, many of the most famous giants have all had acromegaly. So the tallest person of all time was a guy named Robert Wadlow who was still growing when he died at the age of 24 and he was 8 foot 11. He had acromegaly. Do you remember the wrestler André the Giant? Famous. He had acromegaly. There's even speculation that Abraham Lincoln had acromegaly. Anyone who's unusually tall, that's the first explanation we come up with. And acromegaly has a very distinct set of side effects associated with it, principally having to do with vision. The pituitary tumor, as it grows, often starts to compress the visual nerves in your brain, with the result that people with acromegaly have either double vision or they are profoundly nearsighted. So when people have started to speculate about what might have been wrong with Goliath, they've said, "Wait a minute, he looks and sounds an awful lot like someone who has acromegaly." And that would also explain so much of what was strange about his behavior that day. Why does he move so slowly and have to be escorted down into the valley floor by an attendant? Because he can't make his way on his own. Why is he so strangely oblivious to David that he doesn't understand that David's not going to fight him until the very last moment? Because he can't see him. When he says,

> "Come to me that I might feed your flesh to the birds of the heavens and the beasts of the field," the phrase "come to me" is a hint also of his vulnerability. Come to me because I can't see you. And then there's, "Am I a dog that you should come to me with sticks?" He sees two sticks when David has only one. So the Israelites up on the mountain ridge looking down on him thought he was this extraordinarily powerful foe. What they didn't understand was that the very thing that was the source of his apparent strength was also the source of his greatest weakness. (May)

3. Jacobson takes further note of the fortuitous fact that the first name of Ben-Gurion, Israel's first prime minister, was David, "thereby suggesting in a subliminal way to his fellow Israelis that the Kingdom of David was in some sense reestablished with the founding of the State of Israel. This identification of political leaders with King David survived into the period of the ascendance of the right-wing Likud party to political power beginning in the late 1970s, when it became customary for supporters of Likud leaders such as Menachem Begin and Ariel Sharon to chant the declaration that their leader is the King of Israel: '*Begin melekh yisra'el*'" [Begin, King of Israel] (84).

4. It seems altogether typical of Gauld's understated approach to this duality that Gauld wryly observes, "I just find it funny to imagine how people would really have spoken in these situations—I am not sure I quite believe how it is always written down" (Alderson).

5. Here I have in mind Scott McCloud's classic continuum of graphic facial representation that encompasses the following categories: complex to simple, realistic to iconic, objective to subjective, specific to universal. See McCloud, *Understanding Comics*, 46.

6. Notable examples of antiwar graphic narratives include Joe Haldeman's *The Forever War* (NBM 1990); Anthony Lappe and Dan Goldman's *Shooting War* (Grand Central 2007); Brian K. Vaughan and Niko Henrichon's *Pride of Baghdad* (Vertigo 2008); Joe Sacco's *The Great War: July 1, 1916: The First Day of the Battle of the Somme* (W. W. Norton 2013); and Jacques Tardi and Jean-Pierre Verney's *Goddamn This War!* (Fantagraphics 2013).

7. In another interview it becomes clear that Gauld was not interested in vilifying David: "David is not a character here, he is a force of nature. . . . You think it's a small boy against the giant but actually it's the giant against the small boy and the all-powerful creator of the universe. He is bound to lose" (Alderson).

8. Considering growing unease in the Diaspora, the growing inadequacy of the David and Goliath paradigm over Israel's sharp lurch rightward, Todd Gitlin writes: "The Israeli victory in the Six Day War for a while re-cemented the salience of the Holocaust. David had crushed Goliath. But in the conquest of the Territories lay demon seeds. The statehood of Israel had the sanction of international law. It still does. But when Israel became an illegal occupier of the territories it conquered in 1967, it forfeited its universalist mantle" ("Chosen People").

9. An award-winning short film by Avi Dabach, a kind of cinematic midrash and meditation on Amichai's lyric, may be viewed here (its spare imagery bears close comparison to Gauld's rendering of the David and Goliath myth): https://www.youtube.com/watch?v=4RhXI4kV5wE.

10. In her own illuminating critical reading of the poem's antimilitarist values, Glenda Abramson considers the grotesque metaphor of the "birds of blood" to suggest that their

wandering, or migration, "confirms the fact that one victory does not ensure others or the cessation of bloodshed, for the birds migrate, or wander far away" (46).

11. The novelist Avner Mandelman acerbically observes in relation to his own critically imaginative engagement with the contemporary reverberations of scripture: "I would like to acknowledge the ancient fictioneers who anonymously wrote the all-time bestseller, and who, astonishingly, managed to convince half of humanity that it is entirely normal to live one's life according to antique fictions. Without this marvelously original con job, I would have little to write about" (42). In Gauld's vision, the past and present are similarly imbricated. All the heartbreak, hilarity, and horror in his *Goliath* seem to arise from a corresponding epiphany.

BIBLIOGRAPHY

Abramson, Glenda. *The Writing of Yehuda Amichai: A Thematic Approach*. Albany: State University of New York Press, 1989.

Alderson, Rob. "Tom Gauld: *Goliath*." *It's Nice That*. January 18, 2012. http://www.itsnicethat.com/articles/tom-gauld-goliath. Accessed June 13, 2017.

Alter, Robert. *The David Story: A Translation with Commentary of 1 and 2 Samuel*. New York: W. W. Norton, 1999.

Amichai, Yehuda. *Shirim 1948–1962*. Jerusalem: Shocken, 1977.

Baden, Joel. *The Historical David: The Real Life of an Invented Hero*. New York: HarperCollins, 2013.

Brueggemann, Walter. "Trajectories in Old Testament Literature and the Sociology of Ancient Israel." In *The Bible and Liberation: Political and Social Hermeneutics*, edited by Norman K. Gottwald and Richard A. Horsley, 201–26. Maryknoll. NY: Orbis, 1993.

Dabach, Avi (dir.). *Young David*. Israel. Micha Shagrir, 2005.

Doré, Gustave. *The Holy Bible with Illustrations by Gustave Doré*. London: Cassel, Petter, and Galpin, 1866.

Gauld, Tom. *Goliath*. Montreal: Drawn & Quarterly, 2012.

Gitlin, Todd. "Chosen People? The Break-Up of American Jewish Identity." *Tablet* March 28, 2016. http://www.tabletmag.com/jewish-news-and-politics/198681/breakup-american-jewish-identity. Accessed June 13, 2017.

Gladwell, Malcolm. *David and Goliath: Underdogs, Misfits, and the Art of Battling Giants*. Boston: Little, Brown, 2013.

Jacobson, David. *Does David Still Play before You? Israeli Poetry and the Bible*. Detroit: Wayne State University Press, 1997.

Kirsch, Jonathan. "Foreword." In Michal Lemberger, *After Abel and Other Stories*. Altadena, CA: Prospect Park Books, 2015.

Kronfeld, Chana. *The Full Severity of Compassion: The Poetry of Yehuda Amichai*. Stanford: Stanford University Press, 2016.

Mandelman, Avner. *Talking to the Enemy*. New York: Seven Stories Press, 1998.

May, Kate Torgovnick. "David, Goliath and the Appeal of the Underdog: A Q&A with Malcolm Gladwell." *TedBlog*: September 30, 2013. http://blog.ted.com/david-goliath-and-the-underdog-a-qa-with-malcolm-gladwell/. Accessed June 13, 2017.

McCloud, Scott. *Understanding Comics*. New York: William Morrow, 1994.

Miller, Sam. "Review: *Goliath* by Tom Gauld." *KidSpirit*, March 4, 2013. http://kidspiritonline.com/2013/03/a-review-goliath-by-tom-gauld/. Accessed June 13, 2017.

Oz, Amos, and Fania Oz-Salzberger. *Jews and Words*. New Haven: Yale University Press, 2002.

Packer, George. "Home Fires: How Soldiers Write Their Wars." *New Yorker*. April 7, 2014. http://www.newyorker.com/magazine/2014/04/07/home-fires-2. Accessed June 13, 2017.

Phillips, Julie. "Out of Bounds: The Unruly Imagination of Ursula K. Le Guin." *New Yorker*. October 17, 2016: 38–45.

Remnick, David. "The Spirit Level: Amos Oz Writes the Story of Israel." *New Yorker*. November 8, 2004. http://www.newyorker.com/magazine/2004/11/08/the-spirit-level. Accessed June 13, 2017.

Reznikoff, Charles. *Poems 1918–1975: The Complete Poems of Charles Reznikoff*, edited by Seamus Cooney. Santa Rosa: Black Sparrow Press, 1976.

Spurgeon, Tom. "CR Sunday Interview: Tom Gauld." *Comics Reporter*. January 22, 2012. http://www.comicsreporter.com/index.php/cr_sunday_interview_tom_gauld/. Accessed June 13, 2017.

Chapter Eight

TRANSRENDERING BIBLICAL BODIES

Reading Sex in *The Action Bible* and *Genesis Illustrated*

SCOTT S. ELLIOTT

> The magic of comics is that there are three people involved in any comic: There is whoever is writing it, and whoever is drawing it, and then there's whoever is reading it, because the really important things in comics are occurring in the panel gutters, they're occurring between panels as the person reading the comics is moving you through, is creating a film in their heads. You're giving them magic, you are allowing them in, and they are contributing and they are creating the movement, they are creating the illusion of time passing. . . . In film, a lot of the time you're not as engaged, it is all being given to you, and you're accepting it as it comes in, but in comics, as a reader, you are going to have to work, your imagination needs to do an awful lot.
>
> —NEIL GAIMAN, *FRESH AIR*

THE EPIGRAPH ABOVE, TAKEN FROM A RECENT INTERVIEW WITH NEIL Gaiman on National Public Radio, encapsulates wonderfully the difference between what Roland Barthes dubbed "writerly" and "readerly" texts. The latter concern themselves with the appearance of transparency: "They open themselves freely to the reader, seemingly withholding nothing . . . and satisfy her desire for meaning" (Aichele 71). They feign to speak plainly in order to ensure—albeit unwittingly—that the only misperception is one that many are already content to embrace for the certainty it provides, namely, that we have ascertained the inherent meaning of the work. Writerly texts, on the other hand, which are not actually things but rather "a perpetual present" (Barthes 5), are those that seem to foreground their materiality. To whatever extent they can be said to speak at all, they do so indirectly. They are unstable, incomplete, fragmented, and even incoherent. Writerly texts are those that excite, frustrate, or irritate the reader, their "gaps and excesses [forcing] readers to become writers, provoking desires for but simultaneously withholding some satisfaction that they may never give" (Aichele 71). As such, they resist meaning and the desire for meaning.

This sense of the writerly text, one that continually frustrates but excites meaning, underpins what is most valuable about the sacred in comics. A variety of contributors to the recently published volume *Classics and Comics*, edited by George Kovacs and C. W. Marshall, demonstrate convincingly that, for a number of reasons, comics engaging classical literature are uniquely positioned as "writerly" texts, "reversing the expected directionality of the reception process" (Kovacs and Marshall xi). Comics and graphic novels that directly render or otherwise reimagine and recast biblical literature, for example, present an intriguing opportunity to sidestep the notion of derivation and to think instead about how earlier and subsequent, or so-called source and target, texts read and, at times, (re)write each other. The two provide fruitful, writerly intertexts for each other.

Elsewhere (Elliott 2011) I have considered an assortment of comics and graphic novels that variously render biblical material centered primarily on the figure of Jesus. Generally speaking, these comics fall into one of two categories. On the one hand are those that are deferential to the Bible itself. These artists seek to transparently illustrate the Bible either to safely entertain devotees or to attract would-be converts (e.g., *The Discovery Bible* [1995] and *The Gospel of Mark* in the Illustrated International Children's Bible series [1996]). Of course, such transparency is a chimera stemming from an underlying theory both of the work and of translation. These productions—and, along with them, *The Action Bible* (Cariello and Mauss), as we will see below—purport an interest in "the Bible" but are, in both practice and effect, concerned foremost with the message the Bible is perceived to contain and secondly with the packaging of that perceived message. The Bible is a delivery device, now shrink-wrapped to fit snugly and precisely that message imagined to precede and to lie outside it. These works render a message the artists distill from the work and then project back upon the work, curating a text already twice removed. Furthermore, while it would seem that such comics "foreignize" (Kirk) the text, to borrow a term from the field of translation studies, they actually appear to domesticate the Bible by doing little to unsettle its familiarity. The "Bible" they (re)present is more or less what one would expect as a "readerly" text.

On the other hand are those comics and graphic novels produced by artists who are not concerned primarily with any "faithful" visual rendering[1] of the Bible. These artists seek instead to interrogate and/or appropriate biblical narrative through their medium in a variety of ways. Borrowing again from the field of translation studies, these comics would appear, at first blush, to "domesticate" the text insofar as they transport the Bible to the world of the modern reader. However, I argued that they ultimately foreignize the Bible by highlighting and capitalizing on its inherent strangeness, and so make it a "writerly" text. I analyzed two examples from this second category: Frank Stack's *The New Adventures of Jesus: The Second Coming* (2006) and Mark Millar and Peter Gross's *American Jesus, Book One: Chosen* (2009). Using these examples, I demonstrated that, whereas comics in the first category ironically fail insofar as they produce something quite unlike the Bible (albeit in guise of a relatively seamless representation of the thing itself), comics in the second category ironically succeed in capturing something fundamentally true of the biblical text and in so doing reanimate the text in productive ways, even as they irreverently play with the story. Although it does not fit perfectly within this category, *Genesis Illustrated* (Crumb) shares similarities insofar as it lingers with the materiality of the Bible, recognizing its inherent gaps (gutters, as it were), and recognizing the Bible itself to be already a "writerly" text. It refuses to abandon—and thus places the Bible in creative tensions with—the artist's own texts.

In what follows, I will further pursue this line of thought by comparing and contrasting *The Action Bible* by Sergio Cariello and Doug Mauss, and *Genesis Illustrated* by R. Crumb, focusing foremost on the ways that each work handles gender and sexuality, particularly vis-à-vis Roland Barthes's concepts of readerly and writerly texts. While something is inevitably lost and gained in every act of "reworking" or hypertext, I argue that the best of comic and graphic art productions of biblical literature do not attempt to replicate the work. Instead, by virtue of the inherently "guttural" language of the comics medium (i.e., speaking between the panels and enlisting readers in the process of writing the story), they highlight the Bible's own fragmentary nature, and thus leave open the possibility of a more "writerly" engagement with the sacred.

. . .

Attitudes and approaches to Bible comics have varied. Beth Davies-Stofka links exegesis, translation, and interpretation: "The Bible in comic book form is a contemporary example of the artist's translation of words into pictures." She describes Bible comics as "works of exegesis. By translating words into pictures, their creators *limit* the possibilities of meaning, stripping away everything non-essential and leaving a focused and purposeful message." On the other hand, David Burke and Lydia Lebrón-Rivera contend that biblical comics and graphic novels resemble the *Targums* and represent a form of midrash by virtue of the ways in which they expand, interrupt, and reinterpret the original. My own inclination is toward the latter, though I go further than Burke and Lebrón-Rivera.

I have previously referred to them as hypertexts, based on Gérard Genette's classification wherein hypertextuality is understood as any relationship uniting a later text to an earlier text, upon which it is grafted in a manner other than commentary, and which it transforms. On the relation of hypertexts to hypotexts, Genette states that "one cannot perceive and appreciate the function of the one without having the other in mind or in hand. This *requirement for reading* forms a part of the definition of the genre and . . . a part of the perceptibility and therefore of the existence of the work" (19). As hypertexts, Bible comics creatively and productively transform the anterior texts upon which they have grafted themselves (recalling the words of Marshall and Kovacs above concerning reversed directionality).

Despite maintaining a relatively high production standard, *The Action Bible* fits firmly within the category of "traditional Bible comics." It is clearly designed to serve as a clever hook for devotees to capture the imagination of the existing flock (particularly the younger members) or to entice would-be converts into the fold. It is concerned primarily with illustrating the biblical narrative, but in a manner I would describe as connecting the dots. In other words, it is not overtly exploratory but aims merely to reveal what it presumes to be present in the Bible already, and to ensure that there is a discernible comprehensive narrative. Finally, it seeks to faithfully render and portray the biblical world of the story, and to bring the reader to the Bible or to the world of the Bible.

Throughout the comic, we encounter characters depicted in period dress and landscapes that presume to match the historical setting (as perceived by particular contemporary artists). It looks "old world" and distant, but remarkably clean, idyllic, bucolic—one might be tempted to describe it as rather middle class and bourgeois. Although the dialogue and narration are not strictly limited to the specific words of whatever particular Bible translation the artist is using, there are key turns of phrase that evoke "scripture" and a table of contents that includes "based on" Bible citations.

Unlike what we will see in Crumb's work, Cariello and Mauss purposefully sidestep any effort to somehow include, or otherwise represent, every word of the text. In fact, their desire to present the whole story—it is, after all, "God's Redemptive Story," according to the book's cover—can only come at a cost to that story and to the work they believe narrates or scripts the Bible. The story *The Action Bible* wants to tell must be rendered in very broad strokes, which can be accomplished only by means of selecting, truncating, reordering for chronological clarity (e.g., tucking Job between Genesis 11 and 12), and opting for what lends itself to visual rendering.[2] Furthermore, Cariello and Mauss rely on a host of extratextual elements. For example, they supply narratorial interruptions (typically acting as a ligament and moving the story forward—though not without theological shaping), clever titles, supplemental material (e.g., imagined dialogue, internal monologues—frequently providing motives), and direct cues to the reader that what she's seeing is explicitly "based on" the Bible, on scripture, with chapter-and-verse references.

The treatment of gender and sexuality in *The Action Bible* is arresting. For instance, on the one hand we see an image of the seductive "whore of Babylon" in the table of contents; Potiphar's wife (Gen. 39:1–20) is what one would likely anticipate; Samson's beloved Delilah, though not as sexualized as one might expect, is depicted as greedy and unintelligent; and "good" women are either elderly and wise, or young and demure (big eyelashes!). Men, on the other hand, generally speaking, are presented with strong, well-shaped physiques. Meanwhile, it is curious to note, I think, that Rahab, who is pointedly identified in the biblical text as a prostitute, is depicted generously. Presumably, this is in part because the intended audience of *The Action Bible* (adolescents, it would appear) dictates that her sex-worker status be downplayed. More significantly, however, she plays a positive role in the story.[3] What is consistent throughout is a pronounced flattening of characters. An especially useful example is Cariello and Mauss's portrayal of John the Baptist's death from Mark 6.

The Gospel according to Mark is not an especially comforting piece of literature. The Jesus at the center of its narrative is abrasive, gruff, and enigmatic. While I would hardly suggest that the narrator "tells it like it is" with regard to any historical reality, he certainly does not pull any punches. Feminist scholars have regarded Mark relatively positively. Elizabeth Struthers Malbon states,

> Mark is seen as really good news to the powerless about a re-visioning of power—and a warning to all, even followers of Jesus, who might be attracted to hierarchical models of power. God's realm is dramatically portrayed in Mark's story as making health and whole-

> ness available to all, but especially to those who have the least access to them under the Roman Empire ruling Jewish Palestine: women, children, the poor, the sick, Gentiles. And God's realm (or kingdom) . . . challenges and enables persons to join that re-visioning of power in confronting the kingdoms of men. (480; cf. Corley 201)

Mark 6:14–29 depicts a flashback episode in which King Herod throws a lavish party that ultimately results in the gruesome beheading of John the Baptist. The scene is both a political indictment of the imperial occupiers and the religious elites who are in collusion with them, and a theological statement concerning the severe risk and costliness of discipleship in opposition to those who think following Jesus is a one-way ticket to triumph and glory.

As the narrator tells it, a rather wishy-washy Herod (e.g., he fears John but protects him; he's confused by John but listens to him; he makes a foolish vow and regrets it afterward but keeps it only partially out of integrity and equally to save face with his guests) is "pleased" by the dance of Herodias's daughter (Salome), who happened also to be his niece and stepdaughter. There is no indication of the girl's age, or the nature of her dance, or why precisely Herod enjoyed it—the reader is left to speculate. The dance is not really the point; it is not the central focus of the passage. The narrator is not inviting the reader to watch the girl dance, but instead to watch Herod watch in order to see the consequences of such voyeuristic behavior on the part of someone already so rotted out on the inside.

The Action Bible tucks this episode into a chapter titled, "A Death in the Family," which is based on Mark 5:38–6:29 and Matthew 10:14–12. In the space of three pages, we view the stories of Jesus raising the daughter of a synagogue official named Jairus, the commissioning and sending out of the disciples, and Herod's feast. In *The Action Bible*'s depiction of this episode, the dancing daughter is the central image, and she appears in three of the four frames on the page, head and shoulders above everyone around her in each segment. Her hair is long, loose, and flowing. Her shoulders, arms, belly, ankles, and feet are exposed. The shape of her body is accentuated by her pose. Men watch with rapt attention, eyes wide, mouths agape or grinning. The comment made by one (viz., "And she's smart, too.") is comical, absurd, empty, and insulting.

It is striking the degree to which Herod is effectively defended in Cariello and Mauss's treatment of the episode. Whereas Mark's narrator renders Herod spineless and pathetic, Cariello and Mauss portray Herodias as the prime mover of the plot from beginning to end, forcing Herod to imprison

Figure 8.1. The dance of Herodias's daughter at Herod's feast from Mark 6:14–29, *The Action Bible*, by Sergio Cariello and Doug Mauss. © 2010 David C. Cook

John, insatiable in her bent toward revenge, hatching an evil plan *together with her daughter*, who is then shown to ask rather sinisterly for John the Baptist's head without any prompting from her mother, as if it were her own idea.

Furthermore, *The Action Bible* explicitly eroticizes Salome. The dance and the female body occupy the dominant frame, despite the fact that the Markan passage offers scant detail, does not focus on this element, and is neither primarily nor ultimately about the dance. So it would appear that *The Action Bible* is actually less concerned about illustrating the biblical text as such than about adapting and rendering something that passes for the Bible, a particular reading of the Bible, from which is distilled a message that is then put forward with biblical validation and authority.

Meanwhile, however, *The Action Bible*'s vision of "God's Redemptive Story" is one that reinforces gender stereotypes, most notably in the eroticization and objectification of female bodies (albeit within a properly restrained sense of "modesty"). While someone might suggest that the artist regards the reinforcement of these stereotypes as redemptive, doing so raises the question of who or what is redeemed and how, not to mention at what cost? Noting that Cariello and Mauss prefer Matthew over Mark (e.g., taking the cues for Jesus's dialogue in the commissioning of the disciples from the former), why include this episode at all? What precisely does it add to this version of "God's redemptive story"?

I think the book of Esther may provide a useful analogy. In the Hebrew version of Esther, God is nowhere mentioned. Esther acts boldly to garner favor with the king and heroically saves her people. In the Septuagint translation and emendation of Esther, however, God appears twenty-four times, and God's role is made explicit. It is difficult to imagine any ancient reader failing to recognize that God was responsible for saving the Jews from Haman's plot, but in their effort to be absolutely sure, the editor(s) of the Greek Esther assert a more conventionally religious interpretation of the story at the expense of Esther's character. Similarly, in *The Action Bible* the reader participates in the viewing; we watch the dance of Herodias's daughter along with Herod and his guests instead of watching Herod himself. For Cariello and Mauss, Salome is a cipher; she functions as sin simplified. Perhaps something valuable comes of this insofar as the episode may condemn such behavior and implicitly reprove any reader who would engage in it, but this works only if readers catch themselves doing it. Meanwhile, in omitting both the story of the hemorrhaging women that Mark inserts into the story of Jairus's daughter, as well as the second half of the story of Jesus commissioning the disciples, Cariello and Mauss's rendering minimizes two of Mark's most fundamental themes: the role of individual faith and agency, and the relationship of suffering to discipleship.

. . .

Though closer to what I have previously labeled an alternative Bible comic, *Genesis Illustrated* does not fit the category perfectly. In the Introduction, Crumb states,

> I, R. Crumb, the illustrator of this book, have, to the best of my ability, faithfully reproduced every word of the original text. . . . In a few places I ventured to do a little interpretation of my own, if I thought the words could be made clearer, but I refrained from indulging too often in such "creativity," and sometimes let it stand in its convoluted vagueness rather than monkey around with such a venerable text.

Despite referring to the work as a "visual, literal interpretation," Crumb's *Genesis* occupies a "transtextual" relationship to the book of Genesis, just as all Bible comics do to their source text(s). Gérard Genette defines "transtextuality" as "the textual transcendence of the text; all that sets a text in a relationship, whether obvious or concealed, with other texts" (Genette 1). Various elements of Crumb's *Genesis* work within Genette's categories of "transtexuality," especially the fourth category of hypertextuality, which refers to

> any relationship uniting a text B (*hypertext*) to an earlier text A (*hypotext*), upon which it is grafted in a manner that is not that of commentary; it may yet be of another kind such as text B not speaking of text A at all but being unable to exist, as such, without A, from which it originates through a process I shall provisionally call *transformation*, and which it consequently evokes more or less perceptibly without necessarily speaking of it or citing it. (Genette 5)

In my judgment, *Genesis Illustrated*, as a whole, fits the profile of a hypertext. To wit, it shares in common certain dimensions or aspects of translation, which Genette also regards as a form of hypertextuality. However, *Genesis Illustrated* neither perfectly transfers nor completely reworks and transforms. I think instead that it curiously—and, in the end, productively—animates the book of Genesis in the sense of breathing life into it; Crumb's illustrating of Genesis resuscitates Genesis, and especially silenced characters therein, as we shall see.

In his "Introduction," Crumb makes it clear that he does not believe the Bible is "the word of God" but rather "the words of men." However, he also regards it as "a powerful text with layers of meaning that reach deep into our collective consciousness, or historical consciousness, if you will." He indicates that he made use of scholarly resources "and found them helpful in enriching the background material for the content of the drawings." He claims that he approached the project as "a straight illustration job." Lastly, in the "Commentary" that follows his illustrations, he states this about the Bible: "What's remarkable about the Torah is the unbroken longevity of its preservation as a book that is used, read, studied, and interpreted. These writings were never buried and then rediscovered later. They are the oldest texts in continuous use in Western civilization. It's no wonder that people believe them to be the word of God." The point I am trying to make is that, despite purporting merely to illustrate, Crumb's posture toward the work is far from simplistic. He takes the text itself quite seriously, and in a manner that differs from the seriousness of Cariello and Mauss's engagement.

Genesis Illustrated reflects degrees of reworking, which I label with the terms *exposure*, *selection*, *interpretation*, and *rendering*. *Exposure* refers to instances where Crumb is making plain what is already present in the text of Genesis. Chief examples are nudity and sex (the genitalia of Adam and Eve in Genesis 1; Adam "clinging" to Eve in Genesis 2; Isaac and Rebekah lying together in Genesis 24) and violence (Cain killing Abel in Genesis 4; victims of the flood desperately gasping for breath as they drown in Genesis 7; the murder of Hamor and Shechem by the sons of Jacob in Genesis 34). These are the sorts of things that no doubt fueled the decision to exploit the term "graphically" in the book jacket's proclamation: "The first book of the Bible *graphically* depicted!" Here, Crumb is "merely" drawing out, making explicit what is already there but too easy to read past in ordinary written versions. Recalling Scott McCloud's description of comics as a participatory medium (60–69), here one does not assist in committing the act of murder per se, but one certainly bears witness to it in a more profound way.

Selection refers to instances where Crumb decides what element or aspect of a verse to illustrate. Sometimes these are relatively simple matters—"Abram invoked there the name of the Lord" and "there was strife between the headmen of Abram's flocks and the herdsmen of Lot's flocks" (Genesis 13). Other times they contribute to or else draw out the mood of the biblical narrative. For example, the depiction of generations, and the passing thereof, in Genesis 36 is fairly straightforward, but a similar narrative sequence in Genesis 11 goes a bit further, varying the activities, but also shading them, as it were, in certain ways—for example, Peleg (drudgery) versus Reu (dancing). Sometimes the visual medium forces Crumb to collapse divergent strands of tradition interwoven in the text. For instance, in Genesis 7, Crumb depicts rain rather than "the wellsprings of the great deep [bursting] forth," and he portrays one pair of animals entering and exiting the ark, rather than the seven pairs prescribed in Gen. 7:2–3.

At one level, every stroke of the pen is an interpretive act. However, there are instances in *Genesis Illustrated* where Crumb engages Genesis in a fashion that manifests the "writerly" and responds to it in kind. And he does so in such a manner and to such a degree that it reactivates the text's cacophony of voices and invites, even provokes, more active writing. Examples include (1) his depictions of the strange, surreal, and visionary, such as Abram's "great dark dread" in Genesis 15—not to mention the figure of God; (2) supplying information, effectively voicing interior monologues (Genesis 17) or transforming free indirect discourse (Genesis 45), including the words, "and he said," which is redundant in a comic; and (3) adding visual representations of foreign tongues in the Tower of Babel sequence in Genesis 11, and Joseph "playing the stranger" to his brothers in Genesis 42–43, speaking to them through an interpreter prior to their recognition of him. Graphic novels are not translations in the sense of linguistic transpositions, but they are forms of translation vis-à-vis adaptations and transmediations. Decisions like these are unavoidable when one adapts writing to an alternate medium and different narrative mode. *Genesis Illustrated* is no exception.

Finally, instances of what I call *rendering* are those in which a particular reading of the story is fleshed out and rendered on the faces of the characters in Crumb's illustrations. For example, the facial expressions and actions of those building the Tower of Babel evoke a sense of hubris. This happens with a degree of frequency in his depictions of women. Of particular relevance for this chapter are stories that feature women as central characters. For instance, Sarai is first accompanied by a question mark in a thought bubble, then with a tear on her cheek when Abram explains his plan to pass her off as his sister in Genesis 12. And Rebekah is seen making a melody as she prepares food prior to sending Jacob to secure the blessing from Isaac in Genesis 27.

A particularly intriguing example of Crumb's rendering activity is found in his illustration of Lot's daughters in Genesis 19, which tells the harrowing story of Sodom and Gomorrah. Lot (Abraham's nephew) and his family are at the center of the story, and Lot's daughters feature prominently at the beginning and at the end of the chapter. In verses 1–11, when the men of the city are begging Lot to hand over his guests so that they might rape them, Lot offers his daughters as a consolation prize. Later, after the cities have been destroyed (vv. 12–29), Lot's daughters appear again (vv. 30–38). This time they are depicted as making their father drunk, at the suggestion of the older daughter, in order to sleep with him so they can bear children. Ultimately, they give birth to sons named Moab and Ben-ammi, who grow up to become the patriarchs of Israel's long-standing enemies the Moabites and the Ammonites. I want to focus on this latter episode.

The story is painfully sad and dark. Lot's daughters had been married, but their husbands did not flee Sodom prior to its destruction and therefore perished with the city and its other inhabitants. According to Gen. 19:31, the elder daughter's perception of the circumstances was that not a single man was left with whom to bear children. The narrator portrays her as the one who devises a scheme to remedy the situation: "Come, let us make our father drink wine, and we will lie with him, so that we may preserve offspring through our father" (NRSV). In a manner typical of Hebrew Bible narrative, the story is marked by irony: the daughters "sexually manipulate the man who would have allowed a crowd to have their will with them" (Bellis 67). Lot "becomes the passive sexual object he had determined his daughters should become" (Fretheim 475), and the narrator of the episode does not explicitly condemn the daughters for their actions.

There has been a range of interpretations of this scene, especially among feminist scholars. One I find particularly intriguing, not only for the interpretation itself, but for the reading strategy it reflects, is that of Melissa Jackson, who points out that in their use of their wits to achieve what was expected of them, Lot's daughters subvert the power relationships that otherwise constrained them (cited in Bellis 67; cf. Fretheim 476): "The writers of the patriarchal narratives invite us to step in with them and dream our own dreams of a world turned upside-down. Maybe in this reality patriarchy was not the status quo, men were seen as fools for behaving as if they were in total control, and women were valued for motherhood and also for their intelligence, courage, inventiveness, creativity."

What interests me about this episode is the way in which Crumb's depiction is emblematic of his engagement with Genesis as a whole. As he does in a number of places (e.g., the story of Tamar and Judah in Genesis 38), Crumb here seems to read against the grain of the story in order to interrogate the story, to liberate the female characters, and to pointedly challenge the viewer-reader. The result is that he effectively redeems the biblical narrative itself, but without taking recourse to apologetic.

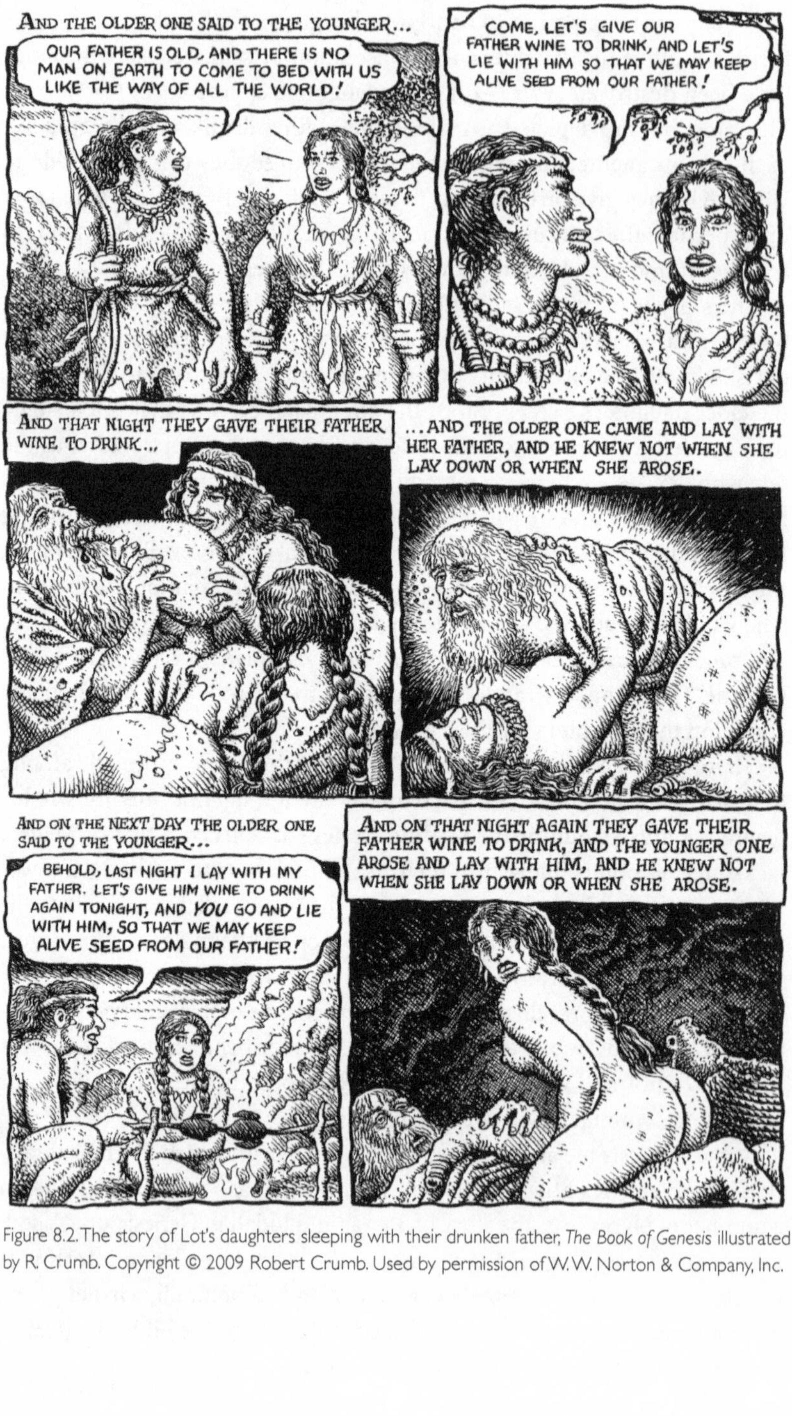

Figure 8.2. The story of Lot's daughters sleeping with their drunken father, *The Book of Genesis* illustrated by R. Crumb. Copyright © 2009 Robert Crumb. Used by permission of W. W. Norton & Company, Inc.

Crumb includes the episode because he is committed to illustrating Genesis in its entirety. However, each scene of the episode is given relatively equal space on the page. The scandalous moments of the story are not sensationalized. Crumb's portrayal imitates the straightforward and stark, flat, atonal mode of the biblical storyteller. At the same time, however, he opts for a feminist reading that neither rejects the Bible nor valorizes it uncritically. Instead, he wrestles with the text. He refocuses the story through the younger daughter. Moreover, forced by and taking advantage of the narrative's sparse detail, Crumb renders on the face of the younger daughter a reading of the narrative that, among other things, gives her a voice that the narrator withholds. The viewer identifies with the feelings of surprise, shock, anxiety, and discomfort written on her face. And, finally, in the climactic moment of the episode, Crumb turns the younger daughter's head away from her father and toward the viewer—suggesting a tear in her eye and a look of shame or disgust as she sleeps with her father at her sister's behest. Crumb's decision to render the image this way reflects what Mieke Bal labels "pictorial narratology," which can function as "a secret code, a subcultural language that facilitates the production of subversive narratives" (2004, 1289). In giving the daughter a voice, he does not silence the text itself in the process. The viewer-reader is drawn into a perpetual feedback loop that allows for critical self-reflection. Despite the potential for images to limit the proliferation of textual meanings and to effectively close texts such that they are made readerly works, such "experiments," as Bal describes them, can just as well thwart any direct and explicit determination of meaning, thereby allowing for writerly engagement (see Bal 2008, 91). Meanwhile, the trajectory of Crumb's redemption of both the daughters and the story appears on the next page, where both daughters teach their young boys their skills with a bow and arrow, while Lot lies wine-sodden and bedraggled in the background.

In the end, it seems to me that *Genesis Illustrated* represents a sort of midrashic transmediation that animates the biblical text by successfully capturing, rendering, and perpetuating the Bible's own writerly nature. My understanding of midrash is that it is not so much about preservation (in the sense of protection) as about curation (a sense of care coupled with keeping alive and in relevant dialogue). To be sure, some portions of biblical literature are more writerly than others. And perhaps it could be argued that individual biblical *scriptures* are more writerly than the biblical *canon*. But the writerly lying within biblical literature is never fully suppressed by its canonical framing, and therefore it always threatens to destabilize and undo the readerly constraints of the canon and the canonical.

. . .

To whatever extent all Bible comics are, in part, midrashic with respect to the ways in which they fill in gaps and extract "extra-textual signifieds," the key difference between *The Action Bible* and *Genesis Illustrated* lies in what these works suggest about the Bible, and in how their respective creators approach the textual gaps. Both begin with scripture as the point of departure, and both seek to adapt it to, or put it in conversation with, the creator's contemporary context. However, the impression one has after reading *The Action Bible* is that the Bible is a readerly text, because *The Action Bible* fills the gaps necessary to create a sense of narrative completeness (while ignoring other gaps that would mitigate against such cohesion) in order to convey and apply a perceived message that serves the purposes of edification and practice. Perceiving it as a work that presents a concrete message plainly, Cariello and Mauss seek to transmit that message in an equally plain manner, as if they were allowing the biblical storytellers to dictate the visual portrayal themselves. The work of commentary is perceived as that of (re)constructing the text as "Bible," and as providing "the reassuring alibi of the 'concrete'" (Barthes 12). The consequence is that, as in the case of Salome's dance, the text's critical voice is silenced, glossed over, and readers of *The Action Bible* are positioned such that the male gaze is reinforced, and the Bible effectively authorizes such a point of view. Crumb, on the other hand, is fiercely attentive to qualities of the text itself, to its materiality, to the subtle complexities that shape the contours of biblical narrative, and to the things that pose obstacles to meaning. *Genesis Illustrated* is not prescriptive but dialogical; the text is one that imitates the Bible as a writerly text in requiring the viewer-reader to occupy the "perpetually present" (Barthes 5) space of writing. Moreover, it invites the viewer-reader to recognize that "the work of commentary, once it is separated from any ideology of totality, consists precisely in *manhandling* the text, *interrupting* it" (Barthes 15). In the end, Cariello and Mauss's Salome is an object, but Crumb's younger daughter of Lot is a subject.

Certainly both artists "read into" the text, as would be expected of any transmediation. But my interests in this chapter have centered on their respective degrees of transparency, their implicit understandings of biblical literature, and the subsequent consequences of their graphic readings. In reference to the book of Esther, Klara Butting claims that "the [biblical] authors testify with their procedure that the Bible wants to be an interlocutor, not an authority" (cited in Bellis 194). I would suggest that the creators of *The Action Bible* and *Genesis Illustrated* similarly testify to how texts function as readerly or writerly interlocutors with readers—not as sources of authority, but as problematic renderings of the sacred.

NOTES

1. The notion of "faithfully rendering" is terribly problematic. All I intend to suggest is that the creators of comics like these seem to take a certain deferential posture toward the canonical text. They do not intend to interrogate, critique, rework, or rewrite the canonical material, but merely to illuminate it in service to its perceived message—both that contained within and that conveyed iconically.

2. It is, after all, the *Action* Bible, so, for example, levitical laws, the messages of the prophets, and the bulk of Paul's letters—to say nothing of those poor "catholic" epistles—are left lying on the cutting room floor.

3. There is an odd paradox inherent in nearly every "children's Bible." In an effort to attract young audience members to the Bible, we offer them a different Bible.

BIBLIOGRAPHY

Aichele, George. *Simulating Jesus: Reality Effects in the Gospels*. London: Equinox, 2011.

Alter, Robert. *The Five Books of Moses*. New York: W. W. Norton, 2004.

Bal, Mieke. "Figuration." *PMLA* 119 (2004): 1289–92.

Bal, Mieke. *Loving Yusef: Conceptual Travels from Present to Past*. Chicago: University of Chicago Press, 2008.

Barthes, Roland. *S/Z*. Translated by Richard Miller. New York: Hill and Wang, 1974.

Bellis, Alice Ogden. *Helpmates, Harlots, and Heroes: Women's Stories in the Hebrew Bible*. Louisville: Westminster John Knox, 2007.

Burke, David G., and Lydia Lebrón-Rivera. "Transferring Biblical Narrative to Graphic Novel." *SBL Forum* (2004). http://sbl-site.org/Article.aspx?ArticleID=249. Accessed December 12, 2016.

Cariello, Sergio, and Doug Mauss. *The Action Bible: God's Redemptive Story*. Colorado Springs: David C. Cook, 2010.

Corley, Kathleen E. "Slave, Servants and Prostitutes: Gender and Social Class in Mark." In *A Feminist Companion to Mark*, edited by Amy-Jill Levine, 191–221. Sheffield: Sheffield Academic Press, 2001.

Crumb, Robert. *The Book of Genesis Illustrated*. New York: W. W. Norton, 2009.

Davies-Stofka, Beth. "The Bible in Comics: Genesis," *Sacred Matters: Religious Currents in Culture* (2014). http://sacredmattersmagazine.com/the-bible-in-comics-genesis/. Accessed December 13, 2016.

Elliott, Scott S. "Jesus in the Gutter: Comics and Graphic Novels Reimagining the Gospels," *Postscripts: The Journal of Sacred Texts and Contemporary Worlds* 7, no. 2 (2011): 123–48.

Fretheim, Terence E. "The Book of Genesis: Introduction, Commentary, and Reflections." In *The New Interpreter's Bible*, Vol. 1, edited by Leander E. Keck, 319–674. Nashville: Abingdon Press, 1994.

Gaiman, Neil. Author interview: "Neil Gaiman on Returning to 'Sandman,' Talking in His Sleep and the Power of Comics." *Fresh Air* (2015). http://www.npr.org/2015/12/15/458319575/

neil-gaiman-on-returning-to-sandman-talking-in-his-sleep-and-power-of-comics. Accessed on December 14, 2016.

Genette, Gérard. *Palimpsests: Literature in the Second Degree.* Lincoln: University of Nebraska Press, 1997.

Jacklin, Mike. *The Discovery Bible.* Carlisle, Cumbria: Paternoster, 1995.

Kirk, Peter. "Holy Communicative? Current Approaches to Bible Translation Worldwide." In *Translation and Religion: Holy Untranslatable?*, edited by Lynne Long, 89–101. Clevedon: Multilingual Matters, 2005.

Kovacs, George, and C. W. Marshall (eds.). *Classics and Comics.* Oxford: Oxford University Press, 2011.

Malbon, Elizabeth Struthers. "Gospel of Mark." In *Women's Bible Commentary*, edited by Carol A. Newsom, Sharon H. Ringe, and Jacqueline E. Lapsley, 478–92. Louisville: Westminster John Knox, 2012.

McCloud, Scott. *Understanding Comics: The Invisible Art.* New York: Harper Perennial, 1993.

Millar, Mark, and Peter Gross. *American Jesus, Book One: Chosen.* Berkeley: Image Comics, 2009.

Neely, Keith R., David Miles, Roberta Neely, Bridget Harlow, and Thomas R. Zuber. *The Gospel of Mark/The Illustrated International Children's Bible.* Nashville: Thomas Nelson, 2006.

Stack, Frank. *The New Adventures of Jesus: The Second Coming.* Seattle: Fantagraphics Books, 2006.

Part III

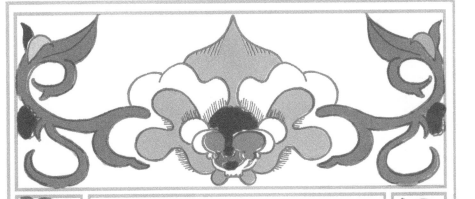

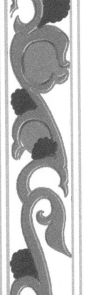

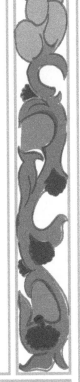

TRANSFIGURED COMIC SELVES, MONSTERS, AND THE BODY

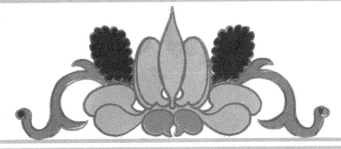

CHAPTER NINE: Samantha Langsdale, "The Dark Phoenix as 'Promising Monster': An Interdisciplinary Approach to Teaching Marvel's *X-Men: The Dark Phoenix Saga*"

CHAPTER TEN: Jeffrey L. Richey, "'Honor the Power Within': Daoist Wizards, Popular Culture, and Contemporary Japan's Spiritual Crisis"

CHAPTER ELEVEN: Samantha Baskind, "Joe Kubert's *Yossel: April 19, 1943*: Faith and Art History's Precedents"

Monsters and wizards are extraordinary humans existing on the edges of cultural norms and expectations. Their powers can be uplifting or grotesque, transformative or destructive. They inform how we think of outsiders, and often arrive as comfort for the boundaries we establish for civilized life. Their bodies, both physical and imagined, are themselves borders of meaning. As embodied, liminal beings, monsters and wizards tell us about ourselves and our beliefs, about what kinds of bodies count as human, and what kinds of belief shape our identities. These displaced bodies, in short, reveal the visual assumptions that underlie sacred bodies. Graphic narratives, and their historical predecessors the editorial and gag cartoons, have often played an important role in establishing these visual assumptions. The grotesque physiognomy of the caricature, the wistful and elastic bodies in the "funny pages" of Winsor McCay and George Herriman, and the virile strongman superhero and the cyborg all inform and undermine assumptions concerning the body. The comic monsters discussed in the three essays of this section are bodies out of place: either transfigured selves from distanced, art-historical periods, or imagined bodies rendered through sacred fantasies, or even repurposed images from popular culture. These liminal bodies are materially rendered in comics as both sacred and monstrous beings: they are the imagined others that visually explore the limits of being human. As comics expand those human limits, they also train us to see and explore the limits of the sacred.

Chapter Nine

THE DARK PHOENIX AS "PROMISING MONSTER"

An Interdisciplinary Approach to Teaching Marvel's *X-Men: The Dark Phoenix Saga*

SAMANTHA LANGSDALE

FEW COMIC BOOK CHARACTERS HAVE UNDERGONE REINCARNATION (literally) as many times as Jean Grey/Phoenix from Marvel's X-Men series.[1] Beginning as the demure Marvel Girl, Jean Grey transforms throughout the comics into various manifestations of the Phoenix, each one more powerful and volatile than the last. For fans and scholars alike, the Phoenix has presented both promising avenues for women in comics and pressing problems associated with sexuality, agency, and identity. Many feminist scholars and bloggers have critiqued the ways in which Chris Claremont and John Byrne's *X-Men: The Dark Phoenix Saga* (DPS) links female desire and female sexuality with psychoses, lack of control, monstrosity, and ultimately destruction. Similarly, when examining the character of the Dark Phoenix, critical questions about agency and identity arise. Her behavior is often characterized as "out of control," and readers are encouraged to understand Jean as being "at the mercy" of the Phoenix Force. Jean Grey's seeming lack of agency precludes the possibility for the Dark Phoenix to be a feminist superhero; further, the ways in which women's sexuality and desires are linked to violence throughout the DPS make a feminist interpretation of the comic unsustainable.

Nevertheless, this chapter argues that mainstream superhero comics have real pedagogical potential and that the DPS in particular might be taught in ways both critical and creative. Through employing an interdisciplinary approach to the DPS—including feminist analysis of Christian mysticism, as well as postmodern theories of corporeality—the character of Jean Grey/Phoenix may be interpreted in ways that critique hegemonic definitions of female sexuality as monstrous and that constructively challenge certain assumptions about agency, identity, and embodiment.

More specifically, I suggest that through teaching the DPS, students might be encouraged to explore theories of religious subjectivity that do not rely solely on definitions of "agency as subversion." Agency is traditionally understood as the ability to act with intention, or for an individual to be able to exert power. Thus, "agency as subversion" would mean that an individual intentionally acts in ways that subvert dominant paradigms or exert power *against* a dominant force. These types of theories cannot be applied effectively to Jean Grey's narrative, owing to the fact that she (like many adherents to religious traditions) is "activated" by a higher, external power. As a result, a different definition of agency must be located, one that does not dissolve because of the ways in which Jean Grey/Phoenix acts both in accordance with and sometimes entirely divorced from the Phoenix Force. One source for alternative models of religious agency that do not fall into this pattern might be feminist historical analyses of medieval Christian mystics. Read alongside the DPS, hagiographies of medieval Christian mystics may be productively referenced in order to provide students with more nuanced ways to think about agency. Further, rather than insist that Jean/Phoenix is or is not a villain, should or should not be read as feminist, it seems productive to frame the character in more complex ways. By engaging with Donna Haraway's theories of corporeality and identity, I suggest in the final section of this chapter that Jean/Phoenix provides a fruitful example of a "promising monster," a figure whose "marked body" demonstrates the fluidity, layeredness, and fragility of identity categories and whose very materiality threatens hegemonic boundaries of gendered embodiment. Ultimately, in taking this interdisciplinary approach, I hope to demonstrate how the DPS may be employed in order to introduce students to expanded definitions of religious agency, to constructively critique normative discourses on female sexuality, to think differently about liminality, and to enable students to creatively engage with dynamic models of embodied subjectivity in visual culture.

. . .

Like many scholars who analyze comics, I initially came to the medium for very personal reasons. Claremont and Byrne's *X-Men: The Dark Phoenix Saga* was the first trade paperback I purchased for myself, because it resonated with me in meaningful ways. Jean/Phoenix seemed to a younger me to embody "girl power"; she was feminine and assertive, part of a team and an individual; she acted with love but also, thrillingly, with fury. My reasons for pursuing this research are rooted in these memories and personal interests, but they have developed further and are also driven by my work as a feminist educator. The proliferation of comic book films and television shows, the increased popularity of comic-cons, and the reinvigoration of the comic book trade industry have undeniably made this medium a dominant part of Western visual culture. Although not all contemporary students may consider themselves fans, box office numbers and purchasing trends seem to indicate that comic book culture is at least relevant to the "typical" university demographic (Syma and Weiner 5). Making use of comic books in classrooms is advantageous, because students are far more likely to retain and synthesize information that seems to them to be personally relevant (Fink 18). Moreover, as comics scholars like Randy Duncan and Matthew J. Smith have argued, "comic books are a unique and powerful form of communication" and can be pedagogically valuable because "reading in the twenty-first century often involves more than the mere understanding of words" (Duncan and Smith 13–14). As both image and text, as the visual and the narrative, comics provide one of the most promising means by which students can develop skills necessary for thinking and communicating in contemporary culture (Syma and Weiner 5).

Further, to a scholar focused on gender, religion, and embodiment in visual culture, there are few other easily accessible media that seem to display and explore these intersections so vividly. In addition to the myriad comics and graphic novels explicitly pertaining to religious traditions, mainstream superhero comics can also be useful in religious studies classrooms. In fact, A. David Lewis and Christine Hoff Kraemer note that as comics have become a more sophisticated medium, creators have begun to address religious issues, "offering their own reflections on traditional religions, criticizing or satirizing those religions, or breaking away from traditional religions in the pursuit of religious innovation" (2). Mainstream comics provide students with the opportunity to investigate how, and in what ways, creators are exploring, interrogating, or inventing religion, and further, how those explorations are demonstrative of, or depart from, dominant cultural discourses. A brief look at the scholarly literature further demonstrates how superhero comics in particular are bound up with religions and the religious (e.g., Garrett; Lewis; Oropeza; Saunders).

It is also the case that mainstream superhero comics are littered with all types of bodies, both fantastic and mundane, of varying genders, racial profiles, and DNA compositions. The varying depictions of bodies in comics are pedagogically fruitful not only because of their diversity, but also because of the ways in which many demonstrate and reinforce particular ideals of corporeality (Bukatman 49). According to John Jennings, the "superhero is an embodiment, but not just of an individual. It is an embodiment of cultural and social values—a *gestalt* of various belief structures in physical form" (59). Thus, students are presented with myriad opportunities to critically question how and in what ways bodies are formed in visual culture by gender, race, ability, and religion.

Finally, while women comics creators and readers are increasing in numbers, and depictions of female characters within comics are diversifying, the history of the industry is androcentric at best, and misogynist at worst (Duncan and Smith 258; Robbins). Current events such as the exclusion of women from the 2016 Angoulême Comics Festival, the persistent creation of "cheesecake" covers,[2] or the continued composition of all-male panels at comic-cons demonstrate ongoing problems related to gender equality and representation. The marginalization and erasure of women creators and readers, and sexist depictions of female characters, not only may be damaging in terms of representation but may also have negative psychological effects. Psychologists Elizabeth Behm-Morawitz and Hillary Pennell state the following: "It is known that people learn about gender norms and expectations from exposure to media. More specifically, gendered media portrayals influence individuals' self-concept, beliefs about traditional gender roles, gender stereotyping, body esteem and eating disordered behaviors, and self-objectification" (79). These effects are of particular concern for girls and women who, when exposed repeatedly to superhero sagas wherein female characters are portrayed as "sexualized, victimized, and objectified . . . internalize the communicated standards of the female body in the media." In other words, say Behm-Morawitz and Pennell, "they generally have lower self-esteem and self-efficacy" (85). To insist on purely "canonical" readings of mainstream comics therefore is to perpetuate these same problems in the classroom. However, to encourage students to creatively reread comics through a feminist lens provides at least some means of expanding inclusion and extracting "women [from] refrigerators" (Duncan and Smith 255).[3] My adaptation of the DPS for the classroom, then, is an attempt to address (in at least one way) the "woman problem" in mainstream superhero comics. That said, the greater aim of this chapter is to enable students to explore the intersections of gender, religion, and embodiment in visual culture in ways that do not replicate marginalization, erasure, and self-doubt, but instead foster and excavate models of whole, multifaceted subjectivity.

. . .

As mentioned previously, the DPS has pedagogical promise not only because it allows for creative rereadings, but also because it can be employed to familiarize students with the ropes of critique. In guiding students first through a discussion of what problems manifest in the DPS with regard to gender, religion, and embodiment, one can effectively introduce multiple strands of feminist philosophy and theories of corporeality. For example, the DPS, like the majority of mainstream superhero comics, is replete with what Scott Bukatman has called "mutant musclemen and the big-titted women who love them" (48). Embodiment in the DPS, for both male and female characters, is hyperbolic and heteronormative. Male characters are hypermasculine and virile, with imposing physical presences (e.g., Cyclops, Angel, or Sebastian Shaw), while female characters are in corsets, skin-tight uniforms, and varying degrees of nudity (e.g., Emma Frost and Jean as the Black Queen). This type of representation sexualizes both male and female characters: male characters become models of masculinity and virility for the intended "typical" heterosexual male reader to emulate, and female characters are turned into objects of desire—objects of the male gaze. The problems resultant from this type of representation are many; not only do these corporeal ideals restrict the valued or admirable body to the overmuscled or oversexualized, but they also have the potential to alienate and marginalize women as readers. Moreover, as noted above by Behm-Morawitz and Pennell, because of "the portrayal of female characters in superhero stories as sexualized, victimized, and objectified," the self-concept of female readers in particular "may be negatively impacted" (85).

Relatedly, female sexuality is treated in the DPS in worryingly Freudian ways. In a general sense, psychoanalyst Sigmund Freud believed that psychosexual desires were innate in all human beings and that libidinal desires were one of the primary drives in the lives of all subjects. As a human being grows from infancy to adulthood, some libidinal desires must be, and are, repressed—repression being a necessary aspect of developing a healthy, normal subject position. Female desire, however, according to Freud, *must* be repressed if a "normal" (read: heterosexual) woman is to materialize; in other words, originary female psychosexual desires are necessarily repressed desires. In this way, female subjects repress and turn away from their originary libidinous desires—they repudiate the feminine—and come to realize that they now lack or feel loss. Freud suggests that women compensate for this loss of originary desire by seeking out "phallic sexuality"; they seek meaning, and because the penis is the "universal signifier," women envy and desire to have a penis. This manifests culturally in women submitting first to their fathers, and then to husbands in the hope of eventually giving birth to male sons—the only way women may truly fulfill their feelings of (phallic) lack (Flax 77–84). As numerous feminist scholars, including Simone de Beauvoir, Julia Kristeva, Luce Irigaray, and Hélène Cixous have argued, this account of "human" sexuality problematically reduces women to nothing, to lack, to being abnormal copies of men with no psychosexual subjectivity of their own (Hekman 27–47). In the DPS, the villainous Mastermind, Jason Wyngarde, uses a special telepathic device to project visions into Jean's head and to slowly gain control over her. When she finds out what has been done to her, she attacks Wyngarde with fury, fuming: "You came to me when I was vulnerable. You filled the emotional void within me. You made me trust you—perhaps even love you" (Claremont and Byrne 107). She goes on to say, once she has discovered the means of Wyngarde's control, "This device enabled you to tailor your illusions to fit my most private fantasies—the repressed, dark side of my soul. You gave me what I secretly wanted" (107). The nature of Jean's visions and fantasies is twofold: on the one hand, she sees herself in historical settings as a hyperfeminine noble woman hopelessly in love with, and in total submission to, Jason Wyngarde (8). In this way her repressed fantasies involve a reverting to the feminine, as well as a desire for submission.

On the other hand, once inside the Hellfire Club, Jean's visions shift—something Freud said female subjects were more prone to, owing to their inherent instability—so that she manifests as the Black Queen, a highly sexualized, corset-clad dominatrix with a whip and a penchant for corporal punishment (Claremont and Byrne 32). This shift in Jean's fantasies and appearance represents what Jordan Phillips has aptly named the Phoenix Complex, an "anxiety and abjection of feminine power" and of female sexuality. Lenise Prater affirms this characterization in her analysis of the early-2000s X-Men films, noting that Jean's sexuality is framed not only as rapacious (in her interactions with Wolverine) but also as treacherous and dangerous (in the death of Cyclops). Prater states that this amounts to a "representation of the mutant woman as monstrously feminine," a point to which I will return later in this chapter, and that the "combination of women's bodily pleasures and power is represented negatively in all of the versions of the Phoenix narrative" (167–68). I would suggest that this is evident in the comics not only in Jean's appearance as the Black Queen but also in her seductive kiss with Angel, and in a subsequent love scene with Cyclops, which Jean initiates (Claremont and Byrne 60–62). Because these overtly sexual acts take place after Jean's repressed desires surface, and after she has summoned the

Phoenix Force in order to defeat Emma Frost (another highly sexualized, dangerous female character), they, like Jean's power, take on the trappings of being out of control at best, and deadly at worst. Thus, the treatment of female sexuality in the DPS contributes to a well-established, persistent belief within Western culture and thought "that explicitly associates women with danger, particularly in the spheres of sexuality and maternity" (Shildrick 30). The pedagogical merit of this insight is, again, the ways in which it fosters an opportunity to introduce students to the history of this type of anxiety, and the various ways feminist critics have sought to question such characterizations.

Much of the anxiety surrounding female sexuality and embodiment is rooted in aversion to limitlessness and a lack of control. As Margrit Shildrick demonstrates, this kind of alignment of femininity with chaos is historically rooted and has traditionally served to marginalize women as subjects:

> The theme of the essential excessiveness of women can be traced like a leitmotif throughout western history. In a tradition dating at least from the Pythagorean Table, the masculine has been associated with the limit, the feminine with the limitless, where the latter implies a failure of the proper, an unaccountability beyond the grasp of instrumental consciousness. . . . Women are out of control, uncontained, unpredictable, leaky: they are, in short, monstrous. (31)

This dichotomous alignment has reinforced man as most akin to light, as most capable of reason, and as a master of control, while simultaneously positioning woman as most akin to darkness, as irrational and emotional, and in need of mastery. Man has been firmly lodged in the Western imagination on the side of mind and woman on the side of body, man on the side of spirit and woman on the side of worldliness (Ortner). In the DPS, Pythagorean dualism is readily apparent in the treatment of Jean/Phoenix. Everything, from the appearance of Jean's speech bubbles—which, when she manifests as the Phoenix, have a certain menacing liquidity—to her increasingly Medusa-like hair, to the dark, blood-red shade of her uniform, places her firmly in a traditionally feminine, and therefore degraded, column. Jean's positioning is thrown into even sharper relief against Professor Xavier, the consummate mind. Nowhere is this dichotomy clearer than in the battle between the two characters: Jean, cocooned in the power of the Phoenix Force yells, "I am what was, what is, what will be—the black angel, the chaos-bringer! I am power!" Xavier responds by stating, "Power without restraint—knowledge without wisdom—age without maturity—passion without love. I must *fight* you, Jean! I must—I *will*—win!" (Claremont and Byrne 145). Here, Jean implies that she is time itself, limitless and fluid; she is death and she is chaos; she is the impersonal and relentless force of power.

Professor X's retort points to the classically Pythagorean mandate that all these things--time, power, knowledge, and passion--are good, are made useful to us, are allowable *only* if they are limited, controlled, and put in the service of reason. The need for (masculine) control is further reinforced by the conclusion of the book in a panel where the Watcher reflects on Jean's fate:

> All beings carry within them a capacity for good and evil. All our actions result from the interaction of these two fundamental forces. Our *reason* makes us aware of these forces and likewise gives us the responsibility of choosing between them. . . . This child achieved a level of power that placed her as far above humanity . . . as they are above [the] amoeba. She had only to *think*, and that thought would become instant reality. But the Phoenix is also a force of *primal passion*. . . . Jean could not help but respond to it, be changed by it, and in time, *overwhelmed*. So, she briefly became the *dark side* of Phoenix: the black angel, chaos-bringer. (Claremont and Byrne 183)

The Watcher (a male character) insists that by our very nature we are subjected to binaries, made up of only two columns, one of which is ruinous and destructive. Jean, while in the sway of the Phoenix Force (and out of the reach of Xavier's psychic control), became the manifestation of evil because she turned away from reason and became passion, unbridled chaos, and darkness. Professor Xavier and the Watcher act in the text as strong examples of what Genevieve Lloyd has identified as "the Man of Reason," the Western ideal of rationality. Despite this figure's supposed "humanness," Lloyd deftly demonstrates his maleness such that "[when] the Man of Reason is extolled, philosophers are not talking about idealizations of human beings. They are talking about ideals of manhood" (149). In addition to the ways in which this figure has perpetuated Pythagorean dualism, it has had more material effects. Lloyd writes, "[The] impoverishment of woman through the imposition of sexual stereotypes is obvious. Exclusion from reason has meant exclusion from power" (164). Although the concluding conversation is framed in "human" terms, it still reinforces the superiority of male reason, order, and limits over female limitlessness, darkness, passion, and chaos. It is no wonder, then, that the representatives of reason and control in the DPS are men, and Jean, the manifestation of all subordinate traits, is destroyed, leaving the Watcher to declare that the X-Men "have won perhaps the greatest victory of their young lives" (Claremont and Byrne 183). Read uncritically, the DPS serves to reinforce the supremacy of men over women and endorses the violent erasure of the feminine in the service of maintaining masculine order.

Certainly one might form a critique of the ways in which Jean lacks agency when embodying the Phoenix Force. Myriad comics scholars have noted the historical tendency of mainstream superhero comics to victimize female characters, be it through physical violence used to spur on their male counterparts or by positioning female characters as damsels in distress (e.g., Bukatman 65; Duncan and Smith 255–57; Gibson 138). In either case, female characters have very little, if any, agency and instead become objects upon which other, more assertive male subjects may act. Interestingly, while Jean Grey does fall prey to Jason Wyngarde's mental manipulation (and arguably, to Charles Xavier's), she does not suffer "victimization" in relation to male characters only; rather, her lack of agency can also result from her relationship with the Phoenix Force. Jean's lack of agency is so obvious that a fan page on Tumblr takes as its title *Jean Grey Has Agency* and describes the need for such a page in the following terms:

> Jean Grey is one of the worst examples of the representation of females in comics. She is literally tossed around from man to man and treated as nothing more than an object. She's basically Helen of Troy. Sure, she supposedly has infinite abilities when coupled with the Phoenix Force, but the Phoenix Force is just another entity tossing her around like a puppet. . . . Jean never gets to act of her own free will.

Throughout the DPS, Jean is described in observably passive ways in relation to the Phoenix Force. Cyclops increasingly remarks on Jean's behavior as being uncommon and not "like her" as the narrative progresses; during a visit to her parents, Jean exasperatedly realizes that she "can't help reading their minds"; and again, at the conclusion of the book, the Watcher describes how Jean was "overwhelmed" by the Phoenix Force, she "could not help but respond to it" (Claremont and Byrne 57, 137, 183). Central to so much of feminist theorizing is the desire to firmly establish women as full subjects and, further, to recognize women's capacity to act as active agents. That said, some feminist scholars have not limited their theoretical critiques to patriarchal depictions of women as passive victims but have also problematized women's behaviors and women's representations of themselves. This has proven to be particularly contentious within the context of women's religious subjectivity.

From radical feminists like Mary Daly, who called for women to abandon organized religion because she saw it as irredeemably patriarchal, to more contemporary, liberal theorists who operate on the (somewhat misguided) assumption that feminism is (or should be) secular, multiple voices within feminist movements and scholarship have outwardly suggested, or tacitly implied, that religious subjectivity and women's agency are mutually exclusive. This is largely because many religions such as Christianity have historically encouraged passivity, submission, and silence in women adherents. Therefore, women who cultivate those types of traits in their own practice have come under fire from certain feminist critics of religion. Women whose subjectivity seems in line with the status quo established by religions like Christianity—rather than in opposition to it—are denied agency because of their failure to act/think in ways subversive of their patriarchal context. The ramifications of this type of response are such that women who claim to be motivated, inspired, or moved by a "higher" power in their thoughts and actions are positioned as having false-consciousness, as perpetuating their own subordination, or as not having a "will of their own." However, scholars like Saba Mahmood have begun to question the equation of agency with subversion in some strands of feminism. She argues "that despite the important insights it has provided, this model of agency sharply limits our ability to understand and interrogate the lives of women whose sense of self, aspirations and projects have been shaped by non-liberal traditions" (15). The pedagogical promise of this particular aspect of the DPS is twofold: on the one hand, in focusing on female subjectivity and women's agency, students can come to appreciate the gravity of feminist critiques of the tendency for superhero comics to objectify and victimize female characters. On the other hand, however, when religious subjectivity is brought into the discussion, students may be further invited to explore how certain assumptions about human agency—even assumptions held by some feminists themselves—may actually further victimize female subjects. The issue of agency in the DPS is one that can fruitfully evoke an analysis of the ways gender, religion, and embodiment intersect in superhero comics.

. . .

Given the problems outlined above, it is necessary to ask how this text may still be positively utilized in a feminist classroom. What resources might be employed in order to help students re-read the DPS such that female embodiment and sexuality are not understood as chaotic, out of control, and dangerous—or finally, as monstrous? How might Jean's relationship with the Phoenix Force be interpreted differently so as to avoid "victimhood" or a total lack of agency? Pedagogical research on active learning environments suggests that students are most productive in tackling research questions when they are first presented with successful case studies. That is, if students are first given the chance to "observe" studies that have successfully answered research questions similar to their own, they will be more productive doing their own research and analysis (Fink 105–10). As such, I suggest that the next step in teaching the DPS is to introduce students to feminist studies of medieval Christian female mystics in order to provide them with examples of how gender, religion, and embodiment intersect in complex, yet positive ways.

Studies of mysticism across traditions are fertile grounds for analyzing gender, religion, and embodiment generally, but they are also a rich source for students examining the DPS in particular. Scholars like Jeffrey Kripal, in *Mutants and Mystics: Science Fiction, Superhero Comics, and the Paranormal*, have made convincing connections between the X-Men and mysticism. While he focuses on Grant Morrison's run of the X-Men—and thus concludes that Jean Grey/Phoenix performs her mystical connection to the Divine in observably "eastern" ways, owing to Morrison's own proclivity for Hinduism and Buddhism—his analysis of the impact of mysticism on the writers at Marvel is compelling (Kripal 173–216).[4] Further, as I shall shortly demonstrate, interpreting portions of Jean's narrative through the lens of Jewish mysticism also provides a solid backdrop against which students may come to better understand certain types of religious subjectivity. As constructive as these analyses are, I suggest that a focus on studies of medieval Christian mysticism in particular will provide students with the strongest examples for their rereadings of the DPS. While by no means the only source for more woman-centric manifestations of the intersections of gender, religion, and embodiment, feminist analyses of medieval Christian female mystics are relevant to the DPS for a number of reasons. First, and most practically, the amount of feminist scholarship we now have on medieval Christian mystics is well developed and provides a wide field of material.[5] Second, and relatedly, while not exactly profuse, the hagiographies and written accounts left by medieval Christian women like Angela of Foligno, Marguerite Porete, or Hadewijch of Antwerp, are substantial enough to provide students with concrete examples of mystical expression of relationships with the Divine (Hollywood 7). Finally, the language in the DPS itself mirrors this expressive relationship among medieval women mystics.

One parallel reading of mysticism alongside the DPS can be seen after Jean has fully succumbed to the Phoenix Force and manifests as the Dark Phoenix (Claremont and Byrne 123). Here we see her recalling a dream of herself as the "Tiphereth," or "heart and soul of the mystic Tree of Life." The concept of Tiphereth, or *Tiferet*, is relevant to both Christian and Jewish mysticism. In the context of Jewish Kabbalah, *Tiferet* (often translated as "Beauty") is the sixth of the ten *sefirot*, "a group of divine entities" that constitute part of "the essential structure of existence" (Green 33). At the center of the *sefirot*, or kabbalistic Tree of Life, *Tiferet* combines *Chesed*—"the grace or love of God"—with *Gevurah*, "the judgment of God, and . . . the bastion of divine power" (Green 42–43). The proper balance between these two *sefirot* is of crucial importance as an imbalance of one, particularly *Gevurah*, can lead to the birth of evil. Arthur Green explains that the combinatory power of *Tiferet* is relevant not only to the structure of the cosmos, but to human beings as well: "Evil resides within each human being, as it exists in the cosmos as a whole. Our temptation to do evil is the result of the same imbalance of inner forces that exists within the divine cosmic structure" (45).[6] While this mystical framework resonates strongly with the DPS and with Jean's narrative in particular, it does run the risk of reinforcing the text's Pythagorean character and may not result in an alternative reading of Jean/Phoenix. Further, I would suggest that the conclusion of Claremont and Byrne's book requires an investigation of the Tree of Life within Christian mystical, christological readings.

Jewish Kabbalah began to manifest in Europe, principally in Provence, Spain, and Italy, as early as the thirteenth century, and while a distinctly Christian version of Kabbalah did not begin to form until the early Renaissance, an earlier cross-pollination of mystical hermeneutics of the Divine is almost certain (Scholem 17–51). Christian interpretations of Kabbalah departed significantly from Jewish kabbalistic interpretations chiefly because, for many Christian thinkers, what they found in "esoteric Judaism [were] demonstrations of the truth of Christianity" (McGinn 16). For instance, the *sefirot* in Jewish Kabbalah appeared to Christian thinkers as confirmation of the Trinity and the Incarnation, rather than as evidence of the structure of the cosmos or the oneness of God. *Tiferet*, as the center of the Tree of Life, came to be associated by Christians with Jesus specifically, with his incarnation as both human and divine, with his ability to bind God to his worldly creation, and with divine love, as expressed through Jesus's sacrifice (Nash 51). Jesus as divine love was a particularly potent metaphor for medieval women mystics. Further, owing to theological definitions of woman as

Figure 9.1. Jean recounts a vision wherein she saw herself as Tiphereth, *X-Men: The Dark Phoenix Saga*, page 123, by Chris Claremont and John Byrne. Copyright © 1980 and 2006 Marvel Characters, Inc.

being more material, more earth-bound, and more human, many medieval women related strongly to Jesus's humanity, for they were able to access an otherwise precluded pathway to God (Newman). This Christian framework is constructive for students because for Jean, a being both human and god-like, the ultimate act of love is one of self-sacrifice, one she must make in order to atone for previous "sins," and to save those less powerful than she. It is not only important that Jean failed to manifest as Tiphereth (because she willfully tipped the balance of love and power), but it is also necessary to note the theme of sacrifice as love attached to Jean's character. The framework of mysticism in interpreting Jean's dream and ultimate sacrifice is one which can aid students in analyzing human relationships with the Divine, which can encourage synthesis with other aspects of the lesson (e.g., Pythagorean dualism, or the role of the feminine), and which may open the door to a comparative study of religions.

Jean's expressions of her desires and feelings in association with the Phoenix Force also strongly recall those used by medieval Christian female mystics. As scholars like Caroline Walker Bynum, Grace Jantzen, and Amy Hollywood have shown, medieval Christian mystics often used language that recalled feelings of hunger, of being consumed by the Divine, of affective joy or rapture, and of intensely corporeal experiences. In terms of hunger and consumption in medieval mystical expressions, Bynum writes: "When medieval writers spoke of eating or tasting or savoring God, they meant not merely to draw an analogy to a particular bodily pleasure but, rather, to denote directly an experiencing, a feeling/knowing of God into which the

Figure 9.2. Cyclops reminds Jean of the sacrifices she has made out of love, *X-Men: The Dark Phoenix Saga*, page 143, by Chris Claremont and John Byrne. Copyright © 1980 and 2006 Marvel Characters, Inc.

entire person was caught up" (151). She goes on to note that "because of the central place of the eucharist in the liturgy," verbs like "*esurire* (to hunger)" were common and "came naturally to late medieval spiritual writers" (151). As Bynum demonstrates in her seminal work *Holy Feast and Holy Fast: The Religious Significance of Food to Medieval Women*, these types of expressions—while used by mystics of both genders—were particularly significant for, and prominently used by, medieval women. Incorporating sensory experience and bodily affect did not stop with language related to hunger but was also evident in the ways medieval women mystics performed their

Figure 9.3. Jean describes her feelings in relation to the Phoenix Force, *X-Men: The Dark Phoenix Saga*, page 143, by Chris Claremont and John Byrne. Copyright © 1980 and 2006 Marvel Characters, Inc.

devotion. Extreme asceticism, experiences of stigmata, and even levitation were not uncommon experiences for mystic women. This kind of affective, ecstatic devotion was not always well received, however. Like Jean's embodiment of the Phoenix Force, many female Christian mystics performed their devotion in ways that were perceived as destructive—either to their own persons or to others—and as dangerous, as evidenced by the execution of mystics like Joan of Arc or Marguerite of Porete (Hollywood 12). Finally, like Jean Grey/Phoenix, female medieval Christian mystics were not trusted to tell their own stories, and so while their narratives were women's stories, and meant to be "feminine" stories, they were recorded and transmitted by men (Jantzen 157–92).

The point for feminist scholars of these hagiographies is that while established Church hierarchies might have seen these women in damaging ways, the women mystics saw themselves as being "brides of Christ," as inextricably linked to the Divine, as living vessels of God's love. Female medieval Christian mystics have been reread by feminist scholars such that women's religious agency, while complex and sometimes paradoxical, comes to the fore. Scholars like Bynum, Jantzen, and Hollywood have sought to illuminate how mystics understood their female corporeality—not as a danger, but as a gateway, as a point of contact between themselves and God. Making use of these studies in order to provide students with examples of successful analyses of gender, religion, and embodiment that do not perpetuate the degradation of female corporeality or the marginalization of certain types of religious subjectivity would not only encourage more-nuanced readings of the DPS, but it would also allow for constructive study of mysticism.

. . .

The final step in productively utilizing the DPS in a feminist classroom is to revisit the question of whether Jean/Phoenix is hero or villain. While feminist analyses of medieval Christian mystics may help us to think better about the intersections of gender, religion, and embodiment, they do not necessarily provide students with a vocabulary for thinking differently about the DPS. Medieval mysticism may indeed aid students in reconceptualizing Jean's relationship with the Phoenix Force, but she herself is not a medieval mystic, and so the question arises: what *is* she? Is she god or woman? Is she good or bad?

In order to form an alternative way to think about the DPS, and to enable a creative rereading of Jean's character, I suggest that Jean Grey/Phoenix be recognized as a model of Donna Haraway's "promising monster." In her essay "The Promises of Monsters: A Regenerative Politics of Inappropriate/d Others," Haraway argues that part of engaging theory in our navigations of the world is "to produce a patterned vision of how to move and what to fear in the topography of an impossible but all-too-real present, in order to find an absent, but perhaps possible, other present." Attempting to find an alternative is, according to Haraway, the attempt to illuminate the "effects of connection, of embodiment, and of responsibility for an imagined elsewhere that we may yet learn to see and build there" (295). In the terms explored in this essay, we are faced with dominant patriarchal norms of religion, embodiment, and gender, but we are responsible for discovering alternative modalities of relation.

Building on Trinh Minh-ha's ideas of "inappropriate/d" others, Haraway sees the promising monster as representative of something other than the "dominant, modern Western narratives of identity and politics": "To be inappropriate/d is not to fit in the taxon, to be dislocated from the available maps specifying kinds of actors and kinds of narratives, not to be originally fixed by difference. To be inappropriate/d is to be neither modern nor postmodern, but to insist on the amodern" (300). These figures, the inappropriate/d, the promising monster, and its cousin the cyborg, make us aware of the inseparability of "the technical, organic, mythic, textual, and political threads in the semiotic fabric of . . . the world" (329). Promising monsters are those who transgress borderlands, who demonstrate the porousness of boundaries, whose corporeality is not One, but undeniably bound up with text, myth, nature, and the political. The promising monster is not one who asks, "Who am I?" but "Who are we?" They reside in the borderlands, which "suggest a rich topography of combinatorial possibility" (328).

Although Jean Grey/Phoenix seems, in some sense, to be a failed superhero, we should understand her as representing the promises of monsters. Like female Christian mystics, Jean/Phoenix is bodily, she is mythical, she is textual, she is divine, and she is human woman. In the last pages of the DPS, Jean says of herself: "Two beings—Jean Grey and Phoenix—separate . . . unique . . . bound together. A *symbiote*, Peter; neither can exist without the other" (Claremont and Byrne 181). Jean/Phoenix performs both at and beyond the borders. She demonstrates the boundaries of patriarchal discourses of gendered embodiment and religious agency because she transgresses both. Indeed, as Scott Bukatman argues, "[mutant] bodies are first and foremost, subjected and subjugated and colonized figures. If they are victims, however, they are also valuable sources of disruption and challenge—transgressive, uncontrollable, and alternative bodies" (73). In introducing students to Haraway's theoretical model, Jean Grey/Phoenix can be read in complex, polyvalent ways. Rather than being read only as a monological patriarchal narrative about the threat of female sexuality and corporeality, and the dangers of mystical religious subjectivity, the DPS, through the lens of promising monsters, might instead be interpreted as a text "full of cacophonous agencies" (Haraway 297)—including that of Jean Grey.

NOTES

1. I have chosen to limit my analysis in this chapter to Chris Claremont and John Byrne's *X-Men: The Dark Phoenix Saga* specifically for reasons of clarity and because of space constraints. Endeavoring to include *all* of Jean Grey's iterations would make a finite, coherent discussion almost impossible. Thus, this text will work strictly within the bounds of *X-Men* #129–137, published as *The Dark Phoenix Saga*.

2. Covers that depict women in highly sexualized poses with little to no clothing.

3. As Duncan and Smith explain, this phrase, coined by comics creator Gail Simone, refers to the overwhelming tendency for comics to treat female characters solely as plot devices. More specifically, in making reference to a particular issue of the Green Lantern comics, Simone explained that female characters were frequently violently killed or mutilated in comics in order to provide a catalyst for male superheroes to spring into action; rarely would women be treated as valuable characters in their own right.

4. I am grateful to Jeff Richey, who has suggested that Morrison's run might also be productively analyzed in a feminist classroom, in ways similar to what I am proposing here, by reading the comics alongside studies of the Goddess tradition in South Asian religious cultures. Namely, Richey has suggested pairing Morrison's comics with works such as Erndl and Hiltebeitel's *Is the Goddess a Feminist?* (2000) or McDermott and Kripal's *Encountering Kali* (2003).

5. It is worth mentioning that feminist interpretations of these hagiographies are important, because while other historical analyses are available, such as *Holy Anorexia* by Rudolph Bell, medieval mystic women were often reduced to being inflicted with psychoses or disorders and so would not be a corrective to the reading already outlined.

6. My thanks to Leah Hochman for helping me to clarify this discussion on Kabbalah.

BIBLIOGRAPHY

Beerman, Ruth. "The Body Unbound: *Empowered*, Heroism and Body Image." In *Superheroes and Identities*, edited by Mel Gibson, David Huxley, and Joan Ormrod, 159–71. New York: Routledge, 2015.

Behm-Morawitz, Elizabeth, and Hillary Pennell. "The Effects of Superhero Sagas on Our Gendered Selves." In *Our Superheroes, Ourselves*, edited by Robin S. Rosenberg, 73–93. Oxford: Oxford University Press, 2013.

Bukatman, Scott. *Matters of Gravity: Special Effects and Supermen in the 20th Century*. Durham: Duke University Press, 2003.

Bynum, Caroline Walker. *Holy Feast and Holy Fast: The Religious Significance of Food to Medieval Women*. Berkeley: University of California Press, 1987.

Claremont, Chris, and Byrne, John. *X-Men: The Dark Phoenix Saga*. New York: Marvel, 2006.

Duncan, Randy, and Matthew J. Smith. *The Power of Comics: History, Form & Culture*. New York: Bloomsbury, 2013.

Erndl, Kathleen M., and Alf Hiltebeitel (eds.). *Is the Goddess a Feminist? The Politics of South Asian Goddesses*. New York: New York University Press, 2000.

Fink, L. Dee. *Creating Significant Learning Experiences: An Integrated Approach to Designing College Courses*. San Francisco: Jossey-Bass, 2003.

Flax, Jane. *Thinking Fragments: Psychoanalysis, Feminism, and Postmodernism in the Contemporary West*. Berkeley: University of California Press, 1991.

Garrett, Greg. *Holy Superheroes! Revised and Expanded Edition: Exploring the Sacred in Comics, Graphic Novels, and Film*. Louisville: Westminster John Knox Press, 2008.

Gibson, Mel. "Who Does She Think She Is? Female Comic-Book Characters, Second-Wave Feminism and Feminist Film Theory." In *Superheroes and Identities*, edited by Mel Gibson, David Huxley, and Joan Ormrod, 135–46. New York: Routledge, 2015.

Green, Arthur. *A Guide to the Zohar*. Stanford: Stanford University Press, 2004.

Haraway, Donna. "Promising Monsters: A Regenerative Politics for Inappropriate/d Others." In *Cultural Studies*, edited by Lawrence Grossberg, Cary Nelson, and Paula A. Treichler, 295–337. New York: Routledge, 1992.

Hekman, Susan. *The Feminine Subject*. Cambridge: Polity Press, 2014.

Hollywood, Amy. *Sensible Ecstasy: Mysticism, Sexual Difference, and the Demands of History*. Chicago: University of Chicago Press, 2002.

Jantzen, Grace. *Power, Gender and Christian Mysticism*. Cambridge: Cambridge University Press, 1995.

Jean Grey Has Agency. Blog. Web. 28 July 2016.

Jennings, John. "Superheroes by Design." In *What Is a Superhero?*, edited by Robin S. Rosenberg and Peter Coogan, 50–63. Oxford: Oxford University Press, 2013.

Kripal, Jeffrey. *Mutants and Mystics: Science Fiction, Superhero Comics, and the Paranormal*. Chicago: University of Chicago Press, 2011.

Lewis, A. David. *American Comics, Literary Theory, and Religion: The Superhero Afterlife*. New York: Palgrave Macmillan, 2014.

Lewis, A. David, and Christine Hoff Kraemer (eds.). *Graven Images: Religion in Comic Books & Graphic Novels*. New York: Continuum International, 2010.

Lloyd, Genevieve. "The Man of Reason." In *Women, Knowledge, Reality: Explorations in Feminist Philosophy*, edited by Ann Garry and Marilyn Pearsall, 149–65. New York; London: Routledge, 1996.

Mahmood, Saba. "Agency, Performativity, and the Feminist Subject." In *Pieties and Gender*, edited by Lene Sjørup and Hilda Rømer Christensen, 13–46. Leiden: Brill, 2009.

McDermottt, Rachel Fell, and Jeffrey Kripal (eds.). *Encountering Kali: In the Margins, at the Center, in the West*. Berkeley: University of California Press, 2003.

McGinn, Bernard. "Cabalists and Christians: Reflections on Cabala in Medieval and Renaissance Thought." In *Jewish Christians and Christian Jews: From the Renaissance to the Enlightenment*, edited by Richard H. Popkin and Gordon M. Weiner, 11–34. Dordrecht: Springer Science+Business Media, 1994.

Nash, John F. "Origins of the Christian Kabbalah." *Esoteric Quarterly* 4, no. 1 (Spring, 2008): 43–58.

Newman, Barbara. "Gender." In *Wiley-Blackwell Companions to Religion: The Wiley-Blackwell Companion to Christian Mysticism*, edited by Julia A. Lamm, 41–55. Hoboken: Wiley, 2012.

Oropeza, B. J. (ed.). *The Gospel according to Superheroes: Religion and Popular Culture*. New York: Peter Lang, 2005.

Ortner, Sherry. "Is Female to Male as Nature Is to Culture?" In *Women, Culture, and Society*, edited by Michelle Zimbalist Rosaldo and Louise Lamphere, 68–87. Stanford: Stanford University Press, 1974.

Phillips, Jordan. "'She Has to Be Controlled': The Monstrous-Feminine and The Cinematic X-Women." *Inter-Disciplinary*. Web. Accessed July 28, 2016.

Prater, Lenise. "Gender and Power: The Phoenix/Jean Grey across Time and Media." *COLLOQUY: Text, Theory, Critique* 24 (2012): 159–70.

Robbins, Trina. *Pretty in Ink: North American Women Cartoonists 1896–2013*. Seattle: Fantagraphic Books, 2013.

Saunders, Ben. *Do the Gods Wear Capes? Spirituality, Fantasy, and Superheroes*. New York: Continuum International, 2011.

Scholem, Gershom. "The Beginnings of the Christian Kabbalah." In *The Christian Kabbalah: Jewish Mystical Books & Their Christian Interpreters*, edited by Joseph Dan, 17–36. Cambridge: Harvard College Library, 1997.

Shildrick, Margrit. *Embodying the Monster: Encounters with the Vulnerable Self*. London: Sage, 2002.

Syma, Carrye Kay, and Robert G. Weiner (eds.). *Graphic Novels and Comics in the Classroom: Essays on the Educational Power of Sequential Art*. Jefferson, NC: McFarland, 2013.

Chapter Ten

"HONOR THE POWER WITHIN"

Daoist Wizards, Popular Culture, and Contemporary Japan's Spiritual Crisis

JEFFREY L. RICHEY

ON MARCH 11, 2011, WHAT HAS BEEN KNOWN EVER SINCE AS THE "GREAT East Japan Earthquake" (*Higashi nihon daishinsai*) shook the homes, nuclear power plants, and cultural confidence of Japan's northeastern Tōhoku region to their foundations. The magnitude-9 earthquake and the devastating tsunami that it triggered took almost 16,000 lives, rendered some 230,000 people homeless, and resulted in approximately 300 billion US dollars' worth of damage (Oskin). Writing in the wake of this catastrophic event, the Japanese cultural critic Azuma Hiroki remarked that "in the present situation, our society is dealing with something that goes beyond the rationality related to practical matters. Here, we must become humble. . . . [T]here are disasters in this world that go beyond the limits of human rationality" (Azuma). The "triple disaster" occurred at a pivotal moment in Japanese postmodernity, having been preceded by the collapse of the "bubble economy" that boosted consumer confidence and the political establishment from 1986 to 1991, the sense of cultural crisis occasioned by Japan's declining birthrate and diminishing global power, and the ascendance of right-wing, nationalist leaders such as prime minister Abe Shinzō, whose government has responded to contemporary Japan's pervasive sense of decline by promising economic revitalization and military rearmament (Kingston). While Abe's policy-makers resort to typically modern, technocratic solutions such as centralized banking, constitutional revision, and targeted investment, ordinary Japanese—particularly youth—appear to be fulfilling Azuma's seemingly prophetic words by turning away from the secularism, modernism, and cosmopolitanism that have characterized postwar Japan, and toward sources of meaning and modes of identity that hark back to Japan's premodern past: spirituality, traditionalism, and nativism. In short, a monstrous cultural-historical moment has given rise to a renewed cultural fascination with monstrosities from Japan's deep past: the Heian period (794–1185) wizards known as *onmyōji* 陰陽師 ("*yīn* and *yáng* masters").

Comics (*manga*) and their animated film and television spinoffs (*anime*) play a prominent role in both expressing and shaping this discursive shift in contemporary Japanese youth culture. In particular, comics and other expressions of visual culture focused on how *onmyōji* (i.e., early medieval Japanese occult adepts rooted in Daoist traditions) function, like "monsters" (instances of the anomalous and/or grotesque) across cultures and texts, as "the embodiment of a cultural moment" (Cohen 4). This chapter describes and analyzes the ways in which Japanese youth interest in *onmyōji*—particularly the disproportionate interest shown by young Japanese women—engages the social realities of contemporary Japanese life. Unlike previous scholarship on *anime* and *manga*, this chapter synthesizes a variety of disciplinary approaches to culture—among them those of anthropology, gender theory, history, literary criticism, and religious studies—in order to produce a fresh look at how the *onmyōji* "boom," now some thirty years in duration with apparently enduring appeal, is relevant to contemporary concerns about cultural authenticity and identity, gender and sexuality, and spirituality and religion in Japan.

For contemporary Japanese, the "cultural moment" that apparently finds its "embodiment" in *onmyōji* is one that is defined by "loneliness, isolation, and disconnectedness . . . a precariousness felt by everyone and not just those (precariat, unemployed, socially solitary or withdrawn) on the underside of a bipolarized, divided society" (Allison 37, 50–51). This pervasive and dreadful sense of "precariousness" is all the more overwhelming given Japan's transformation in recent history into "a nation-state of high economic growth, sustained productivity, and global acclaim as a postindustrial power" (Allison 36) during the decades following its catastrophic defeat by the United States in 1945. Although Japan functioned as a global icon of futurity as late as a decade or so after Japan's fall from postwar economic power (Anders), what once was the future now has become the past. Japan's "system that socialized people into wanting and expecting a certain stability in everyday life whose reference point was the future" (Allison 36) has crumbled from within, and various expressions of cultural nostalgia have arisen to help the Japanese cope with their suddenly expired dreams of prosperity, stability, and meaning (Chakraborty and Chakraborty 59).

This chapter argues that, under such circumstances, *onmyōji*-themed cartoons and comics answer a need for an infusion of premodern, non-Western, nonrational, ethnocentric wisdom in response to the decline of modern, westernized, rational, cosmopolitan Japan. By examining how these kinds of visual culture are received by young people in contemporary Japan, especially young women, one can learn much about how today's Japanese youth imagine their cultural past, negotiate their cultural present, and envision their cultural future. The reception of such media, in turn, reveals much about the role played by spirituality in twenty-first-century Japan and, perhaps, beyond.

. . .

Recent theoretical discussions of the categories of "religion" and "religious" have led to critical reappraisals of seeing religious cultures as systematic, orthodoxy-driven wholes. Instead, some theorists invite us to view religious cultures as "repertoires of resources . . . rather than treating them as fully integrated systems and as containers into which persons, ideas, practices, and texts may be fit without remainder" (Campany 317). This concept of "religion as repertoire" describes not only how Japanese religious culture traditionally has functioned, but also how the contemporary popular-culture phenomena of *manga* and *anime* function in relation to Japan's extensive and heterogeneous repertoire of texts, images, artifacts, historical figures, and structures, as well as how Japanese religious culture and *manga/anime* relate to each other as repertoires.

On the one hand, given the intensely pluralistic and relatively rapid fashion in which Japan acquired its primary religious traditions through the somewhat indiscriminate infusion of Korean and Chinese cultural products between the third and ninth centuries, it should not be surprising to learn that religion in Japan has tended to function precisely in this way—that is, as a cultural repertoire, from which cultural actors have felt free to pick, choose, and recombine in order to play out diverse parts, purposes, and scenarios, rather than as a set of discrete, self-contained "-isms." The cultural repertoire known as "Daoism"—a broad category that encompasses literary and philosophical texts concerned with the ubiquity of change and transformation in nature and the human condition, medical and occult lore focused on identifying and manipulating patterns of change and transformation in the body and the cosmos, and liturgical and magical practices intended to maximize the benefits of such patterns while minimizing or eliminating their costs to human individuals and communities (Barrett 8–10; Robinet 5–8)—has exerted an enduring influence on Japanese religious culture, leaving its mark on institutional traditions such as Buddhism and Shintō but also permeating aspects of folk culture and daily life (Richey 2–3). Daoism, itself a hybrid repertoire, has—along with other imports to Japan—given rise to a hardy and flexible cultural repertoire that continues to shape the Japanese imaginary.

On the other hand, *manga* and *anime* originated and continue to develop as heterogeneous media drawn from repertoires as diverse and different from one another as seventh-century Buddhist temple graffiti, Edo period (1603–1868) travel narratives, British and French political cartoons, and Walt Disney's films and other American cartoon media (Ito 458–63). As a cinematic and televised medium, the repertoires that sustain *anime* are even more heterogeneous and include Edo period *ukiyo-e* (woodblock print) and *kabuki* (costumed drama) as well as modern film and photography (Napier 4). It is important to note that both *manga* and *anime* have their roots in Japanese religious repertoires, especially Daoism and esoteric Buddhism, each of which is a tremendously iconodulistic (as opposed to iconoclastic) tradition. In other words, *manga* and *anime* originated in and as the cultural space between sacred texts and comics. The hybridity of the repertoires out of which *manga* and *anime* have arisen, like the genetic hybridity of successful plant and animal species, helps explain their massive commercial success: today, in a print media market that generally is on the decline, *manga* represents a growth niche, with sales in Japan increasing each year since 2013 ("Japanese Manga Book Market Rises to Record 282 Billion Yen"), including nonfiction *manga* such as histories (Shiohara), while *anime* accounts for half of all movie theater ticket sales in Japan (Napier 7).

Foremost among the items imported to Japan from the Daoist repertoire during the first millennium of the Common Era was the vocation of the *onmyōji*, a Chinese-derived term that literally means "master of *yīn* and *yáng*." *Yīn* and *yáng*—a binary whole, expressive of the universe at rest and at play, receptive and active, hidden and revealed, etc.—are fundamental categories in traditional Chinese cosmology and form the basis of Daoist aesthetics, cuisine, governance, medicine, and so forth—a body of knowledge known in Japanese as *Onmyōdō* 陰陽道 ("the Way of *yīn* and *yáng*"). From the seventh through the eleventh centuries, *onmyōji* were employed by the Onmyōryō 陰陽寮 ("Bureau of *yīn* and *yáng*"), a department of the Japanese imperial government, in order to exploit their knowledge of *Onmyōdō* for the benefit of the regime and the nation (Masuo 19–20). This meant that *onmyōji* were highly educated, cosmopolitan elites who participated in the shared literary and religious culture of metropolitan East Asia during the early medieval period—a world of classical Chinese literacy, imperial politics and bureaucracy, and a pluralistic spirituality that freely combined Buddhist, Confucian, Daoist, and folk elements (Holcombe 105–7). Shintō, the supposedly indigenous primal religion of Japan, had not yet emerged as a distinct tradition; when it did, around a thousand years later, it would do so by both borrowing and separating itself from esoteric Buddhist and Daoist traditions (Kuroda 20).

By far the most renowned *onmyōji* in both history and legend was Abe no Seimei (921?–1005?), who was employed during six imperial reigns from the mid-900s through the early eleventh century. Seimei, the all-time undisputed master of the repertoire of *Onmyōdō*, posthumously gave rise to both literary and religious repertoires of his own, becoming a central figure in both classical texts and popular dramas as well as the object of a cult based at what now is the Shintō shrine known as Seimei jinja in Kyōto, which was founded two years after his death by imperial command (Cali and Dougill "Seimei jinja," 136–38). During his lifetime and for much of the next millennium, Seimei was identified as a conventionally wise and powerful upper-class Japanese male: bearded, preternaturally middle-aged (he was said to be the immortal scion of a *kitsune*, or shape-shifting fox spirit, and a member of the elite Abe clan, one of whose ancestors famously left Japan to serve at the Táng dynasty court in China during the 700s), portly in physique, and deeply learned in continental East Asian scholarship. As an *onmyōji* par excellence, Seimei was regarded as being particularly adept at controlling and expelling demons (*oni*), which in premodern Japanese literature and folklore are closely associated with women's emotional tensions and outbursts (Ambros 90), even though most premodern texts and art depict *oni* as male (Reider 2003, 135). His descendants became the hereditary heads of the Onmyōryō, which endured in increasingly attenuated form until 1870 (Elacqua). In short, the Seimei of both history and legend was a thoroughly elite, masculine, conservative, and cosmopolitan figure who wielded virtuosic power over demonic forces that were, at least in part, associated with the feminine. These traditional characteristics are important to bear in mind in light of the ways in which contemporary Japanese *manga* and *anime* tend to depict Seimei and the type of audience that most avidly consumes such depictions.

Although prominent in contemporary *onmyōji*-based *manga* and *anime*, the Seimei of the comics and films is not quite the same as his pre-modern incarnation. Nor are his appearances in *manga* and *anime* the first instances of his second life as a modern, pop-culture celebrity. He appears in stories and novels by mid-twentieth-century authors such as Mishima Yukio (1925–1970) and Aramata Hiroshi (b. 1947), for example, but in these works,

Figure 10.1. Statue of Abe no Seimei (921?–1005?) on grounds of Seimei Jinja, the shrine at which he is worshiped as a Shintō deity (*kami*), in Kyōto, Japan. Photo by Jeffrey L. Richey

Seimei is depicted as the older, unquestionably masculine, typically cosmopolitan pre-modern sage with which medieval Japanese audiences were familiar (Recchio 22–23). The Seimei who is recognizable to contemporary audiences—youthful, androgynous (*bishōnen*, a colloquial Japanese term that literally means "pretty boy"), and wholly identified with Japaneseness—first emerged in 1988, when the science fiction author Yumemakura Baku (b. 1951) began to utilize him as a central character in light works of fiction aimed at *shōjo* (young female) readers—an audience that grew prodigiously after Yumemakura's novels were adapted into best-selling *manga* by Okana Reiko (b. 1960) (Reider 2007, 109, 121 n. 21). Moreover, it is not only Seimei who is transformed in Yumemakura's novels, but also his demonic antagonists, who are presented sympathetically as "creature[s] oppressed by mainstream society rather than . . . outright evil creature[s] bent on performing malevolent

Figure 10.2. Abe no Seimei as depicted in the *anime* version of the *manga* series *Otogizōshi*. Copyright © AnimeWorks 2004

acts"—not "evil creature[s] bent on harming people but [entities] who just want to receive simple acknowledgement" (Reider 2007, 110, 115). A typical *oni* in Yumemakura's work is a woman whose anger and shame transform her into a demonic threat with which only Seimei can cope (114). These characterizations of both Seimei and his foes are perpetuated and developed further in the *anime* series that followed the work of Yumemakura and Okana. For the purposes of this chapter, the *anime* series that are most illustrative of what might be called the *bishōnen*-ization of Seimei are *Otogizōshi* (2004–2005), *Shōnen Onmyōji* (2006–2007), and *Mushibugyō* (2013–present). All three depict, in different ways, Seimei as a figure associated with youth, femininity, and a Japaneseness that must be invoked to protect the nation from malevolent outsiders.

Both the *anime* series *Otogizōshi* and the *manga* series based on it take their name from a genre of literature popular in Muromachi period (1336–1573) Japan, which was based on oral narrative traditions about vengeful spirits, monsters, and similar supernatural threats (Kimbrough and Glassman 201, 203). In the "Heian Chapter" (*Heian hen*) episode arc of the series, set in the year 972 during Japan's Heian period, the imperial capital is in a state of rapid decline due to famines, epidemics, and the internecine warfare of *onmyōji* and samurai (Production I.G.). A *bishōnen*-like Seimei appears as a character but turns out to be a masked disguise assumed by the female protagonist's estranged lover, who conspires to purify and destroy the imperial capital by exploiting the combined power of five *magatama*—comma-shaped jade pendants associated with ritual power in the late Jōmon period (c. 1000–300 BCE), the era just prior to Japan's contact with civilizing influences from China and the Korean peninsula (Naumann 18). The number of the magical *magatama* corresponds to the five "elements" or "processes" (Chinese *wŭxíng* 五行, Japanese *gōgyō*) of classical Daoist cosmology—metal, wood, water, fire, and earth—whose interactions with, and transformations into and out of, one another are responsible for the constant, dynamic state of cosmic change. In episode 13, the final episode in the "Heian chapter" arc, this pseudo-Seimei—whose mask blinds him, forcing him to rely on young girls to act as his eyes—is thwarted when his estranged lover (herself disguised as a male samurai, who unsuccessfully attempts to stab him) plays her flute for him, reminding him of their lost love. The flute somehow destroys the fire *magatama* and brings about the sudden apotheosis of the lovers, who rise above the devastated but ultimately reprieved capital and ascend to the heavens in a blissful tableau of opposites in union, rather like *yīn* and *yáng* personified. The couple's attire even mimics the black-and-white color scheme of Daoist iconography, even as it echoes the meanings of the characters' names while inverting the traditional gender associations with each cosmic component: the female Hikaru 光 ("bright," a *yáng* quality) wears mostly white, while the male Seimei/Mansairaku ("ten thousand years of happiness," a name that may echo traditional depictions of Seimei as immortal or quasi-divine) wears mostly black. (Unlike the other *onmyōji* characters discussed in this chapter, in the *anime* version of *Otogizōshi*, Seimei/Mansairaku is voiced by unambiguously male actors Tokumaru Kan [Seimei] and Miki Shin'ichirō [Mansairaku].) All the while, typically emotive *anime* music plays, and a female singer intones:

> There is a distant memory that's kept secret in my heart.
> The indelible mistake has left an unspeakable wound in our hearts.
> . . .
> Ah, the sun rises and the sky grows light.
> . . . .
> For us, this broken-down capital is our home. ("Otogi Zoshi engsub Ep 13")

The cumulative effect of all of this concealment and transformation is to present the capital's salvation as the result of a renewed cosmic wholeness that fuses previously divided opposites in order that the human community may find new life amidst the ruins of the past. Furthermore, this salvation is accomplished by a young woman who bravely and self-sacrificially confronts and appropriates the power of the past. This resonates deeply with two of

Figure 10.3. Abe no Masahiro as depicted in the *anime* version of the *manga* series *Shōnen Onmyōji* [Boy Onmyōji]. Copyright © Studio Deen 2006.

what Susan J. Napier has identified as the three major modes of *anime*: apocalypse and elegy (the other mode being festival, which seems conspicuously absent in this and other *onmyōji* media) (Napier 14). These apocalyptic and elegiac modes give shape to the other two *anime* series discussed in this chapter, as well.

Mitsuru Yūki and Sakura Asagi's *manga* series *Shōnen Onmyōji* (*Boy Onmyōji*, 2001–present) and its *anime* version (2006–2007) depict Seimei as an elderly grandfather who is initiating his young grandson (whose voice in the *anime* is provided by the female actor Kaida Yuki), Abe no Masahiro, into the *onmyōji* arts. Masahiro is said to have been born with such extraordinary spiritual powers that Seimei temporarily curbed them until his grandson was old enough to use them properly under the guidance and protection of Mokkun, also known as Guren ("Red Lotus"), a flying dragon (Chinese *Téng* 螣) found in Chinese mythology who conceals his true identity by assuming the form of a foxlike *yōkai* (supernatural monster). However, the inexperienced and somewhat effeminate Masahiro frequently encounters obstacles that he and Mokkun cannot overcome on their own, which is why Seimei often intervenes—appearing in his youthful, *bishōnen* incarnation, which suggests that his true form is that of a sexually ambiguous, lovely youth—to rescue and chide his grandson into reaching new heights as a novice *onmyōji*. Typical of this narrative pattern is episode 5 of the *anime* series *Takeru youi o shirizokero* (Forcing Back the Ferocious Monsters), in which Kyūki, one of the "Four Monsters" (Chinese *Sìxiōng* 四凶) of Daoist mythology, menaces Japan. Kyūki is depicted as explicitly foreign: a rapacious power from the West (which, in the Japanese context, connotes both China and the Euro-American West) who seeks to replenish his spiritual resources by devouring Masahiro's prodigious vital energy. Of course, Seimei saves the day, which serves to remind Masahiro of how much he has yet to learn from his grandfather and, by extension, Japanese tradition ("Shounen Onmyouji—Episode 5"). This and every episode of the series begins and ends with a theme song, performed by a female vocalist, which includes lyrics such as the following:

> I seek boundless strength.
> I continue to rise with what I believe in.
> I want to protect—I want to believe.

The verb *mamoritai* 守りたい ("to want to protect") shares a common root with *omamori* 御守, the term for the Daoist-style apotropaic amulets sold at Shintō shrines. Given that Masahiro's destiny, which he eventually embraces, is to enter the Heian emperor's service and become the supernatural protector of Japan like his grandfather before him, the viewer is left with the unmistakable impression that the only way to defeat the foreign threats to Japan is to apprentice oneself to the lore and discipline of Japan's deep past. Here, just as in *Otogizōshi*, the salvific action is accomplished by an androgynous, vaguely feminine magical savior, who in turn mentors an androgynous, vaguely feminine messianic figure. And, once again, this longing for a supernatural redemption by means of reconnection with the past is expressed in apocalyptic and elegiac narrative modes.

. . .

Mushibugyō (*The Insect Magistrate*), the most recent of the series discussed in this chapter, is set closer in time to the present and also takes the *bishōnen*-ization of *onmyōji* still further. Seimei has disappeared altogether. In this *manga* (originally published from 2009 through 2010, and ongoing in resumed form since 2011), an alternate-universe Edo period Japan is under siege by giant insects who prey upon humans. In response, the Japanese government deploys a special task force led by Tsukishima Jinbei ("Lunar-Island Humane-Soldier-Guardian"), the filial son of a crippled samurai who was forced to amputate his own leg to atone for a crime that he did not commit. The somewhat *bishōnen*-like Tsukishima recruits an even younger and more androgynous male, the *onmyōji* Ichinotani Tenma, to serve on this task force ("TVアニメ『ムシブギョー』公式サイト"). "Ichinotani" plays on words by suggesting a famous battle in the civil war that brought the Heian period to an end—the battle of Ichi no tani on March 20, 1184—while "Tenma" echoes the name of Dr. Tenma, creator of the futuristic robot Atomu or Astro Boy, one of the most famous heroes in all of *manga* and *anime* (Schodt 36–38), thus associating this character with both Japanese antiquity and youthful, forward-looking heroism. Although quite diffident, Ichinotani Tenma—whose youth is emphasized by the bamboo-shoot green of his attire, and whose androgyny extends to the point of outright effeminacy (like Masahiro, this character also is voiced by a female actor, the singer Serizawa Yū)—overcomes his fear of the giant insects and uses his *onmyōji* powers and resources to help defeat them as part of Tsukishima's team. It is as if *Shōnen Onmyōji*'s Masahiro has somehow survived from the Heian period into the Edo period in order to take his grandfather's place as Japan's supernatural defender—yet Ichinotani Tenma demonstrates none of the maturity and confidence that Masahiro longs to make his own. The masculine yet effeminate protagonists in this series all exist in the shadow of some lost or incapacitated father figure; for Tsukishima, it is his crippled and disgraced samurai *paterfamilias*, while for Ichinotani Tenma, it is his unspoken role model, the ur-*onmyōji* Seimei.

Once again the theme song from the *anime* version (2013–present)—which, unlike the somewhat turgid ballads that accompany *Otogizōshi* and *Shōnen Onmyōji*, is performed in a punk-thrash metal style—offers insights into the deeper subtext of the *anime*, as seen in the following excerpts from its lyrics:

> I have a dream. . . .
> I saw the unchanged passion. . . .
> I saw the purity that does not change. ("Mushibugyo opening 1")

These lyrics underscore the apocalyptic and elegiac tone of the series, which simultaneously projects a science-fictional end-of-the-world scenario onto the distant Japanese past while mourning that past's disappearance with the advent of modernity. Viewers thus are invited to nostalgically treasure a vanished world of samurai and *onmyōji* while watching it be valiantly defended from attack by inhuman predators whose insectoid appearance suggests the mechanized terrors of the twentieth and twenty-first centuries at

Figure 10.4. Ichinotani Tenma as depicted in the *anime* version of the *manga* series *Mushibugyō* [The Insect Magistrate]. 2013

the same time that it evokes the more organic *yōkai* of Japanese tradition. As in both *Otogizōshi* and *Shōnen Onmyōji*, the basic narrative pattern is clear: Japan (always some kind of "traditional," premodern Japan) is threatened by inhuman or monstrous outsiders, to which the only effective response is a connection with the vitality and knowledge of Japan's past. What makes this pattern even more interesting, however, is the way in which it is replicated by young women—both within and without Japan—who ritually costume themselves and role-play as characters from these series.

. . .

The largely female phenomenon of "cosplay" (*kosupure*, a portmanteau word created from the English terms "costume" and "role-play") originated in Japanese appropriation of the kind of costumed role-playing in which US science fiction fans engaged during the 1970s. Japanese fans, particularly of historical fiction and period dramas, embraced the practice and extended it to the costumed portrayal of characters found in *anime*, *manga*, and video games of all genres (Okabe 225). At this point in time, the practice has been reintroduced to the West through its Japanese exponents, such that cosplay is widely practiced in the United States, where some 75 percent of participants are female, making it "one of the few areas in geek culture where women dominate" (Granshaw). Research on young female identification with fictional characters suggests that many girls deviate from their initial pattern of identification with female characters and begin to identify with male protagonists between the ages of twelve and thirteen (Lonial and Van Auken 4, 9). This may help explain why Japanese cosplayers, the majority of whom are young women, so often choose to take on the roles and appearances of male characters (Okabe 238), but it does not necessarily explain why young Japanese women are attracted to cosplaying as androgynous or feminized male *onmyōji* such as Seimei, Masahiro, or Ichinotani Tenma. To understand this particular phenomenon, attention must be paid to the *onmyōji* as signifier.

Within the three series profiled above, *onmyōji* occupy a hegemonic yet interstitial position in their semifictional worlds. That is to say, *onmyōji* are endowed with power, yet this endowment renders them out of place with regard to the social and symbolic structures that surround them. Seimei (Figures 10.1, 10.2) is human, yet inhuman, by virtue of his alleged *kitsune* heritage as well as his extraordinary command over the spirit world. Masahiro (Figure 10.3) is young, yet ancient, insofar as he both resembles the *bishōnen* for which his female audience pines (and which his male audience presumably wishes to emulate) but also exists within the über-antique realm of Heian period Japan—and this is even truer of the youthful Seimei who comes to Masahiro's aid in each episode. Ichinotani Tenma (Figure 10.4) is effete yet efficacious, insofar as his childlike appearance and naked anxieties belie his underlying power to defend and destroy. They are *yáng*, yet yīn; empowered, yet disempowered. The heterogeneous, interstitial quality that *onmyōji* in these series share "is destructive to existing patterns . . . [and] also . . . has potentiality. It symbolizes both danger and power" (Douglas 95). This dual capacity to both shock social and symbolic structures and wield power within them may well be what makes cosplay as male *onmyōji* so attractive to young Japanese women.

To borrow another insight from Mary Douglas, "ritual recognizes the potency of disorder. . . . The danger [of such potency] is controlled by ritual" (95, 97). Female cosplay as male characters is nothing less than the ritualization of dangerous yet potent disorder. It has the paradoxical effect of transgressing gender boundaries (women becoming men) while simultaneously affirming them, albeit in a fictionalized, ritualized reiteration:

> Female cosplayers who cross-dress seek to convey masculinity in the fictional or parodied sense and not in the conventional mainstream sense. . . . [C]osplayers are referencing the cross-dressing model constructed by the cosplay community, and they express the idealized masculinity that the community has created. Cosplayers adore and respect cosplayers who succeed in cross-dressing according to these community standards. (Okabe 239)

A cursory search of worldcosplay.net, a social networking and image sharing website aimed at cosplayers, yields a steady stream of photographs capturing young Japanese women in the act of cosplaying these characters. Moreover, it also reveals that young women from Japan are not the only cosplayers who are embracing these characters. Photos posted by young women from China, Hong Kong, and the Philippines, among other nations, also appear on the website. In one case, a young woman cosplays as Seimei, coyly meeting the viewer's gaze from behind her half-on, half-off *kitsune* mask. The implication seems to be that she is conscious of a kind of double play at work (in the character and, perhaps, in herself): she is both female masquerading as male and human masked as fox spirit. In another case, the cosplayer appears to have gone to the trouble of posing as Masahiro on the grounds of Heian jingū, the Shintō shrine to the Heian period emperor Kanmu (r. 781–806) and the Edo period emperor Kōmei (r. 1846–1867), the first and last emperors to rule from Kyōto, respectively, which is a 5/8-scale replica of the original Heian palace structure built in 1979 after the 1895 original burned down (Cali and Dougill, "Heian jingū," 104–5). Here again, a kind of double play apparently is at work, underscored by the cosplayer's direct gaze at the viewer: she is conscious, perhaps, that she is a twenty-first-century woman disguised as a tenth-century man amidst a twentieth-century reproduction of a site that ceased to serve as the center of power almost 150 years ago, yet she does nothing to betray her awareness of the ruse. The fact that the setting for her photo happens also to be a sacred site, where dead emperors are worshipped as gods, does nothing to undermine the pageantry.

. . .

This free yet highly structured play with the repertoire of gender, using the repertoire of *onmyōji*, mirrors the way in which female masculinity functions in other cultural contexts, such as that of "drag kings" or male impersonators in LGBTQ subcultures, or female Javanese dancers who perform in male styles and as male characters. "[S]tereotypical constructions of variable masculinity mark the process by which masculinity becomes dominant" (Halberstam 2). In other words, if we want to see what masculinity—what power—looks like, then we must look not at men, who hold power generically by virtue of "a naturalized relation between maleness and power" (2), but rather at interstitial entities and activities, such as women performing masculinity in its stereotyped, stylized forms. Such "distinct senses of masculinity expressed by females . . . [keep] their femaleness visible and audible. . . . [A] performed gendered role is noticeably superimposed—layered—onto an actor's own gendered self . . . showing that women could be like men . . . without being men" (Sunardi 43). Young Japanese women live in one of the most rigidly patriarchal societies among developed nations, in which "the rise of a 'weak male' discourse at a time when advocacy for gender equality seems to be competing for attention with concern over economic disparity . . . suggests a lack of social consensus about the state's goals and means of achieving gender equality" (Kano 87–88). Yet it is these very women who are "are powerful consumers whose aesthetic tastes have shaped contemporary spirituality" (Ambros 170), particularly the sort of do-it-yourself, individualized spirituality that treats religion (or, for that matter, popular culture) as repertoire rather than as "-ism":

> [Women] have . . . taken active and varied roles in this [cultural] debate [about gender roles]: from Japanese feminists challenging traditional norms to conservatives nostalgically promoting traditional values. It remains to be seen how Japanese religious organizations will reshape themselves to respond to the gendered challenges of the coming decades and what places Japanese women will claim in this new order. If trends continue, religious groups and specialists who stress an individualized spirituality will remain particularly appealing to women. (Ambros 171)

The "individualized spirituality" that enables young Japanese women to construct identity and project power by reassembling components of popular culture, such as images and characters drawn from *onmyōji* media, may well prove to be a point of robust connection between women and Japanese religious culture as Japan's "precarious" future unfolds. Indeed, the astounding emergence of Abe no Seimei from moth-eaten cultural obscurity to popular celebrity status in the early twenty-first century is a powerful testament to "the power of the girl market" (Miller 31). In repeated personal visits to Seimei's shrine in Kyōto, it has become apparent to this author that the proliferation of Seimei-themed products—amulets, cell phone charms, *manga*, even a dedicated Twitter feed with matching photo opportunities made available on site—aimed at young female consumers shows no sign of stopping any time soon.

. . .

The repertoire of motifs associated with *onmyōji*—binary complementarity, transgressive hybridity, the imported as indigenous—and the thematic repertoire associated with the young Japanese women who cosplay as these characters—dangerous potency, deliberate anachronism, invented tradition—converge in a process by which ancient traditions may speak afresh to contemporary audiences. Elaine K. Chang describes this process as "green-washing": a form of cultural production in which "boundary confusions [are transformed] . . . into new forms and combinations possibly better adapted to the shifting demographics of the contemporary world" (292–93). Such boundary confusions may operate in both progressive and reactionary modes, and such is the case with ancient wizards' appearances in contemporary Japanese comics and cartoons. On the one hand, the spectacle of a young Japanese women attired as a Heian period sorcerer may suggest female emancipation from outmoded gender roles. On the other hand, the deep antiquity of the costume and the authoritative persona assumed by the cosplayer may reinforce the value of patriarchal traditions despite contemporary critiques, and thus belie such emancipation. One may interpret the *onmyōji* cosplayer as a boundary confuser, disrupting rigid gender binaries with transgendered identities and blurring the border between tradition and modernity. Alternatively, one may interpret such a cultural performance as a boundary enforcer, affirming the timeless value of masculinity-as-authority and gendering tradition, nation, and the sacred as male. The latter function is more typical of the monstrous across cultures, which "polices the borders of the possible . . . [such that] to step outside . . . is to risk attack by some monstrous border patrol or (worse) to become monstrous oneself" (Cohen 12).

Regardless, such "green-washing" comes across as quintessentially postmodern, insofar as postmodernity typically is characterized by pastiche (imitative collage rather than original creativity), a kind of cultural mask that "displaces 'real' history" and replaces it with a highly stylized mimicry devoid of irony (Jameson 17, 20). Moreover, these "green-washers" and the cultural productions that they seek to inhabit through ritual masquerade appear to be typically postmodern insofar as

> many postmodern texts are shot through with and even shaped by spiritual concerns. . . . [T]hey make room in the worlds they project for magic, miracle, metaphysical systems of retribution and restoration. . . . [T]heir political analyses and prescriptions are intermittently but powerfully framed in terms of magical or religious conceptions of power. . . . [T]heir assaults on realism, their ontological playfulness, and their experiments in the sublime represent a complex and variously inflected reaffirmation of premodern ontologies—constructions of reality that portray the quotidian world as but one dimension of a multidimensional cosmos, or as hosting a world of spirits. (McClure 143–44)

For McClure, these "very features of fiction which secular theorists have singled out as definitively postmodern must at least in some cases be understood in terms of a postsecular project of resacralization" (144). In other words, the "green-washing" of young Japanese women cosplaying as ancient *onmyōji* may in fact be an expression of the postmodern quest for the recovery of wholeness—a cosmos in which male and female, age and youth, the sacred and the profane, *yīn* and *yáng*, still fit together in harmonious but mutually distinct unity. In this way, all of the series discussed here fit into Jolyon Baraka Thomas's category of "aesthetic" religion-related *manga* and *anime*, which (unlike "didactic" media) "show" rather than "tell" religion by

> us[ing] religious vocabulary and imagery cosmetically . . . to mobilize religious concepts, characters, and images in the service of entertaining their audiences, although their products can elicit increased intellectual interest in (and affective responses to) that content. They can also incidentally give rise to religious sentiment or practice. Examples of such products include adventure stories featuring sacerdotal or divine protagonists, ghost stories, and horror tales. (58)

Recall once more the lyrics to the theme songs of the series profiled above, which seem to voice just this sort of postmodern longing for resacralization, if only to entertain:

> There is a distant memory that's kept secret in my heart.
> The indelible mistake has left an unspeakable wound in our hearts ("Otogi Zoshi engsub Ep 13")
>
> . . .
>
> I seek boundless strength.
> I continue to rise with what I believe in.
> I want to protect—I want to believe. ("Shounen Onmyouji—Episode 05 [English Subbed]")
>
> . . .
>
> I have a dream. . . .
> I saw the unchanged passion. . . .
> I saw the purity that does not change ("Mushibugyo opening 1").

Of course, this is what the fantastic, no matter what its guise in any culture, tends to do:

> Fantastic literature points to or suggests the basis upon which cultural order rests, for it opens up, for a brief moment, on to disorder, on to illegality, on to that which lies outside the Law, that which is outside dominant value systems. The Fantastic traces the unsaid and the unseen of culture: that which has been silenced, made invisible, covered over and made 'absent.' . . . Since this excursion into disorder can only begin from a base within the dominant cultural order, literary fantasy is a telling index of the limits of that order. Its introduction of the 'unreal' is set against the category of the 'real'—a category which the fantastic interrogates by its difference. (Jackson 4)

Much has gone unsaid and unseen in Japan since the country entered modernity so forcefully and quickly almost 150 years ago. Like the ancient Horikawa River that still runs near the Seimei shrine in Kyōto's Kamigyō ward, the *onmyōji* and their transgressions against the order of nature, society, and the cosmos once were prominent features of Japan's cultural landscape. Just as the Horikawa was slowed to a trickle and then buried beneath concrete drainage ditches in a fit of postwar construction, so too were the *onmyōji* concealed beneath layers of modernity, rationality, and westernization. But now, even as the Horikawa's waters, retrieved by subterranean obscurity by more environmentally friendly municipal planning in recent decades, flow once again near the shrine to the wizard who exorcised demons within its precincts, the *onmyōji* have reappeared in startling new form to speak and be seen once more, to shock, amaze, and inspire the Japanese—and, given the incredible global popularity of *manga* and *anime*, perhaps those outside of Japan, as well.

BIBLIOGRAPHY

Allison, Anne. "Precarity and Hope: Social Connectedness in Postcapitalist Japan." In *The Precarious Future*, edited by Frank Baldwin and Anne Allison, 36–57. New York: New York University Press, 2015.

Ambros, Barbara R. *Women in Japanese Religions*. New York: New York University Press, 2015.

Anders, Charlie Jane. "When Did Japan Stop Being the Future?" *io9*. June 18, 2009. Web. Accessed December 29, 2016.

Azuma, Hiroki東浩紀. "The Era of Disasters and the Words of Critical Thought." In *Genron: Portal on Critical Discourse in Japan*. Translated by John Person. April 18, 2012. Web. Accessed October 25, 2012.

Barrett, T. H. "Daojiao." In *The Encyclopedia of Taoism*, edited by Fabrizio Pregadio, vol. 1, 8–10. London: Routledge, 2008.

Cali, Joseph, and John Dougill. "Heian jingū." In *Shinto Shrines: A Guide to the Sacred Sites of Japan's Ancient Religion*, edited by Joseph Cali and John Dougill, 104–7. Honolulu: University of Hawai'i Press, 2013.

Cali, Joseph, and John Dougill. "Seimei jinja." In *Shinto Shrines: A Guide to the Sacred Sites of Japan's Ancient Religion*, edited by Joseph Cali and John Dougill, 136–38. Honolulu: University of Hawai'i Press, 2013.

Campany, Robert Ford. "On the Very Idea of Religions (in the Modern West and in Early Medieval China)." *History of Religions* 42, no. 4 (May 2003): 287–319.

Chakraborty, Abhik, and Shamik Chakraborty. "*Satoyama*: A Landscape Conservation Discourse of Romantic Nostalgia and Reflexive Modernity in 'Post Growth' Japan." *Japan Studies Association Journal* 11 (2013): 46–64.

Chang, Elaine K. "Spaghetti Eastern: Mutating Mass Culture, Transforming Ethnicity." In *Revisioning Italy: National Identity and Global Culture*, edited by Beverly Allen and Mary J. Russo, 292–313. Minneapolis: University of Minnesota Press, 1997.

Cohen, Jeffrey Jerome. "Monster Culture (Seven Theses)." In *Monster Theory: Reading Culture*, edited by Jeffrey Jerome Cohen, 3–25. Minneapolis: University of Minnesota Press, 1996.

Douglas, Mary. *Purity and Danger: An Analysis of Concepts of Pollution and Taboo*. London: Routledge, 1966.

Elacqua, Joseph. "Onmyōryō 陰陽寮 (The Bureau of Yin-Yang)." In *Digital Dictionary of Buddhism*. May 15, 2016. Web. Accessed July 12, 2016.

Granshaw, Lisa. "Investigating the 'Psychology of Cosplay.'" *Daily Dot*. November 11, 2013. Web. Accessed July 13, 2016.

Halberstam, Judith. *Female Masculinity*. Durham: Duke University Press, 1998.

Holcombe, Charles. *The Genesis of East Asia, 221 B.C.-A.D. 907*. Honolulu: University of Hawai'i Press, 2001.

Ito, Kinko. "A History of *Manga* in the Context of Japanese Culture and Society." *Journal of Popular Culture* 38, no. 3 (2005): 456–75.

Jackson, Rosemary. *Fantasy: The Literature of Subversion*. London: Routledge, 1981.

Jameson, Fredric. *Postmodernism, Or the Cultural Logic of Late Capitalism*. Durham: Duke University Press, 1991.

"Japanese Manga Book Market Rises to Record 282 Billion Yen." *Anime News Network*. January 23, 2015. Web. Accessed December 29, 2016.

Kano, Ayako. "The Future of Gender in Japan: Work/Life Balance and Relations between the Sexes." In *Japan: The Precarious Future*, edited by Frank Baldwin and Anne Allison, 87–109. New York: New York University Press, 2015.

Kimbrough, Keller, and Hank Glassman. "Editors' Introduction: Vernacular Buddhism and Medieval Japanese Literature." *Japanese Journal of Religious Studies* 36, no. 2 (2009): 201–8.

Kingston, Jeff. "Extremists Flourish in Abe's Japan." *Asia-Pacific Journal* 12, no. 44.2 (2014). Web. Accessed July 12, 2016.

Kuroda, Toshio 黒田 俊雄. "Shinto in the History of Japanese Religion." Translated by James C. Dobbins and Suzanne Gay. *Journal of Japanese Studies* 7 (1981): 1–21.

Lonial, Subhash C., and Stuart Van Auken. "Wishful Identification with Fictional Characters: An Assessment of the Implications of Gender in Message Dissemination to Children." *Journal of Advertising* 15, no. 4 (1986): 4–11, 42.

Masuo, Shin'ichirō 増尾伸一郎. "Chinese Religion and the Formation of Onmyōdō." *Japanese Journal of Religious Studies* 40, no. 1 (2013): 19–43.

McClure, John A. "Postmodern/Post-Secular: Contemporary Fiction and Spirituality." *Modern Fiction Studies* 41, no. 1 (1995): 141–63.

Miller, Laura. "Extreme Makeover for a Heian-Era Wizard." In *Mechademia 3: Limits of the Human*, edited by Frenchy Lunning, 30–45. Minneapolis: University of Minnesota Press, 2008.

"Mushibugyo Opening 1." Online video clip. *YouTube*. April 8, 2013. Accessed July 13, 2016.

Napier, Susan J. *Anime from Akira to Howl's Moving Castle: Experiencing Contemporary Japanese Animation*. New York: Palgrave Macmillan, 2005.

Naumann, Nelly. *Japanese Prehistory: The Material and Spiritual Culture of the Jōmon Period*. Wiesbaden: Harrassowitz, 2000.

Okabe, Daisuke. "Cosplay, Learning, and Cultural Practice." In *Fandom Unbound: Otaku Culture in a Connected World*, edited by Mizuko Ito, Daisuke Okabe, and Izumi Tsuji, 225–48. New Haven: Yale University Press, 2012.

Oskin, Becky. "Japan Earthquake & Tsunami of 2011: Facts and Information." *LiveScience*. May 7, 2015. Web. Accessed July 12, 2016.

"Otogi Zoshi (お伽草子 Otogizōshi?) engsub Ep 13." Online video clip. *YouTube*. January 31, 2016. Web. Accessed July 13, 2016.

Production I.G. プロダクション・アイジー. "Otogo Zoshi—Overview: Heian Chapter." *Production I.G*. 2016. Web. Accessed July 13, 2016.

Recchio, Devin T. "Constructing Abe no Seimei: Integrating Genre and Disparate Narratives in Yumemakura Baku's *Onmyōji*." PhD diss, University of Massachusetts at Amherst, 2014.

Reider, Noriko T. "*Onmyōji*: Sex, Pathos, and Grotesquery in Yumemakura Baku's *Oni*." *Asian Folklore Studies* 66, no. 1–2 (2007): 107–24.

Reider, Noriko T. "Transformation of the *Oni:* From the Frightening and Diabolical to the Cute and Sexy." *Asian Folklore Studies* 62, no. 1 (2003): 133–57.

Richey, Jeffrey L. "Introduction: Conjuring Cultures: Daoism in Japan." In *Daoism in Japan: Chinese Traditions and Their Influence on Japanese Religious Culture*, edited by Jeffrey L. Richey, 1–8. London: Routledge, 2015.

Robinet, Isabelle. "Daojia." In *The Encyclopedia of Taoism*, edited by Fabrizio Pregadio, vol. 1, 5–8. London: Routledge, 2008.

Schodt, Frederik L. *The Astro Boy Essays: Osamu Tezuka, Mighty Atom, and the Manga/Anime Revolution*. Berkeley: Stone Bridge Press, 2007.

Shiohara, Ken. "Manga History Books Appeal to All Ages and Defy Retail Sales Slump." In *The Asahi Shinbun*. September 20, 2016. Web. Accessed December 29, 2016.

"Shounen Onmyouji—Episode 05 [English Subbed]." Online video clip. *YouTube*. May 5, 2013. Web. Accessed July 13, 2016.

Sunardi, Christina. *Stunning Males and Powerful Females: Gender and Tradition in East Javanese Dance*. Champaign: University of Illinois Press, 2015.

Thomas, Jolyon Baraka. *Drawing on Tradition: Manga, Anime, and Religion in Contemporary Japan*. Honolulu: University of Hawai'i Press, 2012.

"TVアニメ『ムシブギョー』公式サイト [TV *Anime 'Mushibugyō'* Official Site]." Web. Accessed July 13, 2016.

Chapter Eleven

JOE KUBERT'S *YOSSEL: APRIL 19, 1943*

Faith and Art History's Precedents

SAMANTHA BASKIND

IN THE SIXTIETH ANNIVERSARY YEAR OF THE WARSAW GHETTO UPRISING, war comics pioneer Joe Kubert (1926–2012) published a graphic novel about that legendary revolt and the possibility, sidestepped by his fortuitous immigration to the United States at a young age, that Kubert himself could have participated in it. Indeed, *Yossel: April 19, 1943* revolves around how Kubert's life might have unfolded, told through the eponymous protagonist's eyes, if his family had remained in a Eastern European shtetl rather than arriving in the United States when Kubert was two months old. Yossel's story allowed Kubert to explore his "'what-if' thoughts . . . [in] a work of fiction, based on a nightmare that was a fact" (Kubert, np). Knowing the persecutions he would have surely endured as a Jew in Poland during the war years, Kubert mused, "If my parents had not come to America, we would have been caught in that maelstrom, sucked in and pulled down with the millions of others who were lost. . . . The experience [of researching and making *Yossel*] was very personal, a little scary, and sort of cleansing. It was something I felt I had to do."

This chapter argues that the 1943 uprising only peripherally propels the story forward, despite the book's title. That is, the book's title specifically references the best-known Jewish revolt during the Holocaust, when a small band of Jewish partisans stockpiled arms and rose up against the Nazis. Modest numbers and meager weapons notwithstanding, against all odds this determined group of Jewish militants held off two thousand well-armed SS men for twenty-eight days, when the entire Polish army had fallen to the Nazis in a comparable amount of time a few years earlier. Yet in *Yossel* the fight, and the attendant heroism typically emphasized in scholarly accounts and historical fictionalizations of the uprising (e.g., Leon Uris's *Mila 18* [1961] and Jon Avnet's NBC miniseries *Uprising* [2001]), is not much of a focus except at the denouement, whereupon the rebels engage in a short battle and Yossel dies. Nor does Kubert's tale about his alter ego reign solely supreme, even as concern about Yossel's welfare in the festering ghetto factors into how readers receive the story. I am more interested in a third theme that runs through the graphic narrative, as important but more subtly conveyed: one of faith during the Holocaust, and consequently how Kubert employs tropes from art history to make points about the challenges of belief and the agony of its loss. While doing so, Kubert upends those visual tropes in order to expose how the Holocaust mercilessly upended humanity, transforming and displacing even the most devout.

Born Yosaif in a Polish shtetl, Kubert gained fame as a cartoonist for *Hawkman* and *Sgt. Rock*, whose titular figure remains the best-known character in the war comics genre. Kubert, who served as DC Comics director of publications and founded his own comics school in 1976, is deemed by many as the premier war comics artist and stands as one of the key figures from the Silver Age of comics. His early audience typically comprised adolescents and young men—frequently those enlisted in the service, contemplating joining up, or recently released from duty—apropos the adult theme of deadly combat intrinsic to war comics. Issues of *Sgt. Rock* and *The Unknown Soldier* often were set during World War II and at times explored some specific horrors of the Holocaust. For example, a year before the first run of the series ended (it has since been reprised twice), the Unknown Soldier infiltrated the Warsaw Ghetto in an issue dubbed "A Season in Hell" (#247, January 1981), which described Nazi violence toward Polish Jews. Part 1 of the story depicts Nazi savagery and trucks filled with heaps of corpses. Kubert's cover imparts an explicit rendering of a frightening episode inside the comic. It pictures the moment in the story when the Unknown Soldier helps a young girl escape the ghetto in a wagon piled high with dead, skeletal bodies. The soldier places his hand over the innocent girl's mouth to keep her from shouting in terror as her tiny head peeks from the side of the wagon, blue eyes wide with fear. Both the girl's and the Unknown Soldier's ruddy, peachy flesh contrasts with the rotting, brownish-gray toned, loose-limbed corpses haphazardly surrounding them.

Late in life, after a career making traditional comics, Kubert wrote three graphic narratives: *Fax from Sarajevo* (1998), concerning the 1990s Balkan conflict; *Jew Gangster* (2005), drawn in a distinctive film noir visual style and about a Jewish boy in Depression era Brooklyn who takes up with mobsters;

and of course his work of documentary fiction and the subject of this essay, *Yossel: April 19, 1943*. Kubert aimed this personal sliding-doors story, in which he imagines himself not as an immigrant in Brooklyn but rather as a child remaining in Poland during World War II, to mature teenagers and adults, and so to a different audience than his war comics and other undertakings. He thereby felt emboldened to tell an especially disturbing story devoid of any catharsis. Although unrelated to this chapter's focus on the place of faith in *Yossel*, it is instructive to point out that Kubert stuns the reader at the end of the book when he kills off Yossel. Certainly, Kubert's choice was partially affected by working in a darker comics universe, one inhabited by such bleak comics as Alan Moore and Dave Gibbons's *Watchmen* and Frank Miller's *The Dark Knight*. It would have been inauthentic to let Yossel live; in 2003 one is allowed to write a graphic narrative where no one gets out alive. Moreover, Kubert's earlier comics about the Holocaust were, to a degree, softened, in part because of the time they were written but also because of their sometimes younger audience. *Yossel* stands in stark contrast to these endeavors, and so one must also consider how the book's themes influenced Kubert's shocking iconography, and reciprocally how his shocking iconography propels forward the book's themes. The protagonist's death provides one of many instances when readers register distress, as Kubert unremittingly pictures the Holocaust's revulsions through a litany of terrible details, especially in his storyline about faith.

Kubert's reflection comes from his position as a secondary witness rather than a primary one, a man on the margins of annihilation rather that at its center—the very space of the monstrous. Namely, he could only imagine what life was like in the Warsaw Ghetto as opposed, for instance, to fine artist Samuel Bak, a child survivor of the Vilna Ghetto who has spent the majority of his career painting canvases addressing his lived memories. Another graphic narrative about a child caught in the maelstrom that was Hitler's Europe, Miriam Katin's *We Are on Our Own* (2006), conveys the artist's firsthand account of her experience with her mother as the pair faked identities, left their hometown of Budapest after Nazis occupied the city, and lived in disguise as peasants in the countryside. Explicitly Jewish graphic memoirs have become especially popular, due in great part to Art Spiegelman's earlier, groundbreaking, Pulitzer Prize–winning *Maus* (1986, 1991), a meta-narrative acknowledged as one of the most distinguished works about the Holocaust in any genre. Bernice Eisenstein's *I Was a Child of Holocaust Survivors* (2006) explores the Holocaust from the same perspective as Spiegelman's. The cover of Eisenstein's memoir, for example, vividly articulates the author's second-generation, or "hinge generation," experience, as Eva Hoffman terms the children of survivors, of which she is one (Hoffman xv). Specifically, the cover reveals the extent to which Eisenstein's parents' ordeal informs her identity. Against a blood-red background, a black-and-white portrait of Eisenstein as a child does not cast a shadow; instead, Eisenstein's parents provide the dark shadows behind her tiny body.

Yossel opens with the title character, at age sixteen, hiding in the sewers beneath the ghetto with a few remaining resistance fighters, observing that the partisans "have lived a hundred years of hell in the Warsaw Ghetto" (4). Most pages comprise a collage of sketchy black-and-white pencil drawings as if Yossel himself made them, often hurriedly as the events occurred. Kubert's choice to execute the story in pencil, forgoing ink entirely, provides a perfect confluence of form following function; the colorlessness evokes the immediacy of the moment as well as the cold emotional darkness of the time as well as the frequently severe, gloomy climate. Further, as Brad Prager so aptly observes, Kubert's "unerased pencil markings also serve as a metaphor for the persistence of the past: it cannot be erased, nor can it be presented cleanly" (118). Kubert's collaged images are not constrained by gridlike panels, but rather extend, undefined and often heavily shadowed, across the book's pages, which are grayish in tone, not a traditional white. The book's thick-stock pages and their muddied hue contribute to the sense that the drawings were made in the time they portray, and add depth to the subtle gradations of the raw graphite, at times supplemented with white highlights. In what amounts to a long flashback, bookended by the uprising and Yossel's death, the young artist describes his family's journey from a life of freedom to their travails in the ghetto, his privilege as an artist for the Nazis, and involvement with the resistance. Dialogue and descriptive information appear not encapsulated in standard circular speech bubbles emanating from a character's mouth but within sketchily lined, blocky squares and rectangles, circumscribing a font known as CCKubert, a crisp lettering style of the artist's invention.

Following the introduction of a rabbi (the second-most prominent character after Yossel), faith plays a significant role in the story. A quarter of the way through the book, the rabbi, who has escaped the camps—coincidentally Yossel's rabbi from his hometown—arrives in the ghetto to tell of his ordeal. Thirty-eight pages (39–76) are dedicated to the rabbi's didactic recitation of the death camps, his untenable position in the gray zone as a member of the Sonderkommando at Auschwitz, and loss of faith. The rabbi's extensive dissertation stuns the reader in its unrelenting detail. He tells of deportation and cattle cars, wherein "babies suffocated" and the stench overwhelmed him (40), selections and the treatment of prisoners, and specifications of the barracks down to dimensions. A full page attempts to impart the scope of the mass killings by channeling one of the most difficult exhibits at the United States Holocaust Memorial Museum (USHMM): Kubert portrays a mountain of shoes, but he takes this further by also showing piles of hairbrushes and combs, luggage, glasses, and bundles of hair (51). Visually engaging with these objects, translated in Kubert's graphic narrative from authentic displays into artistic representations, causes disquiet, but obviously not as forcefully as the much larger actual piles of shoes at the USHMM, which overwhelm in size and stench. The museum's literature employs the shoes in their collection to similar effect. One museum guide cover features a photograph of a pile of dirty, discarded shoes, presented in a close-up and tilted on an angle so that, disturbingly, the mound of shoes seems to spill into the reader's space. While in graphic novel form we cannot react to the smell of shoes or the physical reality of them before our eyes, we still feel relatively besieged by their depiction, and consequently the rabbi's disillusionment, because Kubert augmented the types of objects to signal the enormity of Nazi cruelty.

As the rabbi's harrowing account unfolds, readers learn about his faltering conviction, vividly recorded by Yossel's drawings. Just when the rabbi in *Yossel* thought things could not get worse, he witnessed the gas chambers, peering through a peephole (readers are not privy to what he sees): "How can I describe what I saw? People were being gassed, murdered. Some crawled over one another in an attempt to breathe. It was horrific. Revolting. . . . Bodies everywhere locked in a struggle with death" (58, 60). Near the end of the rabbi's narrative, Kubert gives readers a break from the camp's specific terrors but he does not provide respite. Occupying the center of a page, with only one small additional drawing in the upper right corner so as not to distract the reader from this emotive moment, the rabbi covers his face and forehead with oversized hands. It is as if the larger his hands, the better he can shield himself from the torturous memories that gut him, a pose Kubert used in three distinctive portraits of the rabbi (46, 63, 77). With his head bowed in sorrow, his faith eroded by his Nazi oppressors and the sickening actions that he has seen and undertaken, the rabbi despairingly utters: "Rebbe no more. No more Torah. N-no more teaching, I have seen things . . . done things. I have learned. There is no God" (77). As wrenchingly, in one of the earlier drawings of the rabbi covering his face and head in misery, he similarly states: "God had forsaken us. Leaving only pain and no salvation. There was no God" (46). By concentrating on the rabbi's weary, distressed face, Kubert adapts a technique he often employed for his earlier Sgt. Rock stories; these

Figure 11.1. The Rabbi's anguish, *Yossel: April 19, 1943*, page 77, by Joe Kubert. © Joe Kubert 2003. Reproduced with permission of the Joe Kubert Estate

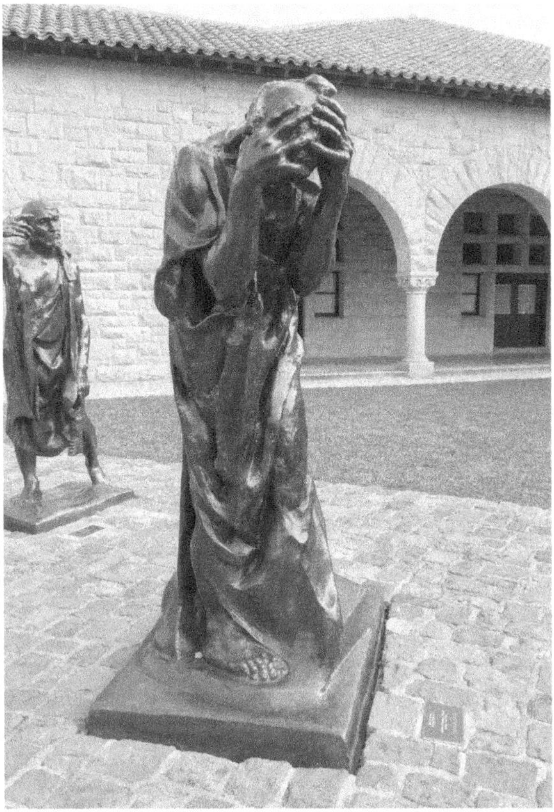

Figure 11.2. Auguste Rodin, *The Burghers of Calais*: detail, 1884–89. Bronze, 6'10½" × 7'11" × 6'6" at base

life-or-death battle scenarios stressed the emotional consequences of war through the expressions of Sgt. Rock and other gritty members of the platoon Easy Company, as much as portrayals of war itself.

Body language throughout *Yossel* communicates the high anxiety and tension of the story. Readers see this vividly in Kubert's oversized expressionistic rendering of the rabbi's anguish. Here, Kubert adopts the pose of a figure in the far right background of Auguste Rodin's sculpture *The Burghers of Calais* (1884–1889), an icon of resignation that commemorates a different city under siege. Indeed, Rodin's celebrated bronze sculpture memorializes six men from Calais who surrendered themselves to the English king Edward III to save the other citizens of their town during the Hundred Years' War. Rodin depicts the moment when the burghers leave their city to stand before the king, who will order their execution. Each man walks barefoot, in sackcloth, and some wear a rope around their neck, foreshadowing the death by hanging that awaits, although unbeknownst to them the queen will provide a last-minute reprieve.

These righteous, self-sacrificing men are a far cry from the rebbe-turned-Sonderkommando, a member of the unit charged with helping prisoners undress and herding the doomed prisoners into gas chambers. After the gas chamber, the Sonderkommando removed gold fillings from the dead's teeth and collected any other "valuables" (including hair), and then dragged corpses to the crematoria, whereupon they aided in incineration. The men of Calais volunteer to die for their friends and family, whereas the rabbi assists in the killing of his friends and family. Still, extenuating circumstances must be taken into account; the rabbi fell victim to those "choiceless choices" (Langer 72) that characterize the universe of the Holocaust. Some view the Sonderkommando as Nazi collaborators, even as monsters, who betrayed their coreligionists in exchange for privileges and as a way to save their own lives at the expense of others; favors bestowed on Sonderkommando units, and also the *Judenrat* (the ghettoes' Jewish Councils), included alcohol, extra food, and better clothing and mattresses.

Auschwitz survivor Primo Levi's "The Gray Zone," the second chapter of his final book, *The Drowned and the Saved*, addresses the role and plight of the Sonderkommando, as does a 2001 movie titled *The Grey Zone*, unrelated to Levi's book save for the title, although spelled differently. Levi described the Sonderkommando as "akin to collaborators" and asserted that their testimonies should be read with a jaundiced eye, because "they had much to atone for and would naturally attempt to rehabilitate themselves at the expense of the truth." He typically takes this contemptuous tack, but at one point he more sympathetically describes the position of the Sonderkommando, viewing members of the units he saw in Auschwitz as Jews who were forced to become perpetrators. By virtue of their actions, he wrote, they took on "the burden of guilt, so that they were deprived of even the solace of innocence" (Levi 53). Historian Gideon Greif, writing long after the fact, understands the Sonderkommando as "victims," even "the most miserable of the miserable. The workers of the death factory had to witness day by day the extermination of their own people. There was nothing they could do about it. Their hearts and souls were broken by sorrow and despair" (Greif "Between Sanity," 41). Undoubtedly, the Sonderkommando are controversial figures that engender very mixed opinions in Holocaust thought and scholarship; some view the Sonderkommando as victims and others as collaborators. These contradictions permeate Kubert's graphic narrative as well.

Kubert's portraits of the rabbi lean toward sympathy. *The Burghers of Calais* is universally viewed as an exquisite instance of despair, agony, and fatalism—surely a meaning known to Kubert, who studied the old masters and found lifelong inspiration from his art history studies (Schelly 2011, 24). Rodin's unparalleled, powerful artistic precedent served Kubert well. For the rabbi there could be no greater agony than the loss of belief in the God he had served for a lifetime and his role in the death of his coreligionists. The care by which Kubert chose and employed a visual analogue, here and elsewhere, demonstrates the importance of faith, and its loss, in his project, and decidedly augments the potency of the written word.

In subject and form, another strong comparison to Kubert's portraits of the rebbe can be made with Ben Shahn's serigraph *Warsaw 1943* (1963), prompted by a drawing originally conceived for a competition commemorating the Warsaw Ghetto (Prescott 51). This work on paper explicitly memorializes the ghetto, the Holocaust, and the destruction of six million Jewish lives. Rendered in black and brown, with a few precisely and effectively delineated lines, *Warsaw 1943* portrays a distraught figure from his waist up. He covers his face and head with oversized hands that—if we read him as a ghetto fighter—displayed remarkable courage and appear strong, but in reality could only offer a meager defense. In an effort to disappear, to escape from the sorrow that consumes him, the man hunches his shoulders, clenches his hands so tightly that his tendons show, and bows his head. Importantly, most ghetto fighters were Zionists and more secular than not, but Shahn still connects his fighter to the religious elements of Judaism vis-à-vis the text he includes underneath the forlorn figure.

A thirteenth-century Yom Kippur prayer from the Musaf service, called the "ten martyrs' prayer," appears in Hebrew below Shahn's anguished man: "These I remember, and my soul melts with sorrow, for strangers have devoured us like unturned cakes, for in the days of the tyrant there was no reprieve for the [ten] martyrs murdered by the government." Ziva Amishai-Maisels observes that Shahn purposely omitted the word "ten," which in the original refers to rabbis killed in the second century by the Romans at the behest of Emperor Hadrian, to make the quote appropriate for Holocaust remembrance (Amishai-Maisels 1986–1987, 316). Clearly inspired by the grief-stricken poses in this familiar prototype and Rodin's sculpture, Yossel/Kubert's vital illustration of the rabbi provides a capstone to the broken man's shocking revelations, which have been punctuated by equally shocking imagery of death, torture, and the results thereof: piles of bodies, a boy being electrocuted by a barbed wire fence during a failed escape, and the

Figure 11.3. The Rabbi, seen through the crematorium oven's door, *Yossel: April 19, 1943*, page 62, by Joe Kubert. © Joe Kubert 2003. Reproduced with permission of the Joe Kubert Estate

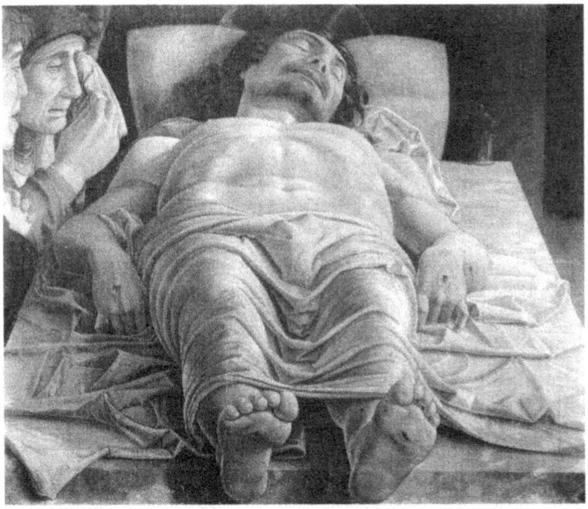

Figure 11.4. Andrea Mantegna, *Dead Christ*, c. 1480. Tempera on canvas, 27 × 32 in. Pinacoteca di Brera, Milan

exterminated inside a gas chamber, all translated by Yossel into drawings. Like Shahn, Kubert also found resonance in the symbolism of martyrdom. To that end, he invokes Jesus in a powerful splash page, once again employing a key model from art history.

Only seven pages in *Yossel* are allotted to a single vignette, including this splash page depicting the rabbi staring at a corpse he has prodded into a crematorium. Sketching the rabbi's words, Yossel shows him surrounded by heavy shadowing and standing in front of the arched furnace door of the camp's oven, looking hollowly at the reader. The disconcerting scene situates the reader on the opposite side of the oven, as if it were the reader's feet facing the rabbi and thus a dead, soon to be incinerated Jew. Distraught, the rabbi laments: "How many bodies did I carry to be incinerated? How many children? How many had I prodded into the furnace? I lost count. And how was it that I continued to live while so many others died?" (62). Most of the drawings in *Yossel* sprawl into the reader's space, pushing off the pages of the book, but only this one incident fully extends into the reader's space. Making striking use of foreshortening, the image positions the viewer in a specific place, known as the station point. Kubert exploits this technique to create an unsettling station point: supine on a slab, it appears as if readers look past their own feet to see the rabbi framed in the doorway of the oven.

Kubert's page evokes Andrea Mantegna's dramatic foreshortening in his iconic and inventive painting *Dead Christ* (c. 1480), with Jesus's feet prominently in the foreground. Kubert turns Mantegna's image inside-out; the reader is not only a dead Jew, he or she is also the dead Christ, the prototypical martyred Jew. In this crucial drawing, Kubert makes a statement about the consequences of prejudice by offering a faceless, genderless victim, such that any reader—of any faith—could assume its identity and consequently its fate. At the same time, Kubert calls upon the tradition of the "Jewish Jesus," engaged by other Jewish artists to comment about the sacrifice (as problematic as that idea may be) of their coreligionists in a larger history as well as the Holocaust—including the sculptor Mark Antokolsky, caricaturist Arthur Szyk, and the painters Abraham Rattner and Marc Chagall.

Some of Chagall's best-known images of persecution employ the trope of the "Jewish Jesus," including *White Crucifixion*. The first of several crucifixion paintings, *White Crucifixion* was painted in the pivotal year 1938, when synagogues in Munich and Nuremberg were destroyed in June and August, respectively, followed by the devastation of Kristallnacht (November 9–10, 1938), the "night of broken glass," the fateful modern-day pogrom when Jewish businesses and synagogues were burned and desecrated by the Gestapo, SS, and Hitler Youth. *White Crucifixion* features a bearded Jesus with a covered head, crucified on the cross in the central foreground amidst a burning synagogue, a Torah scroll unceremoniously tossed on the ground, and panicked, fleeing Jews, among other signs of Nazi brutality. Most obviously, Chagall distinguishes Jesus as a Jew by his *tallit* (prayer shawl) loincloth. Above the cross, the acronym INRI identifies him as "King of the Jews," under which Chagall included the Aramaic translation rendered in Hebrew letters (Iesus Nazarenus Rex Iudaeorum, or Jesus of Nazareth, King of the Jews), thereby marking him as the epitome of Jewish suffering, the idea carried out in the rest of the picture. *Yellow Crucifixion* (1943) takes this symbolism even further, showing Jesus wearing phylacteries (black leather boxes containing scrolls worn around the arms and foreheads of observant Jews during morning prayers) and a *tallit* loincloth. As Chagall described Jesus's presence in his work: "My Christ, as I depict him, is always the type of the Jewish martyr, in pogroms and in our other troubles" (Amishai-Maisels 1982, 104).

Whereas Kubert's earlier portraits of the rebbe pictured him with some sympathy, his portrayal in the splash page communicates the opposite perspective. Kubert's ambivalent view on the Sonderkommando echoes the moral ambiguity of the units, in addition to the two different strands of thought regarding the role of these men in the Holocaust. As we will now see, the splash page and its verso (left page) work together to convey this negative view; in essence, Kubert points a reproachful finger at the rabbi, casting him as culpable and complicit with the Nazis, and a murderer of the Jewish Jesus. Here we witness the rabbi's transformation from a once-sacred man to one who has been desacralized—he has become monstrous.

The white highlights that indicate the oven's fire on the verso page glow in the hinges of the oven door in Kubert's recto (right) splash page of the rabbi performing his Sonderkommando duties. Those same white highlights reflect on the face and hands of the compromised spiritual leader. Throughout art history, light frequently functions as redemptive, especially in Christian art in the form of a halo or even light surrounding a holy figure (e.g., Raphael's *Transfiguration* [1516–1520]). Here light or fire, which also plays around the bottom of the victim's feet and ankles, accusingly links the rabbi to his crimes. Several pages later the rebbe is found hanging from a lamppost (92), his fatal wounds now external as well as internal. The same white accents surround the light source; but even more, white emanates from the tips of all the rabbi's fingers—the very hands that perpetrated the heinous offenses that eroded his convictions. Those fingers appear to be symbolically on fire, an inversion of the light (faith and holiness) that once pervaded the rabbi's life. Kubert's careful use of white highlights opens yet another explicit artistic connection of the rabbi to his crimes—to what Yaakov Gabai, a survivor and Sonderkommando, called "the most terrible things of all . . . the dirty work of the Holocaust" (Greif "We Wept," 205). Also of note, the rabbi's mode of death bears another interesting correlation to *The Burghers of Calais* because all six men commemorated by the sculpture were slated to die by hanging, hence the ropes that Rodin included around their necks. By some idealistic accounts it was their righteousness that saved them, even though in reality it was Queen Philippa's intercession, because she feared that her unborn child would somehow be harmed if she let her husband condemn the men to death.

Circling back to Kubert's haunting splash page, one cannot help but notice that the victim's legs take form with very lightly demarcated lines, the limbs spectral and ghostly. In contrast, the rabbi and his two companions appear much more substantial; Kubert has drawn them heavily, giving the trio a much more solid presence. This unholy triumvirate warrants comparison to the Roman centurions who crucified Jesus. To be sure, the rabbi holding the pole conjures images of Romans holding lances in many images of the crucifixion, rendered in countless paintings from the Early Renaissance through the Baroque period (e.g., Fra Angelico, *Jesus on the Cross*, ca. 1440). Kubert turns the original image on its head by placing a Jew in the position of a Christian Roman. The choice could not be more effective; by utilizing

Figure 11.5. The Sonderkommando at work, *Yossel: April 19, 1943*, page 61, by Joe Kubert. © Joe Kubert 2003. Reproduced with permission of the Joe Kubert Estate

this common pose as his source material, Kubert further associates the rabbi with Christ on the cross iconography, cementing him as a perpetrator of unwarranted and cruel murders.

Looking closely at some of the artist's sources demonstrates that well-known representations from the history of art offered Kubert the means to consider faith vis-à-vis the Holocaust from two perspectives: its loss *and* its consequences. That is to say, uprisings like that in the Warsaw Ghetto were few and far between, predominantly because of the repercussions feared from the Nazis, but in some cases also because the most faithful believed that God would see them through, and thus did not take matters in their own hands. Elie Wiesel remembered that when news of the Nazi genocide reached his hometown of Sighet, Romania, "Our optimism remained unshakable. It was simply a question of holding out for a few days. . . . Once again the God of Abraham would save his people, as always, at the last moment, when all seemed lost" (Wiesel 25). Further, Wiesel recalled that the rabbis responded, "Nothing will happen to us, for God needs us" (124).

Some cultural representations feature characters of this ilk. John Hersey's celebrated historical novel *The Wall* (1950) and Rod Serling's prominent *Playhouse 90* teleplay *In the Presence of Mine Enemies* (May 18, 1960) included characters solely guided by faith. The rabbi in Hersey's novel explained why he remained measured despite knowledge of Treblinka: "We all know that our faith will survive their [the Nazis] persecutions: we are better and stronger than they are. . . . I am calm because I know that any system that is based on love and respect will outlive any system that is based upon hatred and contempt" (369). To the end, the rabbi in *In the Presence of Mine Enemies* tenaciously believes that faith will see the Jews through the war, but his embittered son Paul, whose face has been scarred in a work camp and who has seen first-hand the bestiality of which Nazis are capable, is primed for resistance. Here we encounter the trope of the freedom fighter, and one particularly bent on revenge, versus a man of the book. Angry with his father for his ineffectual supplications, Paul cynically admonishes: "God can't hear you, Papa. God has left the premises. He has new friends now. . . . So Papa, I'd hold up any further prayer till I found a replacement. A God a little more righteous than the one who has moved over to the Germans" (Cook). As Freud contends in *The Future of an Illusion*, the faithful cling to God's existence without tangible evidence—and often in the bleakest of conditions—because to believe otherwise would be too painful. Yet the rabbi in *Yossel*, ostensibly one of the most faithful, falters after his camp experience. He knows how far he has been distanced, even if by horrific circumstances, from the God to whom he was once so devoted. The distraught rabbi who covers his bowed head in misery contrasts with the Sonderkommando who stands upright, face fully exposed, staring at the corpse on the slab. He can never be the man, the spiritual leader, or the Jew he was before the crematorium. The rabbi's body is not dead like the body in the oven, but his soul is another matter.

Miriam Katin's aforementioned Holocaust memoir interweaves a subplot about the young protagonist's, and briefly her parent's, struggle with faith and God. *We Are on Our Own* primarily uses color for scenes in the present day, and black and white pencil for panels describing Katin's experience in Europe. Some of the book's panels are very delicately rendered, and others are strongly expressionistic, a stylistic divergence assumed to help move the story along; the earlier, happier images in cosmopolitan Hungary are softer as compared to the heavier panels describing the emotional, turbulent period when Katin was on the run with her mother. Understandably shaken as a young child on the run amid atrocity, Katin's alter ego—named Lisa in the book—aches for a solid connection to, and belief in, God. However, after two of her dogs are killed, one in front of her by a Russian soldier and depicted gruesomely in a four-panel page (65), followed by additional panels of the bloodied dog lying in the snow with Lisa examining him (67–69), she begins to question: "Maybe God was not . . ." (69). The book's title itself plainly states Katin's perspective, one held by her father as well. When Lisa's (Miriam's) parents reunite after the war, following their separate ordeals, her mother thanks God, to which her father responds, "God has nothing to do with any of this. . . . How can you give thanks to a deadly sky. . . . We are on our own, Esther. That's all there is" (Katin 117–18). Katin's afterword concludes with comments about the divine from the perspective of a woman in her sixties reflecting back on her life: "Perhaps my only regret is that I could not give this kind of comfort, a comfort of faith in the 'existence of God,' to my children. I was unable to lie" (126).

Primo Levi also questioned God after the Holocaust; he stated, in an oft-cited interview, "There is Auschwitz and so there cannot be a God" (Camon 68). Nevertheless, his interviewer explains, Levi wrote in pencil on the transcript of their conversation, "I don't find a solution to this dilemma. I keep looking, but I don't find it" (Camon 68). Elie Wiesel, who post-Holocaust retained some belief in God even as he struggled with that relationship and often indicted the cruelty of a higher power, also lost faith in the specter of the death camps: "Every day I was moving a little further away from the God of my childhood. He has become a stranger to me; sometimes, I even thought he was my enemy" (Wiesel 34). For some, even God can become monstrous.

At the risk of stating the obvious, maintaining faith in the shadow of the Holocaust is not easy for many. If the rabbi in *Yossel* can be besieged by doubt cast upon everything for which he had lived, then where does that leave those of us who have not lived a life that revolved assiduously around the commandments? Many, like Katin, Levi, and Wiesel, along with those who were not persecuted in Nazi Europe, cite a lack of faith in God apropos the horrors of the Holocaust, questioning where a deity could have possibly been as the so-called chosen people—or any people—were systematically killed, close to the point of extermination. Theologian Emil Fackenheim rebuts this perspective so well: to rebuke God, to have one's faith weakened by the Holocaust, would be "to hand Hitler yet another, posthumous victory" (Fackenheim 22–24). *Yossel* addresses the complexities of faith and the limits of humanity during the Holocaust through a marriage of word and image, the latter of which Kubert adopts and adapts from the history of art at critical moments. These precedents provided Kubert with a potent vocabulary to navigate not only his "'what if' thoughts" but also to work through the crisis of faith that he, and perhaps many of his readers, experienced in a post-Holocaust world.

BIBLIOGRAPHY

Amishai-Maisels, Ziva. "Ben Shahn and the Problem of Jewish Identity." *Jewish Art* 12–13 (1986–87): 304-19.

Amishai-Maisels, Ziva. "The Jewish Jesus." *Journal of Jewish Art* 9 (1982): 84–104.

Avnet, Jon (dir.). *Uprising*. CBS, 2001.

Camon, Ferdinando. *Conversations with Primo Levi*. Translated by John Shepley. Marlboro, VT: Marlboro Press, 1989.

Cook, Fielder (dir.). *In the Presence of Mine Enemies*. Written by Rod Serling. *Playhouse 90*, CBS, 1960.

Eisenstein, Bernice. *I Was a Child of Holocaust Survivors*. New York: Riverhead Books, 2006.

Fackenheim, Emil. *The Jewish Return into History: Reflections in the Age of Auschwitz and a New Jerusalem*. New York: Schocken Books, 1978.

Freud, Sigmund. *The Future of an Illusion*. Translated and edited by James Strachey. New York: Norton, 1975.

Greif, Gideon. "Between Sanity and Insanity: Spheres of Everyday Life in the Auschwitz-Birkenau *Sonderkommando*." In *Gray Zones: Ambiguity and Compromise in the Holocaust and Its Aftermath*, edited by Jonathan Petropoulos and John K. Roth, 37–60. New York: Berghahn Books, 2005.

Greif, Gideon. *We Wept without Tears: Testimonies of the Jewish Sonderkommando from Auschwitz*. New Haven: Yale University Press, 2005.

Hersey, John. *The Wall*. New York: Alfred A. Knopf, 1950.

Hoffman, Eva. *After Such Knowledge: Memory, History, and the Legacy of the Holocaust*. New York: Public Affairs, 2004.

Katin, Miriam. *We Are on Our Own: A Memoir*. Montreal: Drawn & Quarterly, 2006.

Kubert, Joe. *Yossel: April 19, 1943*. 2003. Reprint, New York: DC Comics, 2011.

Langer, Lawrence L. *Versions of Survival: The Holocaust and the Human Spirit*. Albany: State University of New York Press, 1982.

Levi, Primo. *The Drowned and the Saved*. Translated by Raymond Rosenthal. New York: Summit Books, 1988.

Prager, Brad. "The Holocaust without Ink: Absent Memory and Atrocity in Joe Kubert's Graphic Novel *Yossel: April 19, 1943*." In *The Jewish Graphic Novel: Critical Approaches*, edited by Samantha Baskind and Ranen Omer-Sherman, 111–28. New Brunswick: Rutgers University Press, 2008.

Prescott, Kenneth W. *The Complete Graphic Works of Ben Shahn*. New York: Quadrangle, 1973.

Schelly, Bill. *The Art of Joe Kubert*. Seattle: Fantagraphics Books, 2011.

Schelly, Bill. *Man of Rock: A Biography of Joe Kubert*. Seattle: Fantagraphics Books, 2008.

Spiegelman, Art. *Maus: A Survivor's Tale*. New York: Pantheon 1986 (vol.1), 1991 (vol. 2).

Uris, Leon. *Mila 18*. Garden City: Doubleday, 1961.

Wiesel, Elie. *Legends of Our Time*. New York: Holt, Rinehart, and Winston, 1968.

Part IV

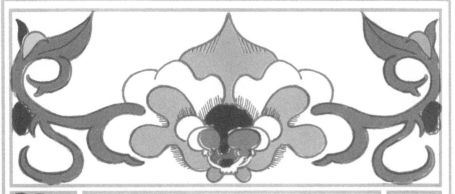

THE EVERYDAY SACRED IN COMICS

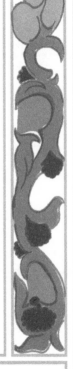

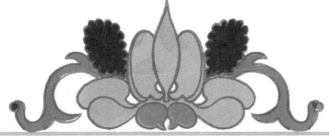

In the previous section we encountered the sacred at the margins; here in this final section we explore through comics the temporal and ontological encounters with the sacred in the ordinary and commonplace. What we find in graphic narratives is the everyday sacred: a holy presence in the mundane, common, and often overlooked features of familiar existence. The comics discussed here make the familiar unfamiliar, where the common becomes uncanny, and where walking itself becomes a sacred stroll through the streets. Artists do this with the basic tools of the trade: refocusing our attention through repetition, furthering the gap between text and image—allowing, requesting, or perhaps even demanding a literal and figurative new point of view. The claim is not that the profane has become sacred, but rather that the profane can always be, or is already, an opening to the sacred. And this opening is distinctly visual: we have to learn to see the sacred in the everyday, and these comics arrive to inform that new vision. It is a kind of educational wisdom, a form of visual learning, in which the pedestrian and local can become windows to revelational encounter. The sacred does not arrive from elsewhere; it remains firmly implanted in the streets we walk and in the homes we build. Graphic narratives both reveal and enable this kind of visual remapping of the everyday sacred.

Chapter Twelve

URBAN REVELATION IN PAUL MADONNA'S POSTSECULAR COMICS

OFRA AMIHAY

SINCE 2004 SAN FRANCISCO-BASED ARTIST PAUL MADONNA HAS BEEN publishing his comic strip *All over Coffee* in the *San Francisco Chronicle*. His work has been collected in two volumes, *All over Coffee* (Madonna 2007) and *Everything Is Its Own Reward* (Madonna 2010). Madonna's comic strips are characterized by sepia drawings of urban landscapes, mostly of San Francisco, and by scenes that are predominantly void of human presence. The visual style is contrasted by a narrative which often describes a poignant human interaction, or an existential meditation, presented in an understated manner, through some mundane activity.

The question of what is seen and not seen, so quintessential to the comics form, is brought in Madonna's work to its extreme, and the postmodern sensibility of disjunction between symbol and reference is given a hypervisual expression. Yet the visual absence of people and the lack of an exclusively observing narrator do not lead to a dearth of meaning. Rather, meaning and significance are constructed by Madonna's readers as equal members in a community of observers.

The diffusion of spectatorship authority points to another significant absence in Madonna's depicted reality, namely that of an observing entity, and hence of a higher power or meaning. I suggest reading this absence in relation to Madonna's visual focus on the tangible reality of the city—buildings, streets, roads, signs—and his textual focus on human interaction, or the lack thereof, and the mundane. Together, these notions suggest a dual philosophical tradition in the background of *All over Coffee*, one I dub as "Durkheimian existentialism."

On the one hand, the manifest absence of a higher meaning in the existence Madonna depicts, comprised only of the tangible and the mundane, links his imagetext work to the French tradition of existentialist writing. Similarly to the prominent texts of this tradition, including Jean-Paul Sartre's *No Exit*, Albert Camus's *The Stranger*, and Samuel Beckett's *Waiting for Godot*, Madonna's depiction suggests that only from within the everyday can meaning be derived. On the other hand, this notion of an internal meaning is often developed in Madonna's work into a strong meditative sense, albeit one which is detached of a higher power or entity. By combining such philosophical mediations with an emphasis on communal spaces, Madonna relates to an earlier French thinker, Émile Durkheim, who analyzed modern religion as a sociological phenomenon, underscoring collective ideals and practices over the belief in a higher entity.

In an afterword for the first collection, Madonna describes this project as an attempt to make comics differently, "to strip down the form to its two fundamental elements: image and text" (Madonna 2007, 165). By using the term "strip" to describe the project's rationale with a meaning that differs from its original usage in comics, Madonna simultaneously acknowledges the roots of his project in traditional comics and notes where he departs from this tradition. In his choice of the comics form stripped down to its fundamental elements, Madonna echoes Durkheim's methodology of identifying the basic principles shared by all religions, captured in the title of his 1912 book *The Elementary Forms of Religious Life*. At the same time Madonna synthesizes Durkheim's conclusions regarding religion's fragile yet foundational role in modernity with an existentialist perception of reality. As such, I argue that Madonna's comics are very much a product of our time, reflecting emerging views of postsecularism through an erudite amalgamation of images and texts.

While preserving the textual and visual hybridity at the heart of the form, Madonna does away with most comics staples, including speech balloons, multiple panels, sequence, progression, and textually and visually depicted actions. He describes his approach to the project as "backwards" from any previous perception he had of comics: "This would be a strip with no characters, highly rendered drawings instead of loose, gestural lines, random pieces of text where the associations had to be deciphered, and no real punch line" (Madonna 2007, 167). Following this, in my analysis of Madonna's work I will refer to it not only as comics but also as an imagetext work, using W. J. T. Mitchell's term intended to describe modes of creation that substitute dichotomist paradigms of word-image relations with a dialectical picture (Mitchell 9). *All over Coffee* is a project that not only strips down the comics form to its bare minimum but also turns this aesthetic choice into a poetic metaphor that becomes even more apparent in the collections. Though seemingly random and dispersed, when collected together Madonna's strips create an intricate comment on modern and postmodern existence, stripped down to its most fundamental elements, institutions, and tensions.

In that sense Madonna's definition of his work as "a strip with no characters" is not entirely accurate. Indeed, the main visual subject of the strip, as Madonna puts it, is "setting, not characters" (Madonna 2007, 166), but since the setting is always composed of different angles of San Francisco, the city becomes a major character. Furthermore, the emptiness of the streets in Madonna's drawings is juxtaposed with human interactions described in the text, with the images and words undermining or complementing each other interchangeably. At times, the visually depicted empty spaces emphasize the foundational loneliness of the individual in the city. This motif is often apparent in the text as well, but even when the text depicts a gathering of friends, the empty scenes highlight an existential loneliness that is not entirely abated by social events. An opaque dialogue between unnamed people adorns the landscape scene with the sense that people were "here," thought and spoke, but no visual trace is left of them, thus coupling the motif of loneliness with a notion of evanescence.

Conversely, by juxtaposing the visual lack of people with their voices constantly floating, Madonna often marks human activity as an omnipresence in the city and as the actual center of all urban commotion. This visual and poetic choice renders people as observing subjects, rather than as objects being observed by an external entity. Indeed, the theme of observing the behavior and lives of others is fundamental to Madonna's storytelling, most notably through the numerous strips portraying conversations between random people overheard by a narrator.[1] Yet, observing others in *All over Coffee* is not an activity unique to the narrator but one shared by all, whether indirectly in conversations about other people, or directly in descriptions of people looking into other people's houses or imagining other people's lives. Furthermore, since no person is represented visually in Madonna's comics, the narrating voice remains as internal and omnipresent not only as the other floating voices but as the reader's internal voice. The result is a narrator devoid of the exclusive status of an external spectator.

. . .

Unlike the many single-paneled strips to follow it, the opening strip of Paul Madonna's first collection, *All over Coffee*, is divided into three panels that show different images. Encased between two different drawings of residential urban rooftops is a drawing of a neighborhood church peering behind trees

Figure 12.1. The opening triptych panel, *All over Coffee*, page 11, by Paul Madonna. Copyright © 2007 Paul Madonna

and electric wires. In his choice of the triptych form for a strip that contains an explicit graphical mention of Christianity, Madonna creates a visual echo for one of its foundational ideas—the Holy Trinity—only to neutralize its holiness altogether. More generally, by equating the church with industrial buildings, this strip offers a visual representation of a central idea to Madonna's comics as a whole—namely, the undermining of classic distinctions between sacred and secular spaces.

This visual sense of a religious institution obscured by urban surrounding is textually matched in an argument between two men depicted in these panels. Though it takes place at a café and concerns San Francisco's weather, the argument nevertheless becomes heated (to the verge of blows, as the narrator notes) and includes religiously charged expressions. "I'm sick of you unobservant transients," exclaims the first interlocutor, Maurice (one of the few recurring named characters), "San Francisco does **too** have seasons!" (Madonna 2007, 11). On the one hand, the topic of the argument and the fact that it is settled over a slice of cake when both men agree that "Kundera can't end a novel" bring to mind the nonsensical conversations and arguments in Beckett's *Godot*. As in the famous absurd existentialist masterpiece, at the outset of his collection Madonna presents two men, arguing vehemently on a minute topic, only to settle it with an absurd conclusion and some food, albeit a cosmopolitan tiramisu substituting Didi and Gogo's raw carrots and turnips (Beckett 12).[2] Furthermore, the non sequitur literary agreement that settles the dispute refers to an author who echoes Beckett in more than one way. The composer of such existentialist books as *The Unbearable Lightness of Being*, Milan Kundera, similarly to Beckett, also identifies as a French author regardless of his origins (Czech in his case, Irish in Beckett's). Far from a coincidental biographic similarity, the latter fact attests to the inherent cosmopolitan potential of existential perception, allowing artists to culturally relocate, much like an Italian dessert casually consumed at a San Francisco café.

At the same time, Madonna charges this mundane scene with a ceremonial aura from the outset—indeed, lifting the scene upwards, as the Italian title of the dessert mentioned in it suggests (*tira mi sù* meaning "lift me up"). By describing the café as Maurice's "favorite," Madonna instantly transforms Maurice's actions—sipping mocha and arguing with someone—into social rituals. In choosing this as the opening strip, Madonna sets the tone for the significance of the café in *All over Coffee* as a central public space of ritual and gathering. Madonna marks the café as an urban alternative to the church, "the living rooms of a city," as he writes in his afterword (Madonna 2007, 167), echoing Durkheim's discussion of religion in modernity. While admitting to some difficulty in "imagining what the feasts and ceremonies of the future will be," Durkheim believes religion is destined "to outlive the succession of particular symbols" since the need for ritual and gathering is so great:

> There can be no society that does not experience the need at regular intervals to maintain and strengthen the collective feelings and ideas that provide its coherence and its distinct individuality. This moral remaking can be achieved only through meetings, assemblies, and congregations in which the individuals, pressing close to one another, reaffirm in common their common sentiments. (Durkheim 429)

An argument about the weather over a cup of mocha and a slice of cake might be an even greater leap than Durkheim envisioned, but Madonna's depiction offers them as relevant candidates for "the feasts and ceremonies of the future." Maurice and his interlocutor debate and reaffirm common sentiments—regarding the weather, regarding literature—through ritual and gathering. Furthermore, the dessert they share speaks not only to Durkheim's discussion of the believer who communes with his god being momentarily "*lifted above* the human miseries" (Durkheim 419, my emphasis), but also to the cosmopolitanism Durkheim identified in modern religions. "The more we advance in history," Durkheim contests, "the larger and the more important these international groupings become" (428).

In this way, Madonna's texts can be associated with what John McClure defines as "postsecular fiction" (ix). In his literary analysis McClure adopts the term coined by Jürgen Habermas to describe the postmodern call for "an interpretation of the relation between faith and knowledge that enables them to live together in a self-reflective manner" (Habermas). In the context of my analysis of the "Durkheimian existentialism" at the heart of Madonna's work, it is not surprising that postsecularism is often associated with Durkheim's theory, what Massimo Rosati calls "the Durkheimian imprint" marking the study of postsecularism (Rosati 6). In his own study Rosati refers to a center-periphery social model which he defines as "strongly resonant of Durkheimian insights" and includes "society's genetic code or deep grammar" while making room not only for solidarity but also for conflict and contestation (6). McClure's literary analysis refers to a similar contestation of spirituality at the heart of postsecularism and his description of novelists Don DeLillo and Toni Morrison accurately describes the salient sentiments in Madonna's work: "These novelists . . . tell stories about new forms of religiously inflected seeing and being. And in each case, the forms of faith they invent, study, and affirm are dramatically partial and open-ended. They do not provide, or even aspire to provide, any full 'mapping' of the reenchanted cosmos. They do not promise anything like full redemption" (ix).

McClure's emphasis on "seeing and being" suggests that Madonna's "backwards comics" is an especially apt medium in which to "invent, study, and affirm" such open-ended forms of faith. Moreover, by creating a textual and visual hybrid that fluctuates between harmony and conflict, Madonna further captures the coexistence of competing perceptions, a notion so central to the idea of postsecularism. In his foreword to *All over Coffee*, Andrew Sean Greer discusses the relation of images and texts in Madonna's work by comparing it to the work of novelist W. G. Sebald: "As in the work of . . . Sebald, neither do the words narrate a picture, nor does the image illustrate the words. Instead, they are each meant to turn the other sideways, pointing not to any specific event or storyline, but to a moment in which the two might coexist" (Madonna 2007, 5). In fact, by using the comics form while challenging its most traditional elements, Madonna connects directly to the postsecular ideas embedded in his work. This is most evident in a strip with a rare direct reference to comics. Relating to a classic comics protagonist, the superhero, this strip quotes an anonymous female speaker saying: "I don't get superheroes . . . if you could see through everything you'd see nothing at all" (19). The two panels accompanying this text juxtapose an indoor scene with an outdoor one, pointing to the limitations of human eyesight while celebrating the unique outlook on reality they afford. Here the playful textual contemplation of the non-realistic aspects of superhero plotlines becomes a comment both on Madonna's divergence from the genre's traditional elements, and on the human condition in a reality diverting from traditional perceptions of God. By implication, the strip challenges the notion of an omnivoyant God, as well as the relevance of such a God in modern and postmodern circumstances, thereby opening the field to alternatives.

The image of the neighborhood church in the opening strip is one of ten other such images included in *All over Coffee*. Similarly, they are often coupled with texts that challenge fixed religious notions or reflect the substitution of such notions with alternative nonreligious discernments. In one case a character named Liz wonders if her parents, when hearing about "the collective unconscious," feel the same as she does when hearing "the president talk about God" (Madonna 2007, 64). This sense of intergenerational competing perceptions is reversibly reflected in the image, which shows an old residential house across a modern style church, with both buildings pulled in opposite directions, as if viewed through a distorting lens. The cross-like television antenna on top of the residential house, which stands in the same line as the cross on top of the church, enhances the sense of cultural competition. Yet while representing a uniting social instrument that competes with the church, an antenna on a residential house also represents the shift from communal to individual and even isolated existence, of which the television is often mentioned as an emblem. An earlier strip in the collection relates precisely to this sense of isolation brought about by the television set, by describing an unnamed woman who watches her neighbors' television through her window (47). The text represents not only an individual's attempt to break this isolation and resist it, but also the physical proximity of urban habitats that should render such an attempt successful. But the image of an almost empty window which accompanies it suggests the futility of such an attempt which only creates an illusion of togetherness, perhaps much like the television, generating a sense of shared content consumed in isolation.

. . .

Alongside the representation of human interactions in urban public spaces that substitute religious spaces of assembly, *All over Coffee* equally concerns the solitude inherent in modern and postmodern urban existence. As in the strip about a woman watching her neighbors' television, Madonna often depicts this solitude through strips that deal with attempts to access the lives of others through spectatorship; attempts that often end in disappointment for both sides.

In his explorations of the spectator's experience, Madonna focuses on the inevitable disenchantment and failure to develop the one-sided spectatorship into a dialogue or a source of comfort. In a strip describing a girl named Sarah browsing windows with the hope "to see something seedy" (Madonna 2007, 73), she ends up ducking and holding her breath only to watch a man across the street pacing with a baby on his shoulder. Similarly, another strip in this volume depicts a couple whose bed's location and heating situation, which requires one of them to stand on the bed and swing a garment for heat circulation, allows them to see into their neighbors' windows. "But," the narrator concludes lamentably, "they never do anything interesting" (115). On the one hand, both strips deliver a sense of irony, with the disappointed onlookers doing what could appear seedy (ducking by a window in the dark) and interesting (standing on a bed and swinging a garment overhead). In other words, Madonna's voyeurs fail to realize the interesting aspects in their own lives, since they are convinced that the source of interest is necessarily in the other. For instance, rather than searching for excitement in windows of others, the man standing on the bed could share with his partner the comic element in his usual position.

At the same time, the trivial reality behind the spectator's behavior in both cases—a false concern of being spotted or an odd heating situation—relocates them in the mundane. It marks "interesting" as a relative notion that is often in the eye of the beholder, placing the lives of the spectators on the same plane as their neighbors': mundane yet potentially interesting. Hence, from a portal to the lives of others, the window in Madonna's work can instantly turn into a mirror of the spectator's own life—as is often the case with windows. This reflective power of the other suggests the source of disappointment to be the inability to accept the everyday for what it is: a collection of casual moments from which pleasure and comfort could potentially be extracted, pending on attention and attitude. Without the expectation to see "something seedy" and without the ducking, the scene Sarah witnesses could be a heartwarming moment. Furthermore, it could be a moment that two neighbors share and through which they connect—rather than ducking, Sarah could make eye contact with the tired dad across the street and smile empathetically at him. In fact, the counterpart panel to Sarah's search for something seedy in *All over Coffee* describes a private affecting experience turned collective through a quiet act of sharing—precisely the kind of leap that Sarah fails to perform: "Inside the bookstore, moved by a song on the radio, a woman sits in a chair provided for reading. For those who have never heard the song before, there is no emotional recall. But the next time they hear it, they'll sit, moved by the memory of her" (Madonna 2007, 72). By juxtaposing these two strips, Madonna creates a spread that contains the tensions at the very heart of the reality depicted in *All over Coffee*: those between the individual and the community, and between solitude and uplifting interactions. As long as the access to the other remains indirect in Madonna's depiction, it does not lead to communication or sharing even when it is mutual. In a strip about Rachel, who knows her neighbors hear her screening calls but "also knows they each have guests when the other isn't around" (123), rather than a source of comfort this mutual access becomes a balance of terror.

While touching on a strong sense of urban alienation, the attempts in Madonna's comics to access the lives of others without engaging with them are also burdened with a personal dissatisfaction with the everyday, making it hard for spectators to part with the notion that "interesting is elsewhere." Such is the strip about a woman who suspects the existence of "secret maps of the city" that chart "seemingly normal sites behind whose doors lives more exciting than hers are led" (Madonna 2007, 149). Put differently, Madonna's spectators fail twice: they fail to acknowledge their need for communication and to act upon it by reaching out to others properly, and they also fail to realize the potential for beauty and interest in their own everyday lives.

Similarly, Madonna's exploration of the person on the other side of the window addresses not just the sense of intrusion but also the need for solitude and the complex balance between public and private. "I thought the best way to keep people out of my business was to stay out of theirs," one of Madonna's first-person narrators exclaims, "but they broke all my windows just to have a look." In an almost direct reference to the many spectators populating Madonna's comics, the narrator concludes: "now I'm open for all the world to see and they avoid me like debt" (Madonna 2007, 55). This strip can be read on three levels. In its exploration of the need for solitude, it joins several other panels in *All over Coffee* that touch on the other side of interaction as reliever of loneliness and the burdens of communication: the woman wishing for dialogue but regretting it when approached by someone (67), the character tired of listening to others and contemplates staying home (70), or the one noting "it's good to leave the flat . . . to remember why I don't like to leave [it]" (110). On another level, the existential hardship in being watched by others and becoming an object connects to Sartre's famous line in *No Exit*, "Hell is—other people!" (Sartre 45). As with Sartre's Garcin, the hellish experience of Madonna's narrator originates in "all those eyes intent on me. Devouring me" (Sartre 45). Finally, Madonna specifically problematizes in this strip the circuitousness so inherent in attempts to access the other

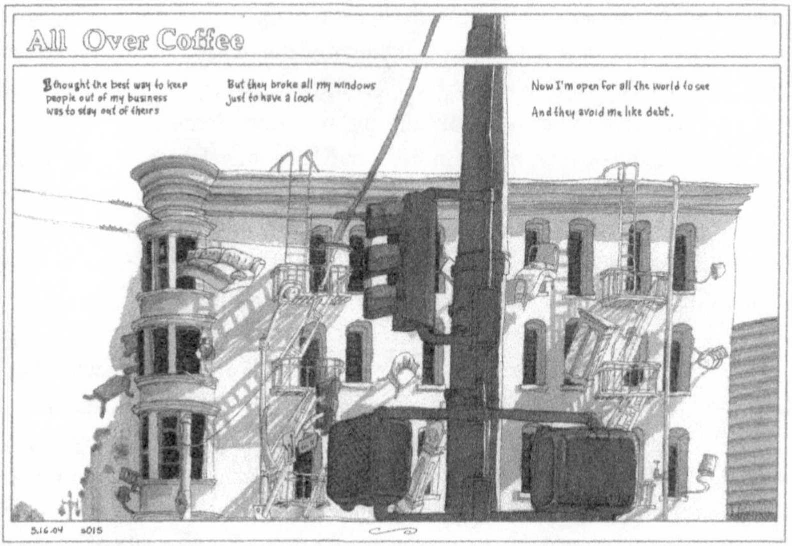

Figure 12.2. A single panel, *All over Coffee*, page 55, by Paul Madonna. Copyright © 2007 Paul Madonna

indirectly, but when made directly it loses its appeal. Unwilling to commit to the debt involved in mutuality, the spectators leave the person on the other side both exposed and abandoned.

The image accompanying this text is outstanding in the context of Madonna's comics, in that it is one of the only images to portray movement, and of a very unusual kind. The single panel shows a corner building and from each of its windows a piece of furniture flies out, arrested in midair. Resting alarmingly between the private sphere of the home and the public domain of the street, the chairs, closets, sofas, and lamps offer a poignant visual representation of the same sense of tautness that the text evokes, which lies between these realms. Madonna locates his imagetext in the space that stretches between the privacy of one's window and the public domains of the café.

The many windows depicted in the "spectator strips" show no such outstanding action as the "flying furniture." Nevertheless, in their very appearance alongside these texts they challenge the textually represented isolation by highlighting not only the plurality of windows in city streets but also their proximity. In one of his café strips, Madonna has an anonymous speaker relate to this urban oddity by failing to make conversation with two reluctant couch fellows. "It's funny," he tells them, "that in the country you can be miles away from your neighbor but still know them intimately, whereas in cities you can go years without even talking to the person right next door to you" (Madonna 2007, 74). It only follows that this strip too, though not dealing with spectatorship, is accompanied by an image of a row of windows. Indeed, windows are present in many of Madonna's images, perhaps even in most of them, but in the aforementioned strips they become the focal point, even lending the single panels—also, far from unique in Madonna's oeuvre—a window-like feel. As Greg Smith contends, the concept of windows in comics, much like frames and panels, is "a usefully orienting inheritance from older media." As in these older forms, it can function both on a symbolic level and on a literal level. As Smith suggests, "at times they float with the abstraction of metaphor, while at other times they act like grounded physical properties of a medium" (221). In *All over Coffee* Madonna employs both levels by joining his narrator, characters, and readers into a community of spectators, looking through windows in search for something interesting, but left with the poetic challenge of finding it in themselves, in the window-mirror duality.

Alongside the window there is yet another square object of vision that seems to equally inspire Madonna's work, namely the photograph. At its very base, *All over Coffee* combines images of a physical setting—the foundation of somatic existence—with words—the building blocks of human communication. The presentation of this fusion in panels with handwritten text unquestionably locates Madonna's work in the realm of comics. Even in turning to photography as inspiration Madonna connects to the growing tendency of comics artists towards photography (see Amihay; Cook; Pedri). Yet in the same way that his work transcends the boundaries of conventional comics, Madonna's visual design is inspired by photography in ways that exceed the influence of photography on comics thus far. Madonna further develops the spreading custom of embedding real or drawn photographs in comics panels by rendering all his panels with a photographic aura; more than comics panels, Madonna's square drawings often look like drawn snapshots of city scenery seen through a window. In creating comics renderings of this common photographic practice, that in itself suggests the window/photograph connection,[3] Madonna adds the comics-panel as yet a third element in this metaphoric field of square objects that can offer a vision of the world.

In constructing this "snapshot comics" with mostly sepia square images of empty urban streets, Madonna visually refers to the very genesis of photography, when lengthy exposure time did not allow one to capture human and mechanic movement in photographs. More specifically, many of Madonna's panels echo a particular photograph of urban scenery taken from a window in 1838 by Louis Jacques Mandé Daguerre, considered the definitive example for this chapter in the history of photography. Although the lighting suggests that this daguerreotype, now known as *Boulevard du Temple*, was taken in midday, of all the commotion that crowded the Parisian street at such an hour—people, carriages, horses—the only visible element is a man having his shoes shined. Unlike the carriages and pedestrians that undoubtedly surrounded him, the anonymous shoe-shining man stood still long enough for Daguerre's camera to capture him, becoming the first photographically documented person. These powerful absences and surprising human presences solicited many interpretations of Daguerre's image, either about the sense of revelation it conveys or the connection it established between photography and deathly absence (Brunet 18–19). In his essay "Judgment Day," Giorgio Agamben develops these early interpretations in presenting this photograph as the ultimate demonstration of photography's ability to capture the last judgment:

> I could never have invented a more adequate image of the last judgment. The crowd of humans—indeed, all of humanity—is present, but it cannot be seen, because the judgment concerns a single person, a single life. . . . And when has that life, that person, been picked out, captured, and immortalized . . . ? While making the most banal and ordinary gesture. . . . And yet, thanks to the photographic lens, that gesture is now charged with the weight of an entire life. (24)

The resonance of Daguerre's image in Madonna's visual grammar charges his work with a similar sentiment. Indeed, Madonna's metaphorical lens allows for no character to be visually captured. In fact, the only visual representation of people in *All over Coffee* is in rare appearances of depicted photographs—for example, a picture of a hugging couple on a living-room wall (Madonna 2007, 21, 106) or a photograph of a feminine face on a refrigerator (125). However, as in Daguerre's image, it is the complete visual absence of people that allows Madonna to truly isolate "the most banal and ordinary moments" in individual lives and through the mere focus on them to expose gestures "charged with the weight of an entire life." Thus, the everyday becomes in Madonna's work the last judgment—the moment when human existence can really be assessed and appreciated. This further explains why photography, with its association to stillness and arrested time, is such a major source of visual inspiration for Madonna.[4] Contrarily to the probable connotation of the visual image of emptied streets, Madonna's comics are not concerned with a world post-judgment, devoid of all people, but with the power and meaning embedded in each and every moment, isolated and examined as closely as possible. To paraphrase Agamben's analysis, in *All over Coffee* the crowd of humans—indeed, all of humanity—is present, but it cannot be seen, because the judgment is concerned with the moment itself, with the philosophical potential of the everyday sacred.

As a form of visual reminder of that potential, Madonna uses sudden appearances of color. "Color is a crucial part of [this work's] beauty," posits Greer in his foreword, making its "secret cameos throughout the work" (Madonna 2007, 5). Whether in the form of cherry blossoms in front of a building (33), colorful clothes on a rooftop laundry line (76), or stained-glass windows at a café (98), the permeation of pigments in *All over Coffee* are more than visual treats. In a surrounding where "there are no people present, no wind, no motors to move them" as Greer writes, color embodies the potential for meaning in the everyday while charging it with the notion of revelation. It is the sense of stillness and arrested time—the signifiers of revelation in religious sources[6]—that make these "color cameos" in *All over Coffee* so powerful. Yet unlike these sources, it is not an external truth or entity that Madonna reveals in his imagetext, but rather an internal truth and beauty revealed equally in flowers, laundry, or windows.

. . .

In an early strip in *All over Coffee*, alongside the image of a Middle Eastern–style complex, there appears a statement in quotation marks: "The world is going the way of satellite-tracking and robot armies, and I'm trying to make something beautiful" (Madonna 2007, 40). Though presented as a quote, this proclamation could well capture Madonna's own stance throughout *All over Coffee*: that of a postmodern urban prophet, warning of modernity's pitfalls while identifying and creating beauty. Tellingly, in addition to the beautiful building, Madonna depicts two small birds flying above it, capturing not only obvious forms of beauty but also the minute and fleeting ones. Like the character who responds to a friend's concern about wasting her hopes on ridiculous things by saying, "sounds like the good life to me" (69), Madonna insists on celebrating the everyday, with all its complexities.

This stance becomes even clearer in the second collection, beginning with Madonna's choice of the title, *Everything Is Its Own Reward*. The Zen style that characterizes several strips in the first volume (but also parodied in one strip[5]) becomes a major writing mode in the second volume. As Madonna attests in his afterword to the second volume, whereas in the first volume he was concerned with "bringing in viewers through one door and leading them out another," in the second volume he "began to define these doors"

Figure 12.3. A double spread, *Everything Is Its Own Reward*, pages 18–19, by Paul Madonna. Copyright © 2011 Paul Madonna

(Madonna 2010, 228–29). In the second volume Madonna also expands the references to the title of his comics which appear in the first volume only sporadically, half hidden on newsstands and within street signs (143, 144, 151). Thus, in a Cervantesian manner of self-reference, the "everything" in the second volume often includes Madonna's comics. To the details composing the strips in both volumes—conversations, telephone wires, buildings, curbs, or, as Greer puts it, all the details edited out from the "carefully revised version" of life (Madonna, 2007, 5)—Madonna adds the title of his comics. Like color, the initials "AOC" (All over Coffee) and sometimes the full title often appear within panels throughout the second volume (including the images chosen for its front and back cover), marking the comic strip as yet another element that offers its own reward. Madonna declares this almost directly by placing the first strip in the volume to display such a reference right after a strip that reads, underneath an image of the de Young museum in San Francisco, "everything is its own reward" (Madonna 2010, 17). As Madonna describes in the afterword, the making of the de Young image was a pivotal moment in continuing *All over Coffee* and creating the second volume, with the line "everything is its own reward" becoming his "call of duty" (225).

The flow from this image and line to a full spread that celebrates the comics itself, with the title appearing alongside Madonna's full name as the only text in the image, captures this process precisely. Indeed, Madonna more fully adopts the stance of the postsecular prophet in the second volume. Printed on a street sign and hovering above a wall of tiles in different colors—the ultimate representation of revelation in the first volume—the title and name join the many messages that appear in the second volume on signs and walls. While these texts could be interpreted as documented graffiti, their design and content of existential wisdom and advice defy this interpretation, rendering them instead as textual epiphanies, revealed like color in the city.

Considering Madonna's own moment of revelation at the de Young museum, it is not surprising that the final appearance of such a message resides on a museum billboard, in the penultimate spread of *Everything Is Its Own Reward*. In this spread Madonna actually depicts a pensive woman, with her face hidden behind her hair, leaning on the railings of a balcony situated in the heart of a rotunda. The bottom image reveals it to be the San Francisco Museum of Modern Art (as the Calder mobile in its right corner suggests), and the billboard message highlights the surprising appearance of a person with a metaphorical meaning. Unlike the declarative style of Madonna's other texts, the billboard reads like an outline for a text, but as such it captures an essence pertaining to all of Madonna's work. In its search for "something about how there is no everywhere" and its conclusion that "in the end, a room will always be a group of people" (Madonna 2010, 219), it reveals the true meaning behind the visual absence of people in Madonna's comics: a celebration of people's centrality and importance in a reality with no external meaning, to the extent that they themselves can become a revelation. Madonna addresses these people in the ultimate strip of his second volume, in a text floating freely in the city skies like a personal note from reality:

> Keep going. There is no destination. If the day of your death is unknown, then do everything for the sake of doing. . . . It will all be forgotten or reinterpreted anyway. So be happy. . . . Nothing has an inherent or permanent value. Every day, every life, every action, every thing is its own reward. (220)

The focus on mundane events of life and fleeting conversations marks *All over Coffee* as a secular work, with very few mentions of religion, God, or the supernatural. Yet its concerns for the human soul and its engagement with questions of existence, particularly in the comics genre, render it an exceptionally musing work in the realm of popular culture and the everyday sacred. Through text and image Madonna's drawn snapshots offer a meditation on urban experience in the twenty-first century, a century already marked by an unmistakable textual-visual hybridity, on the one hand, and postsecularism on the other.

NOTES

1. In his afterword to *All over Coffee*, Madonna emphasizes that contrary to the common assumption, the writing is fictional and not actually overheard conversations. Yet this misconception is partly due to his choice to present many strips as conversations overheard by a narrator. In one strip Madonna even has a first-person narrator compare the voice of a woman behind him to that of Cindy Williams in *The Conversation* (Madonna, *All over Coffee* 34), a film about a surveillance team in San Francisco.

2. The implicit transition between Beckett's text and Madonna's, from raw vegetables to a refined dessert, also calls to mind Claude Lévi-Strauss's theory in *The Raw and the Cooked* of the binary notions behind sociocultural formations.

3. As photographer Stephen Shore writes in his book *The Nature of Photographs*, "a photograph can be viewed on several levels. To begin with, it is a physical object, a print. On this print is an image, an illusion of a window on to the world" (10).

4. In his afterword to *All over Coffee*, Madonna mentions using "reference photos" for completing his drawings (163) and uses the metaphor of photography to refer to the feeling of time standing still. In describing the moment when his *All over Coffee* was accepted for publication by the *San Francisco Chronicle*, he writes, "It's like time itself stopped and said, 'Here, let me take a snapshot for you'" (168).

5. For the relationship of theophany and stillness/silence in religious texts, see for example 1 Kings 19:12 or Revelation 8:1.

6. For example, the text at the bottom of an image of an urban intersection in *All over Coffee* reads, "Though our roads lead to the same place, our stories will be different when we get there" (140). Together they constitute a Zen-like existential observation, typical of several other strips in the first volume. At the same time, in the text accompanying the image of a half-black/half-white cookie bitten on opposite ends in the same volume, a

waitress responds to a customer's complaint with a sardonic reference to Zen philosophy. Examining the black and white dots in his coffee, she remarks: "Cool, it's like yin and yang. Have a Zen day!" (117).

BIBLIOGRAPHY

Agamben, Giorgio. *Profanations*. Translated by Jeff Fort. New York: Zone, 2007.

Amihay, Ofra. "Red Diapers, Pink Stories: Color Photography and Self-Outing in Jewish Women's Comics." *Image & Narrative* 16, no. 2 (2015): 42–64.

Beckett, Samuel. *Waiting for Godot: A Tragicomedy in Two Acts*. New York: Grove, 2006.

Brunet, François. *Photography and Literature* (Exposures). London: Reaktion, 2009.

Camus, Albert. *The Stranger*. Translated by Matthew Ward. New York: Vintage, 1989.

Cook, Roy T. "Drawings of Photographs in Comics." *Journal of Aesthetics and Art Criticism* 70, no. 1 (2012): 129–38.

Durkheim, Émile. *The Elementary Forms of Religious Life*. Translated by Karen E. Fields. New York: Free Press, 1995.

Habermas, Jürgen. "A 'Post-secular' Society—What Does That Mean?" Paper presented at the Istanbul Seminars, June 2008; see resetdoc.org/story/00000000926. Accessed January 27, 2016.

Kundera, Milan. *The Unbearable Lightness of Being*. Translated by Michael Henry Heim. New York: Harper Collins, 2004.

Lévi-Strauss, Claude. *The Raw and the Cooked: Introduction to a Science of Mythology: I*. Translated by John and Doreen Weightman. New York: Harper & Row, 1969.

Madonna, Paul. *All over Coffee*. San Francisco: City Lights, 2007.

Madonna, Paul. *Everything Is Its Own Reward*. San Francisco: City Lights, 2010.

McClure, John A. *Partial Faiths: Postsecular Fiction in the Age of Pynchon and Morrison*. Athens: University of Georgia Press, 2007.

Mitchell, W. J. T. *Picture Theory: Essays on Verbal and Visual Representation*. Chicago: University of Chicago Press, 1994.

Pedri, Nancy. "Thinking about Photography in Comics." *Image & Narrative* 16, no. 2 (2015): 1–13.

Rosati, Massimo. *The Making of a Postsecular Society: A Durkheimian Approach to Memory, Pluralism and Religion in Turkey*. Farnham, UK: Ashgate, 2015.

Sartre, Jean-Paul. *No Exit and Three Other Plays*. Translated by Stuart Gilbert and Lionel Abel. New York: Vintage International, 1989.

Shore, Stephen. *The Nature of Photographs*. New York: Phaidon, 2007.

Smith, Greg M. "Comics in the Intersecting Histories of the Window, the Frame, and the Panel." In *From Comic Strips to Graphic Novels: Contributions to the Theory and History of Graphic Narrative*, edited by Daniel Stein and Jan-Noël Thon, 219–38. Berlin: de Gruyter, 2013.

Chapter Thirteen

THE COMMON PLACE

The Poetics of the Pedestrian in Kevin Huizenga's *Walkin'*

SHIAMIN KWA

THE FIRST PAGE OF KEVIN HUIZENGA'S 1998 COMIC *WALKIN'* PRESENTS THE simple rituals accompanying the narrator's walk in a new neighborhood, on a late summer Sunday morning. Its first panel introduces this information in a text box, showing the lower half of the narrator's body, crouched with left knee bent forward as he ties his laces. The second panel presents the quiet beginnings of departure as he shuts the door, revealing his top half: his back, the back of his head. The final panel on the first page presents the narrator in full from behind, in an aerial view that shows a series of pavement squares diminishing in size as they slide from trapezoid to triangle as they stretch farther away from the viewer. He is walking in a suburban landscape, away from us and toward the perpendicular crossings of tree branches and telephone wires that frame the top of the panel. The second page continues this shifting perspective between above and below; the limitations of the walker to gravity are attenuated by the weightlessness of his line of vision. The reader is sent, on the second page, to look up, and then down. The wires that hang above him transmit the knowledge of unseen actions and movements, electrons coursing back and forth through the wires strung above our walker; he hears only the sounds that surround those wires, from places equally outside the grasp of his vision: "I could hear people's voices comin through a screen door. Birds chirping call and response." The eye is shifted downward, to shadows on the ground: "The sun's low, long shadows and sparkling diamonds in the trees." The comic deploys fragmented language, down to the words themselves ("walkin," "comin"), harmonizing

Figure 13.1. Beautiful big old trees, *Walkin'*, page 2, by Kevin Huizenga. Copyright © 1998 Kevin Huizenga. Image courtesy of Kevin Huizenga

with fragmented images (parts of bodies, parts of moments in time). The crossings in the images, and the crossings of thought and perceived sounds intimate other intersections: between earthbound and avian, between the mundane and the numinous. Most importantly, the crossings intimate them as multiply crossed intersections: a weave that cannot be unraveled. We are looking not at layers, but at tightly bound imbrication; the hatch is created by the two-dimensional flatness of the comics page, which forces the lines to cross each other without the relief that would be accommodated by depth. Drawings on the comics page preclude the possibility of separation, which can occur only by a reader's conscious act: "Those things are not entangled, because I know they are not supposed to be," he thinks.

This chapter shows how Huizenga's comics signal our awareness to that conscious act of supposing. Purposely withholding explanation, and making the reader do the work of parsing the visual assumptions of the surface to understand the basic action depicted in the frame, *Walkin'* models the processes we use when we try to make sense of what we see. We make dozens of these assessments, adjustments, and revisions whenever we look at something. Those processes are each small narratives of meaning, but they are occurring so quickly in our minds that their strangeness is hardly ever noticed. This comic continuously reminds readers of the strangeness of the common, a strangeness that should give them pause. By making readers attend to the intersections of lines on the surface of the page, Huizenga's comics suggest the possibilities of more metaphysical intersections. The careful attention to pacing, and the deliberate parallels between the pace of the walk and the structure of the comic, highlight the requirements of marked space and time in the construction of meaning.

Huizenga's works frequently insinuate the profound relationship between efforts of the bodily and mundane with those of the sublime, and work toward developing an accord between profane and sacred time that conceptualizes a relationship famously defined by Mircea Eliade:

> Religious man lives in two kinds of time, of which the more important, sacred time, appears under the paradoxical aspect of a circular time, reversible and recoverable, a sort of eternal mythical present that is periodically reintegrated by means of rites. This attitude in regard to time suffices to distinguish religious from nonreligious man; the former refuses to live solely in what, in modern terms, is called the historical present; he attempts to regain a sacred time that, from one point of view, can be homologized to eternity. (70)

Huizenga's stories question these distinctions, first by suggesting that nonreligious man, too, occupies both kinds of time, and second by showing how those two kinds of time are mutually generative rather than independent entities. The two kinds of time do not exist separately, these works suggest, but rather exist only because each cannot exist without the other. In Huizenga's work, time outside of time is the direct result of the consistent pacing and deliberate rhythm established by the comics. This is accomplished by the structure of the comics themselves: a successive pattern of squares on the page that draw the eye along the path they create. The steady movement of the eye and the hand as the reader encounters these patterns finds its counterpart within those pages, in the figure of the walker.

. . .

Born in 1977, Kevin Huizenga has been producing some of the most critically acclaimed small-press comics since the 1990s. They have been anthologized in the *Best American Comics* collections and have been awarded five Ignatz awards by the Small Press Expo, which supports comics and cartooning works by small-press or creator-owned projects. Part of a generation of artists creating what can broadly be defined as "art" or "literary" comics, Huizenga creates work that is distinguished by a keen interest in negotiating the gentle balance between sharply astute observation and abstracted and generalized delivery. The frequent protagonist of his works, Glenn Ganges, resembles archetypes of the Sunday funnies, recalling characters in the comics of Charles Schulz (*Peanuts*) and Chic Young (*Blondie*), with their sparely defined hairlines and profiles, their suburban landscapes, and the activities that occupy their quotidian rhythms. They wash dishes, check their mail, read the newspaper, and stroll on their sidewalks. These steady rhythms are precisely what create the impact of their concluding punchlines, which unfold with a combination of inevitability and surprise that lingers in the mind in a time that is equally "reversible and recoverable" only through the careful ritual of the everyday. Our encounters with Ganges involve walks from the mailbox back into the home; walks through suburban neighborhood streets; and walks through the aisles of a suburban megastore. The stories that he has produced over the last two decades vary in subject and storyline; yet they share an aesthetic that relies on the steady and slow. This aesthetic extends from the very lines of the drawing to the lines of the narrative and builds conclusions that reach outside of the mundane and into the metaphysical.

Huizenga's comics build a sympathetic framework that bridges the mundane and the numinous, so that the form itself is the source of the comic's meaning. Stories frequently involve a journey that culminates in revelation.

They all also involve walking. The walk, with its repetitive patterns, its steady and even pace, its unremarkability, is the reason that, when used as an adjective, "pedestrian" signals dullness, monotony, and the absence of interest. The walker, the pedestrian, is common, but in Huizenga's comics, that commonness is the means toward unraveling life's mysteries. The mysteries of reading find their analogue in the mystery of the walker's encounters with the mundane, mystery that he feels as "not merely something to be wondered at but something that entrances him; and beside that in it which bewilders and confounds, he feels a something that captivates and transports him with a strange ravishment, rising often enough to the pitch of dizzy intoxication" (Otto 85). The characters in Huizenga's comics do a great deal of walking, and even spirit quests to search for feathered ogres involve walking through the equally repetitive strip malls that limn the Midwest's exurban sprawl (Huizenga 2006). This chapter examines how Huizenga's comic demonstrates walking as a subject. Walking mimics the structural pacing of the comic, as panels steadily unfold in space in the same way that footsteps proceed in time. The relationship between walking and its desired destination represents a commitment to the physical labor that makes it distinct from waiting; the transition between the sacred and the profane implies a ritual act in between the two that makes access to the sacred possible, but the walker's position suggests that everyday action is the ritual that allows for the access.

The walker does not wait; rather, the walker abides, taking part in a continuous action, a holding pattern that has its own meaning. The pace of walking is also a system of measuring; an extension of the body into space, it measures out time with each movement. Each step is a punctuation point that marks the beginning and endpoint of the measurement, and this essay is not only about those points, but about the movements in between them. In his uses of the panels native to the comics form to direct the reader's movement and pace, Huizenga figures reading as a kind of walking. He exposes the crucial role that this rhythm plays in establishing an achievable suspension of time, the suspension of time articulated as sacred time by Eliade. In Huizenga's formulation, suspended time is instead firmly tied to the profane. A journey is made by the accrual of units that each, individually, is close to senselessness, but that cohere into meaning at the end. There is a human drive, Frank Kermode argues, to make narrative meaning of what comes between beginning and end: "The clock's 'tick-tock' I take to be a model of what we call a plot, an organization which humanizes time by giving it a form; and the interval between 'tock' and 'tick' represents purely successive, disorganized time of the sort we need to humanize" (Kermode 45). Huizenga's comics show how the disorganized time between the tocks and the ticks is precisely meaningful because its disorganization gives definition to the end product. They suggest the productive possibilities of resisting the organizing impulse that Kermode notes, understanding that moments of clarity must emerge from incoherent forms. In these journey stories, Huizenga reframes the distinctions of sacred and profane, placing himself in the tradition of a rich community of walker-philosophers. His comics suggest that it is precisely the rhythms of pacing, and the abiding that it creates, that define how revelation is reached. Revelation, in this model, is not the point of entry but in fact the entire progression, a progression that is defined by the assumption of continuity between fragments: step by step, frame to frame. By connecting the deliberate pacing established between word and image on the comics page with the physical labor of walking, Huizenga redirects readers to a celebration of the processes of typically ignored continuity that connect the inevitable "points of interest" that vie for our attention.

. . .

Comics provide a model for reading practices based on continuity, a continuity that is native to the aura of comics itself. Jared Gardner notes a shared "archival drive" that indexes a "compulsive need to fill in the gaps, to make connections between issues (the serial gap inherent to comic production, mirroring and complicating the gaps between the frames themselves) that drives the collector in search of missing issues," which elides the collecting practice of the comics reader with the reading practice of finding closure between them (Gardner 173). The formal qualities of comics, he argues, are what make them so resistant to easy binary formulations and these qualities are, he argues, better defined as "a bifocal form":

> Like the archive, the comics form retains that which cannot be reconciled to linear narrative—the excess that refuses cause-and-effect argument, the trace which threatens to unsettle the present's narrative of its own past (and thereby of itself). The comics form is forever troubled by that which cannot be reconciled, synthesized, unified, contained within the frame; but it is in being so troubled that the form defines itself. The excess data—the remains of the everyday—is always left behind (even as the narrative progresses forward in time), a visual archive for the reader's necessary work of rereading, resorting, and reframing. . . . It is precisely the inability or refusal to choose

> (between text and image, past and present, graphic and novel, popular culture and art/literature, etc.) that draws creators to this form in the first place. (177)

Gardner astutely categorizes the way that the comic's form is a model for the reading practices of the comics reader and collector himself. The constant balance between the acceptance of the surplus of information in the face of comics' archival quality, and the desire to complete the meaning between sequences, is characteristic of the comics reading process.

Closure has been most famously defined by Scott McCloud in *Understanding Comics*, as the "phenomenon of observing the parts but perceiving the whole" (63). He singles out the gutter, or the space between the panels, as the central defining characteristic of comics. The panel-and-gutter relationship works to "fracture both time and space, offering a jagged, staccato rhythm of unconnected moments. But closure allows us to connect these moments and mentally construct a continuous, unified reality (67). This distinction is pursued by Barbara Postema in her study of not just gutters but other kinds of absences and voids in the comic: making meaning from what is missing. Taking her cues from the semiotically inflected work of Thierry Groensteen (2009, 2013), she offers readings of how comics both create gaps—structural, sequential, narratological—and close them. As she explains, "the same principles are applied for looking at the semiotics of the image, the semiotics of the page and of the narrative, because the same processes are involved in creating narration out of a panel, a sequence, a narrative, revolving around asserting the gaps that are present and then offering ways to erase the gaps (Postema xx). These critics all emphasize the reader's participation in bringing closure to the gaps of meaning in the comics text.

This is not a concept exclusive to comics. Reader-response critics have long argued for the crucial role that the implied reader plays in the construction of meaning from a literary text. Wolfgang Iser suggested that the successes of uncovering "textual structures and structured acts of comprehension" in literary texts relied on the "degree in which the text establishes itself as a correlative in the reader's consciousness. This 'transfer' of text [though initiated by the text] depends on the extent to which this text can activate the individual reader's faculties of perceiving and processing" (107). The "gutters" of the comics find their corollaries in the three dots of the ellipsis, which themselves are a device used in the comic strip, both as a figurative device and as literal punctuation points in text (Lind 251). In her eloquent study of the ellipsis, Anne Toner describes the way that the punctuation mark signals an effort to capture, in writing, the pauses, hesitations, and fraught silences that come with speech. Completeness exists in thought, whereas speech itself is fragmented:

> Unfinished sentences can work productively as a force for social cohesion, rather than standing out as semantic failures. The unfinished sentence can promote intimacy between speakers or show deference towards an interlocutor. It can also have a strong illocutionary force. We can make propositions and give them extra emotional force by failing to deliver them fully. Not saying something often says it better. (5)

The ellipsis marks are visual reminders in written and printed texts of something gone unsaid, and the gutters of the comics page are no less than the constant presence of what is left out from panel to panel. In the absence of language and, in the case of the gutters, action, absence takes on illocutionary force by prompting the reader to draw conclusions about the relationship between the panels. Interruption thus becomes constancy, establishing a pace, which is reinforced by the actions on the page; starts and stops, pauses to think through those shifts, becomes a single action. By drawing the reader into colluding with the pace of the narrator of *Walkin'*, the rhythms draw her also into more intimate collusion by making meaning together with Huizenga's pedestrian heroes. This connection is underscored by Huizenga's device of bringing the reader along with his narrator on the walk, viewing the world from the speaker's point of view so that the reader, too, becomes a pedestrian.

. . .

The remainder of this essay reads the ways that the motif of the pedestrian in *Walkin'* examines the practices of ellipsis that achieve a suspension of time. This suspension asserts the capacity for so-called profane space and activity in continuity with the sacred. A continuum of the sacred of the everyday is a motif that recurs throughout Huizenga's work, and which finds its most direct address here. From the squares of the frames themselves, to the parcels of visual and textual language that they inscribe, to the contemplation of the body as it extends into space, these comics insistently present the reader with these repetitive, and necessarily limited, units that can be understood only at the end of the motion. Curiously, the understanding that comes at the end of the motion is that all the action that came before it was crucial. It is precisely the fragmentation of language and image that arrests the attention of the reader, so that the process of becoming drawn in to the pace and rhythms of the comic and ultimately reaching the expansive conclusion is entirely in step with the walker's progress and experience within the space of the comic. *Walkin'* thus achieves its illocutionary act upon the reader in both content and form, arguing that reading is a kind of walking.

Walkin' resituates the nature walk described by Henry David Thoreau, whose essay "Walking" argued for the necessity of a passage through nature unsullied by the interventions of human civilization:

> When we walk, we naturally go to the fields and woods: what would become of us, if we walked only in a garden or a mall? . . . Of course it is of no use to direct our steps to the woods, if they do not carry us thither. I am alarmed when it happens that I have walked a mile into the woods bodily, without getting there in spirit. (np)

Huizenga instead transplants this ideal walk into the Midwest's residential landscape, with its closely spaced houses, fenced yards, and power lines, but adopting that same urgency of purpose toward linking body and spirit that Thoreau sought in the woods. He walks through the kind of landscape that Rebecca Solnit describes as reflecting "a desire to live in a world of predestination rather than chance, to strip the world of its wide-open possibilities and replace them with freedom of choice in the marketplace" (Solnit 255). Unlike the paths in the woods, these sidewalks transmit an inevitability of passage, controlling the directions that the pedestrian may take. Thoreau requires the woods to create a separation between himself and the "village" that represents the cares and obligations of other people: "In my walks I would fain return to my senses. What business have I in the woods, if I am thinking of something out of the woods?" (Thoreau np).

Walkin' replicates the sense of being, and of being bodily, as the narrator sets off; but, unlike Thoreau, it argues for a link of the spirit with everyday encounter, where the sounds of birds and the sounds of hair dryers are equally able to transform the one who encounters them. By thinking of the streets that he walks on, the narrator reaches a level of illumination that acknowledges, and extends beyond, the cognitive clarity that scientists have recently linked to walking (Berman, Jonides, and Kaplan). Instead, walking is described as a sacred activity, in the sense that it becomes out of time. The subject of *Walkin'* is simple: the speaker has moved to a new neighborhood, and these are the last days of summer. He walks alone on these new streets, taking in the new sights, sounds, and smells as they appear to him. Many of the pages are nearly wordless, simply showing the objects of the walker's observation, and sometimes accompanied by texts that record snippets of sound or fragments of thought. As he progresses in his walk, the drawings within the panels begin to lose definition and detail in places; shapes emerge from between the crossed wires on the page (Huizenga 1998, 7). Bird sounds mimic the sounds of words, and the panels become blurs of impressionistic shapes and fragments that resolve as the walker finds himself in a park, watching a parent and child in the playground. The parent and child become a metonym for the walker's sense of the universe; as he observes them, the pages resolve into a single observation: "I am that kid" (26). This conclusion compresses the impressions witnessed and catalogued in the preceding pages into a sublime moment of identification with an anonymous parent and child, forming less a rejection of the sacred than a repositioning of the sacred into the everyday human world.

The walk takes place on a Sunday morning, but this walker, in his ripped jeans and T-shirt, is not walking to church. The details in his lyrical monologue suggest a deep familiarity with going to church; *Walkin'* takes those recognizable pieces and replaces them with the objects he sees on the street. He thus makes a case for finding the numinous in the surroundings of the everyday world: "Trees cast jigsaw puzzle shadows on the houses and moss grows in-between shingles. / I'm feeling real alive, awake, soaking it all in. Didn't go to church this morning but here you go, a squirrel's Sabbath, the robins saying 'when peace like a sidestreet attendeth' and the trees clap their hands, the Sun of God Baptist Assembly" (Huizenga 1998, 4). The details he sees on the street are part of a neighborhood that is "older than the Brady Bunch suburb and . . . still technically in the city" (4). The trees, wires, objects, and animals in yards and sidewalks form their own church: a "squirrel's Sabbath." The sound of the robins evokes the hymn "When Peace Like a River," and its first verse: "When peace like a river attendeth my way, / when sorrows like sea billows roll, / whatever my lot, thou has taught me to say, / it is well, it is well with my soul." The robins substitute "sidestreet" for "river," and the trees substitute their clapping branches for the hands of human congregants.

The reader being thus established in this church of the "sun of God," the next few pages begin a nearly wordless reverie providing a caesura in the progression of the comic. On page 5, the walk is interrupted as the speaker passes a chain-link fence to observe a dog sleeping on its side in a backyard. The page emphasizes the simultaneous ordinariness and significance of the moment by placing nearly identical panels side by side in three rows. The

Figure 13.2. Detail of "Old hound" panel. *Walkin'*, page 5, by Kevin Huizenga. Copyright © 1998 Kevin Huizenga. Image courtesy of Kevin Huizenga

pairs of panels are thus remarkable for the similarities between them; rather than fulfilling the ellipsis of action, the gutter suggests only the slightest of differences, so that the connection made by the mind is one of profound subtlety. In the first row, the objects framed in the view are the same: the back door, the covered barbecue, the window, and the sleeping dog. The reader looks from left to right, then right to left again, to make sense of the sequence; whereas the image on the left shows the figure's passage arrested by a sight beyond the fence, the image on the right shows him stopped with hand resting on the fence. The action of the ellipsis, then, is the cessation of action: a rest. Likewise, the second pair of images also evokes stasis. The images are identical, except for the thought bubble on the left, which obscures some of the objects in the upper left quadrant. The walker wonders, "Old hound . . . wonder if it'll start yalping in its dreams." The following pair provides the answer: side-by-side close-ups of the sleeping dog, its position unchanged from left to right (Huizenga 1998, 5). What Huizenga accomplishes here is a suspension of time, accomplished in part because of the comics reader's expectation of closure of action between the panels. When there is no action, the reader is forced to think instead about the significance of that fact. In a form where readers frequently do the work of bridging or interpreting absence, where an action has occurred between those panels, they are here confronted with the absence of absence, a device that forces a pause for contemplation. This is, of course, exactly what our narrator does; his forward trajectory is arrested by the sight of the inert dog, and he pauses to observe him. Rather than emphasizing change or difference, the frame represents the absence of movement or change.

This recording of the absence of movement is a reminder to us, the readers, of the gentle balance between the content of the comic, which is the walk to the park bench taken by the narrator, and the making of the comic, which is likely made indoors, perhaps at a table, and long after the fact. The distance of recording finds an easy berth in the motif of the frame, which evokes a conscious capturing. The comics frame evokes the window introduced early on in Sebald's monument to memory and, significantly, to walking: *The Rings of Saturn*. In it, Sebald recalls how he began to write these pages after a walk he had taken in the English countryside; the immobility at the time of writing is inextricably linked to his memory of walking, and the link between the two is created by the frame of his hospital room window: "all that could be seen of the world from my bed was the colourless patch of sky framed in the window . . . all I could hear was the wind sweeping in from the country and buffeting the window; and in between, when the sound subsided, there was the never entirely ceasing murmur in my own ears" (4–5). Sebald's window comes to represent the series of journeys of thought and memory evoked by the remembered walk, the recording of which is also itself encased in memory. *Walkin'* echoes the window evoked by Sebald with the frames on the comics pages, which begin to gesture to their fragmentary nature as if bent by their own "never entirely ceasing" susurrus of memory.

The wordless panels that follow continue to record the crossed lines seen on the first page, and they continue to depict objects from the walker's point of view, but insert greater formal innovation. On page 7, six panels show the street scene as viewed from different angles, intercut with wires, poles, and tree trunks and tops. The twelve syllables "carless moment / the tips of trees / are little trees" appear in the top right panel, and the panels beneath show the scenery leaking out into the gutters, which are described in the top half of the row but breached by a continuous scene across the bottom half (Huizenga 1998, 7). What is seen begins to inform the way that it is presented: the middle panel of the next page shows a central pole from which a mesh of crossed wires emerges, and across which other lines pass; the bottom edge of the panel sinks to the bottom right rather than crossing horizontally on the page, as if mimicking one of the rays of wire depicted within its frames (8). The walker pauses to contemplate the summer he has spent landscaping other people's lawns, and the possibilities in his future that he has imagined: in this recorded moment, he himself is that gutter between past and present. Objects in his path become labeled, creating a taxonomy of his landscape: the red squirrel, the "serious exercise ladies and happy dogs," the sparrows (11); and on the very next page the labels tell what the images do not show. Juxtaposed against images of house fronts, the text boxes read: "fat bees on lilacs," "and butterflies," "millions of ants," "daddy long-legs," "earwigs," "millipedes," and "roly polys" (12). In the remarkable series of pages that follows, the frames become increasingly abstracted and strange, and continue to meditate on the way that the walk accommodates the act of summoning meaning from these minutely captured fragments.

The walk becomes visually syncopated as the walker is progressively absorbed in his surroundings over the course of ten pages. The content of the frames is necessarily a fragment of the whole picture, as emphasized by the unusual angles and focus on specific shapes or objects in a panel. On page 10 of *Walkin'*, little symbols appear in the panels to denote invisible stimuli that are nonetheless perceived: the apple smell of shampoo, the whirring noise of someone's blow-dryer through a window. The walker's nose and ear are unusually pronounced in close-up in complementary panels. This visual emphasis on parts is echoed by the sparseness of the language, sometimes so spare that it has been abbreviated to incomplete words as well as incomplete sentences. Birds on a wire have a conversation in six abstractly drawn panels on page 13, and the listener strains to make sense of their bird sounds. He hears "cheap tea," "Tallahassee," "squeaky clean," "sleep sweetly," "easy," all rhapsodies on the long "e" sound that become increasingly urgent: "freezing scene! Keep sinking!" (Huizenga 1998, 14). Alongside the impenetrable sounds of the birds, the vistas within the panels begin to lose their definition as well.

The silent distortions of panels and their contents are at their most remarkable as the six panel pages become pulled as if into a vortex at the center of the page. Shadow and whiteness are whorled together, and open on to the following page, which bears curves, crossed lines, fragments of the lines describing treetops in previous panels, and the sensation of viewing a glare bouncing off a reflective surface or perhaps of simply looking directly at the sun itself (18–19). These pages could be read as nothing more than a mimetic representation of the walking narrator being blinded by the lambent light of a summer morning, looking up and seeing a whirl of dazzling white dappled with treetop shadows. The reader might also consider that what is represented here is not what the narrator inside the comic sees at the moment; rather, it is a depiction of the artist's experience of trying to remember and capture the moment, which is now obscured by the passage of time. This latter interpretation is supported by the pages that follow, which appear as drawings made over text; the muddle of light and dark splotches laid over a nonsensical typewritten text suggests a surplus of text and image. Again, the panels are separated in orderly fashion in the first page, and then melted

Figure 13.3. Whorls of light and shadow, *Walkin'*, page 22, by Kevin Huizenga. Copyright © 1998 Kevin Huizenga. Image courtesy of Kevin Huizenga

toward one another in the subsequent page (20–21). On the last page of the sequence, the blank space appears as the overlay, reversing the expected process of dark marks made on a white page to white splotches redacting an existing underlayer of dark marks (22).

Frederic Gros writes this about walking:

> Walking is a matter not just of truth, but also of reality. To walk is to experience the real. Not reality as pure physical exteriority or as what might count as a subject, but reality as what holds good: the principle of solidity, of resistance. When you walk you prove it with every step: the earth holds good. With every pace, the entire weight of my body finds support and rebounds, takes a spring. There is everywhere a solid base somewhere underfoot. (94)

The walker cannot help but be aware of his body; each step is an extension away from, and then toward, the ground. Yet, if walking is a matter of truth and reality, so is the narrator's perception of the world and the things left untouched during his passage. The glare of white unreadability blinds the reader along with the narrator. The walker is returned from this blinding white back to the crossed power lines and the conversational birds; their chatter continues as the words careen between the crossed lines and white spaces. This detachment from the blur of black and white in the preceding page asks the reader to consider what makes one more legible and less strange than the other. Finally, as he navigates another hill, he comes upon a place to stop: "As if the morning, the walk, the sights, smells, sounds, feeling weren't enough I stumble on a park in a valley" (Huizenga 1998, 24). He proceeds to a picnic table bench and sits with his back to the table, facing the playground.

The fragmented visuals are again reinforced by the fragmented language. The point of view shifts from behind the shoulder of the narrator to a playground in the distance to a close-up of the slide, its curves set in relief against the straight angles of the swing set's legs. A box that straddles the two top panels contains the words, "Over there's a / parent loving / hearing a child / babble breathless / from the playground," and the bottom panel resolves into another panel in which he is now viewed at a distance and from the side. "I'm that kid," reads the text (26). The word "loving" becomes an object of interpretation as well. If the sentence should read that the parent is loving the sound of the child's babble, the caesura would more properly belong after "parent" instead of after "loving," and, like the fragmented panels in the pages before it, the subtle differences of meaning of those lines become the work of the reader. From the faceless body with bending knee at the beginning of the comic, to the stick figure sitting alone on a bench in the park, something has changed. He has begun with possibility, and he has ended with a magical accord between past, present, and future. What has happened between these two positions has been the walk.

What Huizenga accomplishes by the end of *Walkin'* is an articulation of a question about purposefulness and its relationship to walking. How is it, we are asked, that that which is so bounded by gravity, that which pulls our feet one after the other back to the ground, is also the means by which we reach toward the sky? In this comic, both the passage of the walker through the streets and side streets of his newly adopted neighborhood, and the passage of the reader through the pages, employ the same processes of attending and appraisal. *Walkin'*, in all of its strange hesitations and surprise, anatomizes the experience of walking as not only akin to the experience of reading, but to the experience of perceiving the world around us. By traversing the spaces between, whether one step at a time or one panel at a time, we are broadening our capacities for reaching each time from the terrestrial to the aerial. Rather than trying to apply an order to that space between the "tock" and the "tick" of the progression of our lives, Huizenga suggests a kind of time travel made all the more remarkable because it is achievable by each of us in our profane, but no less magical, world.

BIBLIOGRAPHY

Berman, Marc G., John Jonides, and Stephen Kaplan. "The Cognitive Benefits of Interacting with Nature." *Psychological Science* 19, no. 12 (2008): 1207–12.

Eliade, Mircea. *The Sacred and The Profane: The Nature of Religion*. Translated by Willard R. Trask. New York: Harcourt Brace Jovanovich, 1987.

Gardner, Jared. *Projections: Comics and the History of Twenty-First-Century Storytelling*. Stanford: Stanford University Press, 2012.

Groensteen, Thierry. *Comics and Narration*. Translated by Ann Miller. Jackson: University of Mississippi Press, 2013.

Groensteen, Thierry. *The System of Comics*. Translated by Bart Beaty and Nick Nguyen. Jackson: University Press of Mississippi, 2009.

Gros, Frederic. *A Philosophy of Walking*. Translated by John Howe. Reprint ed. London: Verso, 2015.

Huizenga, Kevin. "28th Street." *Curses*. Montreal: Drawn & Quarterly, 2006.

Huizenga, Kevin. *Walkin'*. Self-published, 1998.

Iser, Wolfgang. *The Act of Reading: A Theory of Aesthetic Response*. Baltimore: Johns Hopkins University Press, 1980.

Kermode, Frank. *The Sense of an Ending: Studies in the Theory of Fiction*. Oxford: Oxford University Press, 2000.

Lind, Stephen J. *A Charlie Brown Religion: Exploring the Spiritual Life and Work of Charles M. Schulz*. Jackson: University Press of Mississippi, 2015.

McCloud, Scott. *Understanding Comics: The Invisible Art*. New York: Harper Collins, 1993.

Otto, Rudolf. "On Numinous Experience as *Mysterium Tremendum et Fascinans*." In *Experience of the Sacred: Readings in the Phenomenology of Religion*, edited by Sumner Twiss and Walter Conser, 77–85. Hanover, NH: University Press of New England, 1992.

Postema, Barbara. *Narrative Structure in Comics: Making Sense of Fragments*. Rochester: RIT Press, 2013.

Sebald, W. G. *The Rings of Saturn*. Translated by Michael Hulse. New York: New Directions, 1999.

Solnit, Rebecca. *Wanderlust: A History of Walking*. New York: Penguin Books, 2001.

Thoreau, Henry David. "Walking." *Atlantic* (June 1862); *Atlantic* Web. August 15, 201.

Toner, Anne. *Ellipsis in English Literature: Signs of Omission*. Cambridge: Cambridge University Press, 2015.

Chapter Fourteen

MARVEL'S *FALLEN SON* AND MAKING THE ORDINARY SACRED

JOSHUA PLENCNER

IN THE WAKE OF MARVEL COMICS' 2006–2007 *CIVIL WAR*, A SEVEN-ISSUE limited series that frames its otherwise recognizably generic superhero punch-up story against the backdrop of post-9/11 American national security state politics, one of even a fictional life's certainties catches up with Captain America: he dies. Abruptly, upon his surrender to government authorities that sought him out as a criminal, handcuffed, and still wearing his near-universally recognizable star-spangled uniform, Steve Rogers (the Captain's secret identity) was assassinated by a sniper's bullet (and finished off with three pistol shots to the belly delivered by a mind-controlled comrade from short range). Captain America, that seemingly solid symbol of heroism—the long-held "dream"—was gone (Millar and McNiven).

Perhaps running counter to a broad public expectation of the character and what he represented as a symbol of American life, Captain America did not perish in battle as a hero, but died rather ingloriously under criminal suspicion and subterfuge. With his hands behind his back, flanked by US Marshals and a thronging crowd of onlookers as he climbed the federal courthouse steps in New York City to an arraignment hearing where he was to stand accused of violating the Superhuman Registration Act—a law passed with the intention of protecting innocents from the dangerous consequences of superpowers—Rogers exited life under a cloud of controversy, offering few answers. What does it *mean* that Captain America is dead? What does his death, at this moment, *tell* us about American life? What does his death *do*?

Outside of the comics, Rogers's death was immediately newsworthy. Even traditionally staid organs like the *New York Times* weighed in, publishing a March 8, 2007, headline stating: "Captain America Is Dead; National Hero

Since 1941" (Gustines). But *Times* readers were offered some solace by way of official explanation. Marvel Entertainment president and publisher Dan Buckley promised that Marvel "delivered a compelling story that made everyone think," adding that "the stories we have planned dealing with Cap's death are really compelling too" (Gustines).

The most primary of the stories "dealing with Cap's death" subsequently published by Marvel is *Fallen Son: The Death of Captain America* (2007), a five-issue limited series written by Jeph Loeb, with art by five separate artists—Leinil Yu, Ed McGuinness, John Romita, Jr., David Finch, and John Cassaday. The series is indeed compelling, designed as an exploration of grief and bereavement, looking in on a small collection of moments unfolding in the wake of Captain America's death so as to trace out the reactions of Marvel's most central characters to the loss of their friend and comrade.

To be clear, so explicit is its exploration of grief and bereavement that the series is structured around the widely recognizable "stages of grief" model of therapeutic psychiatry initially popularized by Elisabeth Kübler-Ross in her successful (if contested) work, *On Death and Dying* (1969). The five emotional stages of grief initially described by Kübler-Ross are denial, anger, bargaining, depression, and acceptance, with acceptance—in its popular understanding—signifying a kind of orderly completion of grief management. While subsequent empirical psychology has sought to challenge and redefine the specific categorical boundaries popularized by Kübler-Ross, even critics acknowledge the resilience of the original formulation (Bonanno et al.; Wortman and Silver), often noting the outsized role the model enjoys within medical education—even despite a dearth of strong affirmative studies demonstrating the theory's precise applicability in treatment (Downe-Wamboldt and Tamlyn). It is, after all, a *popularized* theory; it retains a kind cultural-heuristic power, if a contested medical-explanatory power. For that reason, we can understand why Kübler-Ross is valuable as storytelling guide. In *Fallen Son*, these stages work as chapter titles and governing themes for each issue, signposting each stage in the process, and providing a sense of in-world navigation, and even completion, of grief management in the wake of Captain America's death.

But rather than analyze *Fallen Son* as a demonstration of Kübler-Ross's model of grief and bereavement, I want to suggest that it might be more useful to read the series for the ways that it undermines, in navigating the complex affective territory of grief in loss, the very diagrammatic structure of staged emotional categories it purports to employ as narrative chapters. As many of us might attest with our own personal experience, grief in loss (a term I use interchangeably with *bereavement* and *mourning*) can be intense—even excessive—working in a space that Raymond Williams describes as "the very edge of semantic availability," where feelings themselves are still being sorted through as they happen, in the moment of their greatest intensity (134). That is, amidst the excess of intense feeling, how one actually feels in any given moment of bereavement can move beyond clearly defined categorical boundaries, and into a much more difficult to name space of "immeasurable" feeling (Hardt and Negri). So intense can grief be that it can render the complex feeling of grief itself ineffable, irreducible to "stages" of specific emotional states. Grief in loss can exceed boundaries, surging past them, rendering the familiar unfamiliar.

In acknowledging the excessive potential of grief—and its ineffability—I want to suggest that we can also see how, through that same excess and intensity, the affective registration of grief is an opening to embodied experience of the sacred, where the familiar and unfamiliar collide and demand a new accounting of the self. Feelings beyond "semantic availability," I contend, are grounds of the sacred. By invoking "the sacred" here, I don't mean to mobilize a specific theological understanding of sacredness, or a doctrinal reading of grief in the context of a particular religious history or ritual practice. Instead, I'm interested in investigating the way that ineffable affect—with special attention to its manifestation in ritualized representations of grief and mourning as depicted in *Fallen Son*—mimics what I understand as felt or phenomenological qualities of sacred experience. The sacred is fundamentally ineffable; it is, as Roland Barthes might argue, "obtuse," or beyond semantic description, exceeding the limitations of language as a "signifier without a signified" (1985, 318). Thus, much like affect that moves beyond categorical emotional boundaries, the sacred is irreducibly complex—impacting bodies and senses in ways often difficult to categorize but bearing material, *felt* consequences that structure relations among people and things.

Following the work of psychologist Silvan Tomkins, recent critical conversations on affect theory have engaged pointed, categorical feelings—joy and rage, excitement and shame (Sedgwick; Berlant). However, in linking affect and the sacred I'm inspired by the work of anthropologist Kathleen Stewart, whose analysis filters such excessive, structuring feelings through the lens of the everyday in her evocative book *Ordinary Affects* (2007). There, Stewart employs poetic, autoethnographic close reading to probe the ways that excess affect isn't merely bound up in extraordinary moments of life—those rare instances of peculiar social formation that produce punctuated moments of ineffable experience such as grief in loss. Rather,

Stewart suggests that ineffable affect is spread throughout "circuits . . . [of] the ordinary," or everyday scenes composing that undescribable sense of Barthes's "signifier without a signified." For Stewart, the ordinary is not a stable structure that determines the contextual meanings of affective experience, but a "shifting assemblage of practices and practical knowledges" that helps us navigate an agonistic world where meaning is plural and contested (1). Ordinary affects don't follow schematics; they are not "stages" of discrete emotions, but the "trajectories, connections, and disjunctures" of feeling that give shape to life (3).

Imagined through such trajectories, connections, and disjunctures, I think we can understand "the sacred" as an equally ordinary—and equally ineffable—constitutive element of everyday experience. This is in some ways a stark shift away from traditional conceptions of the sacred and sacredness. As famously conceptualized by Émile Durkheim, the sacred is composed of "things set apart and forbidden," away from the ordinary, routine stuff of daily life—or what he describes as "the profane" (44). For Durkheim, this is a crucial point: the social function of religion is to negotiate the tension between the sacred and the profane, protecting the sacred for extraordinary occasions mediated by specific, controlled, and orderly social practices. The sacred is space aside, or perhaps pointed above, the mortal coil—as much an extraordinary phenomenological preserve and collective teleological end as a physical space reserved for sanctified, hierarchized social interaction.

But as many critics of Durkheim have argued, situating the sacred as a space apart from the ordinary routines of life impoverishes our understanding of how social order is contingent and changing. It isn't enough to conceive the sacred as constitutive of an *a priori* social totality which religion mediates; it can also be understood as a dynamic force that transgresses the boundary of chaotic "inner experience" and ordered society, caught up in the energy of what Georges Bataille calls "being without delay" (47). In Stewart's language, this kind of contingent social order is a "shifting assemblage"—a heterogeneous composition, much of which may be conceived as ordinary or "profane" in Durkheim's view, but should nonetheless be meaningfully understood as constitutive of the sacred, sacredness, and ineffable sacred experience.

Pursuing this line of thought here, I will argue that comic books are one of the many "little *some*things worth noting in the direct composition of the ordinary" (Stewart 48). Even superhero comics—as extraordinarily fantastic and impossible as their narratives might be—when acknowledged as part of our social world, are ordinary things, and thus provide a promising object of analysis for understanding the connections between ineffable sacredness and popular, everyday experience. This chapter takes the first steps toward identifying and elaborating the "ordinary sacred" qualities of comics—those qualities that, by eluding the very narrative structures of meaning around which they are designed, forge provocative phenomenological links between culture, bodies, and power in society.

In the following section I situate *Fallen* Son within the broader context of superhero comics culture, outlining the genre's fascination with themes of death and bodily finitude. From there, I argue that—in employing the Kübler-Ross "stages of grief" model as a structuring device—*Fallen Son* is comparatively unique among examples of superhero comics concerned with bereavement. Such uniqueness, I argue, warrants close reading to demonstrate how exactly the "stages" model is employed, as well as how the narrative's excessive affect skirts the boundaries of staged emotional ground. By tracing that excess of affect, I argue that such suffusion of intensity is not demonstrative of extraordinary irruption but is, rather, an ordinary aspect of the comics, and that *Fallen Son* helps illustrate "the ordinary sacred" as a provocative (dis)organizing force. Speculatively, I argue the ordinary sacred offers the opportunity to think about sacredness and comics together differently, engaging texts not directly interacting with or informed by religiosity yet still composing sensibilities of sacredness that *do* things, that act in the world, creating vibrant social orders and publics in their wake.

. . .

At first glance, *Fallen Son* might register as a lamentation song for a slain hero, a simply constructed elegy that interrupts and decompresses the narrative adrenaline of Rogers's assassination and the ensuing in-world disorder with a pause, a reflection, and an offering of final, contemplative resolution in its four-color *selah* to the seventy-some-odd-year verse of Captain America's story. Ultimately, after all, *Fallen Son* is about bereavement, funeral, and burial—a story structure familiar to longtime comics readers as a kind of episodic break from routine serialization. Death, when it comes in superhero comics, is an opportunity for pause and memorial. Indeed, *Fallen Son* works well as a space for the narrative exploration of grief and mourning, as well as a kind of manual for the social processing of loss, even when—as is so often true in the world of superheroes—the dead are hardly ever *actually* dead.

This phenomenon—of the undead, ever-lurking superhero—has been explored at length in critical academic literatures. Umberto Eco, for instance, convincingly argues that superheroes are "inconsumable," which is to say that death is a specter that haunts superheroes but never fully arrives (16). Death is all *around* superheroes, but does not come *for* them. Moreover, even when death does arrive asking for its receipt, in superhero comics death most often remains temporary (Alaniz).

Thus, even though superheroes are impelled toward serial heroism, they rarely succumb to logics of finitude and expiration. Eco's argument undergirds a broader analytic position that superheroes are a kind of modern mythology, etiologically unbound by human constraints—their inconsumability constituting exactly that which elevates their status as "super," above and outside of ordinary human limitations, up to and including time itself. In this view, mythified superheroes are sacred things, for they are not of nature; their stories do not share our horizons, even if those distinct tracks might occasionally converge.

For many, this myth-critical perspective on superheroes is authoritative, shaping critical interpretation around a pole of analysis that treats as overlapping (if not precisely synonymous) the concepts of "superhero" and "modern mythology" (Coogan; Reynolds). That strength draws on a deep field of thinkers for whom myth plays an important role in stabilizing complex societies. For instance, Roland Barthes famously describes myth as "frozen speech"—an ahistorical discourse that "distorts" the routine lived experience of contingency and uncertainty. As Barthes writes, "*myth hides nothing*: its function is to distort, not make disappear" (1982, 107). Through this distortion of social meaning, myth augments both sources and structures of power. Put differently, the question "Who rules?" can be understood, via Barthesian distortion, as directly linked to another question: "What myths?"

In superhero comics, mythic distortion also extends to the otherwise inveterate rules of human life and death, breaking down the familiar meanings of bodies and lives as finite, substituting instead Eco's premise of the inconsumable superhero. While the history of American superheroes is dotted with various "deaths of," superhero death is notoriously short-lived. Insofar as superheroic mortality represents an unfreezing of myth and an explicit recognition of frailty and finitude, death in superhero comics is most often, with the rare exception, merely "death"—not a coda, but a signature of return.

But it is at this fault-line, between extraordinary death and the routine of short-term "death," that some superhero comics push back against the logic of inconsumable myth. Because the stability of mythic authority always hinges on a consumer's adoption of that logic, for whom each next "death" might actually be the first, superhero comics cannot be said to simply replicate familiar norms; rather, they must create those norms, recombining extant and familiar components into something new. That bid toward "the new" can work to shore up the hegemony of superhero myth, and often does so, but need not. As with any cultural project, things can fall apart. Not all deaths are created equal. And superhero deaths can open up a particular kind of instability; in each creative act, death is potentially removed from its mythic stature as extreme or extraordinary—death, or even "death," can be made ordinary, subject to very human routines and journeys where the real effects of mortality can be, and often are, messy, imperfect, haphazard, and incomplete—or, you know, utterly human.

I read this play along the fault-line of extraordinary and ordinary death in *Fallen Son* as pushing back against the structuring logics of myth, calling into question the timelessness of the superhero. More complex forces are at work—things that don't so easily fall into place. To expand on the first-glance reading of *Fallen Son* offered earlier, it's not a mistake to look at the series as a typical lamentation song for the slain Captain America—a means of Kübler-Rossian mourning and orderly narrative resolution; rather, I argue that that reading is incomplete, unable to account for the ways that, in attending to "how Earth's Mightiest Heroes respond to this shocking and painful loss," the ordinary and extraordinary qualities of superhero death are unfrozen, affectively animated, and shown stepping into time—toward a more compelling, human, and ordinary sensibility.

. . .

In *Fallen Son*, while the layers of processual narrative grief build over the five issues by exploring the titled "stages" in depth, each individual issue/chapter anchors its story in the routine of ritual. For example, when opening the cover of each issue purchased off the comics shop wall or newsstand, consumers are met with a series of visual and textual reminders of Captain America's death. On each issue's title page, situated above an image featuring Captain America's iconic circular red, white, and blue shield spattered with blood, a block of text reads: "He was the greatest soldier the world would ever know. When a devastating Civil War divided the super heroes, he surrendered to end the conflict. Despite his noble sacrifice, he was assassinated. Captain America is dead. This is what happens next" (Loeb et al., 1). That title page is immediately followed, via a page-turn reveal, with an image featuring a red-gloved hand, shackled at the wrist with silver-metallic handcuffs, laid prone over a bloodied newspaper edition of the *Daily Bugle*. Underneath the cuffed hand, two bits of newsprint text remain legible: "Captain America," and "Death of the Dream." This reliance on ritualistic rhythms as readers enter the story serves to anchor the narrative and emphasize to readers that this story is set aside, sacred—that mourning is under way.

In the first chapter of *Fallen Son*, titled "Denial" and written by Jeph Loeb with art by Leinil Yu, readers follow X-Men mainstay and oft-times Avenger Wolverine as he attempts to confirm for himself that Rogers is *actually* dead—that it isn't some ruse, trick, or other means of obfuscating the truth from those who knew Rogers best, longest, and personally. "I don't buy it," Wolverine says. "Things aren't always as they seem" (3–4). Later, meeting with Daredevil, whom he hopes to recruit into his plan, Wolverine reiterates his disbelief: "I'm going to take a look at Cap's body. Those heightened senses of yours could come in handy at peeling back the truth." In response, Daredevil, his incredulity veneered with empathy for a friend, replies, "People die, Logan. You more than most of us know that" (14). Convinced to join in on the plan, Daredevil and Wolverine break into a government-protected holding cell and interrogate the sniper who fired the first shot that felled Rogers, a hired assassin named Crossbones. As Wolverine presses Crossbones—the "bad cop" to Daredevil's "good"—the latter monitors the accused's heart-rate, listening for fluctuations that might betray some subtle untruth from the man who admits he fired on Cap but "didn't get the kill shot" (21).

As a makeshift lie detector Daredevil's heightened senses might be very effective in discerning the truth, adding narrative credibility to the unfolding storyline, but confirmation of Crossbones's truth-telling is delivered best (and most directly) by artist Leinil Yu's red bands of spiking-and-valleying pulse lines, stacked on the pages, that signal to readers what Daredevil presumably senses and Wolverine needs to learn for himself: that Crossbones successfully fired on Captain America but didn't kill him, and that he doesn't know anything more. Crossbones played his part in the assassination, but it was only *a part*. Here at least, in interrogation, there is no piece of conspiracy left to uncover; there is no room for Wolverine's lingering doubt and denial. Crossbones shot Rogers. Wolverine now knows this.

But confirmation of Crossbones's guilt isn't enough—it wasn't Wolverine's goal at the outset to simply confirm the assassination plot; it was to confirm that it was Rogers *himself* who was shot and killed, that Rogers, and not some surreptitious placeholder, is really gone. Dissuading Daredevil from joining him on this last part of the mission ("You've had enough trouble in your life, Murdock. Don't add mine."), Wolverine seeks out the body of Rogers, held somewhere in the same facility (27).

The discovery of the body is a quiet page: Wolverine emerges out of the black background, eyes glowing red. He approaches a flag-draped casket. Panel break. His gloved hand lifts the casket lid. A sound effect—small white

Figure 14.1. Wolverine discovers Steve Rogers's casket. *Fallen Son: The Death of Captain America*, chapter 1, page 30, Jeph Loeb (writer) and Leinil Yu (artist). Copyright © 2007 Marvel Characters, Inc.

letters against the black: SNIF. Panel break. Tight close-up of Wolverine's face, eyes narrowed, head turned. In red, harsh-edged, electronicized text, a voice from off panel: "It's him" (29). Panel break. Wolverine standing over the casket, hands braced against its edges, leaning over an olive-drab uniformed body in shadow. Panel break. Two faces in extreme shadow, Wolverine in the foreground, Iron Man in the background. Same red-electronicized text, "That's why you came here, isn't it? To make sure" (29).

With his confirmation—that "SNIF" suggesting Wolverine's heightened, animal-like aptitude for identifying Rogers—the narrative suggests that denial has been a veil that served only to obscure his actions, to lead him astray. There's nothing left to deny, and Wolverine now understands the truth. Rogers is dead, and with him, "The Dream." Addressing Iron Man, Wolverine realizes his last mission in the story: "You want me to go back and tell them. Anybody who had hope. Who are in denial. . . . That I've got proof" (31). The suggestion is that truth carries its greatest strength not through self-evidence, but through social evangelism. Acceptance of loss is not merely personal; it's oriented toward communities who share their denial, and must overcome it together.

Even when accepting the truth of Rogers's death, some questions still remain for Wolverine. For instance, consider the tension between "seeming" and "knowing" that informs Wolverine's denial to the point where the only kind of knowing that matters is the kind forged through direct subjective experience. As he says at the outset, all is not as it seems, sometimes. He knows loss more than most. That play between seeming and knowing, in tension, is capable of generating intense reactions. Indeed, Wolverine's denial of Rogers's death generates more than an emotive reaction, an affective "stage" of grief marked out on a path to clear acceptance of loss; it generates entire, even conflicting, epistemological orientations to the truth of loss. For Wolverine, in this moment of intense grief, the only way to know, in the end and truly, is to *know*, to experience knowing with one's body and senses. Those senses are alive and searching, never far from the surface. Moreover, they're creative. That is, insofar as the body absorbs sensory experience, those senses help construct and defend the epistemological orientation adopted in the wake of loss. Yet even as Wolverine "accepts" that the body is Rogers, using the direct experience of ritualized grief performed over the open casket, as well as his olfactory confirmation that it was truly his friend lying in that box, to say that he has "completed" a stage of emotional processing misses something much more profound about how affect, senses, and the body can—at least sometimes—do much more than confirm the "truth." In that moment, the affective stage of denial spreads out further, entangling not only what Wolverine knows as the truth, but how he knows it, and with whom he must share it. His special status as a skilled arbiter of the truth thus highlights the epistemological tensions of grief in loss, the inhabitation of multiple standpoints, roles, and responsibilities: the body is shown as a constant vector for ineffable experience—those meaningful moments that both elude rational description and structure knowledge of the world—just as forcefully as it is called into the responsibility of social evangelism, of sharing the truth of loss with others.

Questions linger narratively, as well. In the issue's last panel, Wolverine threatens Iron Man, angrily saying that if he finds out that Iron Man had anything to do with Cap's death, he would kill him. Here, readers are snapped back into the structuring logic of the stages explored by the individual chapters of the series. If the narrative arc of the first issue is one of overcoming denial, Kübler-Ross's model dictates that the resolution of denial leads not into immediate acceptance (and proselytization of the truth), but into anger and bargaining.

The second and third chapters of *Fallen Son* trace "Anger" and "Bargaining" through an account of several new in-world status quos developing in the aftermath of Rogers's death. In these issues, one burgeoning story follows the "New Avengers," or comrades of Captain America who refuse the Superhuman Registration Act and form an underground resistance against state co-optation; another follows the "Mighty Avengers," or those legally complying registrants whose superhuman abilities are marshaled as extensions of state security against unchecked global threats (Loeb and McGuinness); and the last follows Clint Barton, or Hawkeye, who had until the third issue of *Fallen Son* been absent from contemporaneous Marvel Comics storylines, presumed dead, and left without a clear role in the context of a superhero world that moved on after his passing (Loeb and Romita Jr. 8). Here, these layered stories work as a complex staging of grief for which there are no predefined rules of performance. "Anger" and "Bargaining" are visualized on the page in a variety of forms, dynamic and moving, driving characters to lash out physically and verbally, make jokes, openly despair, and plead with one another. For all of the complexity and nuance shown, though, the various demonstrations of grief in loss are presented as risky: self-defeating at best, and even harmful. As characters act out the staged emotional standpoints, they are revealed as inadequate to resolve the pain of bereavement. So, if the rain deluging the final pages of "Bargaining" works as a cue for a shift in the comic's affective mood, we see how anger and bargaining lead directly into the next stage of the Kübler-Ross model—as well as the title of the next issue in the series—"Depression" (Loeb and Finch).

In the fourth issue of *Fallen Son*, depression is staged through Spider-Man's rain-soaked grief, with his iconic "alternate" black suit—often used by storytellers as an outward visual sign of Spider-Man's inner emotional state—demonstrating in some unsubtle terms the depression he feels following the death of his friend.

Depression in the wake of loss is a familiar trope for Spider-Man comics stories, and the issue turns on its ability to present this newest suffering of grief as yet another in a series of devastating losses. Indeed, in 1962's *Amazing Fantasy* #15, Spider-Man's superheroism is famously born through such loss—the death of his beloved Uncle Ben at the hands of a petty criminal whom Spider-Man had, earlier in the issue, elected not to stop when he had the chance. That fatal choice subsequently haunts the character—he always returns to it, beset by the loss even as he tries to move beyond it. Indeed, as an example of this haunting return to origins, "Depression" begins with a page depicting Spider-Man standing, shoulders hunched, over the gravestones of his mother, his father, and—in a panel anchoring the middle of the page, dominating the layout—his uncle, Ben Parker. Inset on the bottom left of the page, a caption box narrating from Spider-Man's perspective makes clear how he situates himself amidst the monumentalization of death around him: "Knowing me, my legacy will be judged by the lives I've lost" (Loeb and Finch 1). He goes on, listing others whose lives have ended around him over the years: "Harry Osborn. Captain Stacy. *Gwen*. And now Captain America is dead. Even though I didn't have anything to do with it . . . I know the role I played in leading up to it made everything . . . worse" (2).

Given the character's long history of constitutive grief, Spider-Man is the perfect human/hero analogue of depression in *Fallen Son*—his heightened, supersensory capacity (or "spider-sense") a kind of resonating drum for his own feelings, as well as a clear sign highlighting the general precariousness of those vulnerable lives around him, for whom he bears "great responsibility." Literally sensitive, his body is constantly made aware of threat and the attendant potential pain of loss. And in that thickly layered registration of *felt* threat, we see drawn the link between exterior social danger and interior psychological pain—a depressive and depressing admixture of anxiety, fear, and certainty that one's own action (taken up in "responsibility") will never be enough to dislodge the cycle of loss.

In "Depression," as the issue presses into conflict, Spider-Man's "spider-sense" triggers in the cemetery while he grieves over his family's gravestones. "Not here," he says aloud. "Not now." Stuck in the cycle of loss, Spider-Man seems to acknowledge the cycle as such—the "not here" and "not now" reading more like "not again," in turn smashing together his dismay with a fantasy of refusal, or walking away from the cycle. But, as the first-person narration of the second-panel caption box shows, Spider-Man understands that such fantasy—of not going on—is just that: a fantasy. "Not like I have a choice," he says—to himself and readers alike (6). The cycle of trauma compels him forward, the "great responsibility" of his superheroic mission, a traumatic duty that *must* be borne.

But as Spider-Man flips and tumbles into action, rather than take measure of the potential threat sensed, he charges headlong into another staging of grief—one that, for all appearances, seems equally valid as Spider-Man's own grief, and equally deserving of contemplative reverence. Rhino, a perennial Spider-Man rogue, is depicted hunched over a tombstone—his enormous body wrapped in a trench coat, his signature horn hidden beneath a broad-brimmed hat. "I know I ain't come to see you as much as I should," he says, alone with his voice, "but things are bad right now."

Yet just as he finishes his sentence, Rhino is punched from behind by Spider-Man. Incensed, Rhino responds: "What're YOU doing here? Why can't you leave me alone?" Spider-Man coolly shoots webbing into Rhino's eyes, incredulous: "What . . . ? You're gonna act like this is a big coincidence that we're both in this cemetery—at night—in the rain?!" Peeling the webbing away from his face, Rhino yells out: "I don't know what the @#$% you're talking about." "S'okay," Spider-Man says. "Nobody ever knows what I'm talking about." He kicks Rhino in the face and goes on: "In fact, I'll just do the talking for both of us. At least that way I'll be amused." Rhino is knocked backward, stumbling, with a mid-page close-up panel focusing on his heel as he barrels through a headstone with an unceremonious "KRAK." "Look what you made me do!" Rhino cries. And here, from above, the engraving on the headstone is seen: "Miriam Systevich [*sic*], Beloved Mother."

Here, "Depression" unveils its darkest implications. Rhino is visiting the gravesite of his mother, his grief interrupted by Spider-Man's own, with the conflict between the two coming to literal blows. But because Spider-Man "screwed up," intervening in a moment of reflection and bereavement that Rhino intended to be private—he repeatedly says that he "wanted to be left alone," screaming, "Why couldn't you leave me alone?!" (14–15)—the consequence of his mistaken sense of threat is a pitch-black hierarchizing of grief, enforcing some mourning as more important than others. In that way, the issue reflects on depression itself as a site of compounded grief and mistakes but goes further in showing how those compounded mistakes can manifest real-time consequences. While a narrative door opens for a more complex Rhino to demonstrate nuance through depression, perhaps even going so far as to link hero and villain together across shared senses of grief, instead the narrative closes down an intriguing opportunity and follows Spider-Man as he simply beats up Rhino, prioritizing his own grief over that of others. The fight is intercut with scenes of Captain America fighting the Hulk, a visual echo of the present fight, and one that seems designed to again reiterate the permanent lack experienced in Rogers's loss. But such lack is especially grim when visually overlying a fight with another whose grief was interrupted. "What are we going to do without you, Cap?" asks Spider-Man, standing victorious over Rhino's now-motionless, defeated body. Whatever the answer to that question might be, in depression it seems only ever receding from view.

At the conclusion of "Depression," Wolverine coaches Spider-Man through his feelings, offering at least a kind of narrative resolution to the issue. "Wanna know why it's called 'depression'?" he asks. "Because it *is* depressing. . . . A death isn't like losing a job or getting divorced. You don't 'get over it.' You have to integrate it into your life. Learn to live with it. But . . . life does get better. Best you can hope for" (32). Wolverine's blunt question-and-answer—a sort of flat-edged argument that things might come around someday—is meant as a corrective to Spider-Man's flailing and unfocused actions throughout the issue's staging of depression. On the surface, there's a great need for this argument to Spider-Man in that specific moment; by "integrating" the loss of Rogers into his life, Spider-Man might come to find, in the very least, the "best he can hope for" at some point in the future. But the felt moment of grief in loss for Spider-Man, yet unintegrated, displays a kind of frightening revanchism, where powerful emotions translate into disturbing exercises of power. Indeed, with Spider-Man in "Depression," excessive affect leads to anxious, excessive recapitulation of traditional generic power hierarchies. The turmoil of Rhino's grief in the cemetery—displayed so violently as *beneath* the grief experienced by Spider-Man—undermines the comic's bid for clear affective resolution of depression as it moves into structured acceptance. Wolverine tries his best to convince Spider-Man that it gets better. But contra the supposed movement toward resolution of loss promised by the series, ultimate resolution is not available to everyone—it is shown to be not a universal end, but a rarefied one. By lashing out at Rhino in his moment of grief,

Spider-Man locks his adversary within a specific emotional stage—binds him in loss—and thus ultimately reinstantiates the hierarchies that have defined their relationship. This suggests that grief itself, while perhaps necessary, offers little in the way of justice. Someday that grief might be "integrated" into life—but maybe not everyone can get there.

Spider-Man's final line of dialogue of "Depression"—"Someday"—should be read as an entrance into the final issue of the series, as well as the final stage of the Kübler-Ross model, "Acceptance" (Loeb and Cassaday). "Someday"—or a future beyond the direct experience of grief, but at the same time not altogether outside of that grief—is made possible in acceptance of the loss, "integrating" it into one's new routines and daily reality. Mourning loss might be permanent, in the sense that it permanently alters those who mourn, but it is not itself a final stage. In the logic of Kübler-Ross, only through acceptance can one really "move on" with a life and open up to the possibility that it gets better, someday.

Before someday can be reached, however, "Acceptance" works through the mourning rituals of eulogization and burial to mark firm closure for Rogers's story. Opening with an extreme close-up panel centered on a single white star against a darkened field, the first page of the story pulls back, panel by panel, to reveal a flag-draped casket, "drawn by a single white horse, *riderless*, a ceremony up until now held only for a president" (3). Proceeding toward the Capitol Building in Washington, D.C., "mourners and fans" have "lined the streets" to honor Rogers one last time, standing in the rain to recognize the passing of someone who many feel, as the final caption box of the page attests, "was even more important than any elected official" (3).

Turning the page reveals that the symbolism of the ceremony is amplified by its ultimate destination. "The journey comes to an end at Arlington National Cemetery," reads the first caption box, where six pall-bearers, "Ben Grimm of the Fantastic Four; T'Challa, the Black Panther; former Captain America partner, Rick Jones; Carol Danvers, also known as Ms. Marvel; Sam Wilson, The Falcon; and of course, Tony Stark who, as we all know, is Iron Man," receive the casket and lay it at the base of the "newly installed Captain America Memorial," a towering figural sculpture depicting Steve Rogers in his Captain America costume, holding a flagpole to his side and raising his iconic shield above his head (4–5). Around the Memorial, masses of mourners are pictured, many huddling beneath black umbrellas guarding them from the saturating rain. The tinted gray palette—gradations of rainclouds and the pall of ceremonial burial—adds a clear visual layer of mourning to the issue, the washed-out color standing in for the felt emotions of those "mourners and fans," as well as former friends and comrades, who usher Rogers's casket toward its final resting place.

Through much of the remaining issue, friend and longtime partner Sam Wilson eulogizes Rogers from a dais situated beneath the Memorial. The story moves through a series of reflections on Rogers's life, with Wilson noting the personal histories of those gathered and their connection to Rogers. It's in these moments of personal connection and remembrance that "Acceptance" shows its greatest force as the narrative resolution of the story arc, as well as its status as the end-stage of Kübler-Rossian grief. This is true because, rather than utilizing a familiar visual storytelling technique for the conveyance of memories past—imagine a typical gray-toned, "times past" code displacing readers from the narrative present—"Acceptance" employs visual cues that move in the opposite direction. Here, the present—in mourning—is awash in gray tones, while memory—in reverence of the ideal once represented—is alive and bursting with color. Indeed, it's in remembrance that Rogers remains most vibrant, ever lurching into action, ever representing the ideal of what could be, and ever inspiring those around him.

Each memory of Rogers constructed in eulogy stands apart from the primary funeral story arc, full-page and double-page splashes that punctuate the issue—the eulogization and collective remembrance of the memorial service working as a pulsing resuscitation of life, or at least resuscitation of what a life can mean again in mourning.

The Falcon, for instance, is shown in the first beat of memory, his original electric green costume popping off the page above a plain-clothed, barechested Rogers as they fight early foes (10). But because Rogers's "real power came from the lives he touched in the *decades* he was with us," Wilson digs further, un-archiving the sedimentary layers of memory within the collective mass of mourners gathered together to honor his passing (11). "I'd like those of you who served with Steve in World War II to please stand up," Wilson says, "those soldiers . . . those Howling Commandos . . . those he saved from the horrors of war" (11). Elderly men and women, in successive panels—some in military dress uniform—are shown rising with Wilson's call, bound together by lives lived alongside Rogers, and sharing in remembrance of Rogers's dynamic, dramatic double-splash-page memory of liberating a Nazi concentration camp. Wilson calls out again, first to the early superheroes who fought alongside Rogers, and then to those who continue their legacy, the "new era of heroes" who defined so much recent history. As each next group stands, adding their beat of memory, each last group remains standing—performing physically the layers of remembrance they share, and opening up generational links between those who share different memories of the same man.

"Now. Look around you," says Wilson:

> Kind of amazing, isn't it? How we usually see differences between us . . . separated by nationality, by color, by religion . . . and yet here we are all connected. Steve Rogers, the skinny blond-haired kid who grew up on the streets of New York showed us that the *ideals* of the American dream—the great *melting pot* that can bring out the best in each of us and bind us all together—actually works! And he can keep teaching us that long after he's *gone*. By telling stories about him . . . to our children . . . to our grandchildren . . . *Steve Rogers, Captain America, will never die*. This doesn't have to be a day of sadness. We can accept it as a gift of *unity* and *hope*. *The kind of day Captain America lived for*. (24–25)

As the structure of "Acceptance" suggests, and the end of Wilson's eulogy of Rogers directly reiterates, the acceptance of loss in mourning need not subsume the memory of those lost to the moldering reaches of the past. Mourning is an opportunity to construct memories of the dead, memories that actively "bind us all together," gifts of "unity and hope" whose promise points to the future. In this way, mourning is shown as an intergenerational transfer of memory, such that the life of the dead is reconstructed again and again, in perpetuity, through storytelling.

And as if to model the iterated memorialization of storytelling, "Acceptance" tells another. At the end of the issue we learn that Rogers wasn't buried at Arlington, and that it will be Tony Stark, in his Iron Man suit, who will deliver the final eulogy for Rogers before his real burial, surrounded by a select few of Stark's closest comrades. "The funeral in Arlington was for the public. Steve Rogers deserves to rest in peace," says Stark.

In his own eulogy—like Wilson—Stark recalls the way that Rogers brought together a set of disparate heroes, united under the common banner of The Avengers. Despite their differences, almost always on opposite sides of the argument until the end, Stark's simple admission, "I miss your battle cry," ushers in the last pulse of collective memory that unites several strands of Rogers's life in "Acceptance," one final call: "Avengers Assemble!" Indeed, in death as he did in life, Rogers assembles The Avengers. Thus remembered, his battle cry is not lost, but re-created for the next generation, and the next.

The memory of Rogers is creative, reassembling those who, compelled by the outstanding ideal he modeled, use his life as a way-marker for where they too may lead.

As Rogers's casket is lowered into the sea, entombed in icy water as he was once before a generation earlier, the star on his casket lid sinks beneath the surface, panel by panel, until his symbolic presence is swallowed up by the blackness of the ocean depths below. Visually bookending the issue, "Acceptance" begins and ends with Steve Rogers. But dancing the line between beginning and ending, of bodily finitude realized and mythic infinitude suggested, The Wasp, one of the few heroes present during Rogers's burial at sea, says to Stark when Rogers's casket sinks into the waters: "One era ends. And a new one begins. We're going to have to accept that now. Right, Tony?" (32).

. . .

For readers, *Fallen Son* does more than catalog the emotions of "Earth's Mightiest Heroes" as they wrestle with loss; insofar as the Kübler-Ross model seeks to describe typical emotional processes of grief in loss through its model of discrete stages, the series practically demonstrates how readers themselves ought to come to terms with mourning Captain America.

But the series is full of tensions that press beyond the structured stages of grief described by the chapter titles. And those tensions, suffusing the narrative with an intensity that juts out beyond the boundaries of discrete emotional standpoints, actively play with the space between extraordinary moments—like individual death in comics—and the messy, flighty, altogether excessively ordinary affective negotiation that happens throughout *Fallen Son* as we watch characters struggle to navigate bereavement. Barriers of distinct emotions are shown melting away, intrinsically saturated with qualities of ineffable sacredness, at the same time they are shored up by chaptered narrative structure. I see those tensions as provocative, and productive; they reveal what comics can *do* in the world, drawing out and revealing affective disjunctures that, in turn, can reconstitute the "shifting assemblage" of society and point our attention toward the altogether ordinary dimensions of sacredness threading the social whole.

Throughout the story, the mythic pretensions of the superhero genre—its timelessness and "inconsumability"—are brought down into the register of what I see as the ordinary sacred. Skirting the structured boundaries of ritualized stages, *Fallen Son* takes familiar elements of superhero myth and reconstitutes them, making myth new and lively, as well as unpredictable. That unpredictability is, following Stewart, eruptive. "Sudden eruptions are fascinating beyond all reason," she writes, "as if they're divining rods articulating something. But what?" (68).

That question—"But what?"—is for me the fundamental draw of the ordinary sacred; it isn't easily articulable meaning, a clearly wrought interpretive tool, but a sense of things that can impel us forward, asking again in each next moment what intense "what" is erupting through the boundaries of structure, impressing on our bodies, *doing* sacred things through feeling and experience. Put differently, and closer to the discussion here, the ordinary sacred is a kind of spider-sense of the world revealed in moments of breakdown—of threat and promise that shy away from the familiar and approach the utterly ineffable.

By making myth lively—playing the dance of structure and creativity through less predictable registers of embodied affect—*Fallen Son* taps into the felt, phenomenological qualities of the sacred. Firmly rooted in everyday experience, the sacred is revealed in the moment where the ordinary and extraordinary congeal in death, in memorialization, the resulting tangle pointing upward off the page, toward the reader, whom *Fallen Son* assembles as feeling subject, and for whom the comics perform a specific kind of feeling-work. Although the Kübler-Ross model suggests the potential of clean, clear resolution for affective distress experienced in loss, *Fallen Son* shows us instead that—through ineffable intensity—comics can work to make the ordinary sacred.

BIBLIOGRAPHY

Alaniz, José. *Death, Disability, and the Superhero: The Silver Age and Beyond*. Jackson: University Press of Mississippi, 2015.

Barthes, Roland. "Myth Today." In *A Barthes Reader*, edited by Susan Sontag. New York: Hill and Wang, 1982.

Barthes, Roland. "The Third Meaning: Research Notes on Some Eisenstein Stills." In *The Responsibility of Forms: Critical Essays on Music, Art, and Representation*. Translated by Richard Howard. Berkeley: University of California Press, 1985.

Bataille, Georges. *Inner Experience*. Albany: SUNY Press, 1988.

Berlant, Lauren. *Cruel Optimism*. Durham: Duke University Press, 2011.

Bonanno, George A., Camille B. Wortman, Darrin R. Lehman, Roger G. Tweed, Michelle Haring, John Sonnega, Deborah Carr, and Randolph M. Nesse. "Resilience to Loss and Chronic Grief: A Prospective Study from Preloss to 18-Months Postloss." *Journal of Personality and Social Psychology* 83, no. 5 (2002): 1150–64.

Coogan, Peter. *Superhero: The Secret Origin of a Genre*. Austin: Monkeybrain, 2006.

Downe-Wamboldt, Barbara, and D. Tamlyn. "An International Survey of Death Education Trends in Faculties of Nursing and Medicine." *Death Studies* 21, no. 2 (March–April 1997): 177–88.

Durkheim, Émile. *The Elementary Forms of Religious Life*. New York: Free Press, 1995.

Eco, Umberto. "The Myth of Superman." *Diacritics* 2, no. 1 (Spring 1972): 14–22.

Gustines, George Gene. "Captain America Is Dead; National Hero since 1941." *New York Times*, March 8, 2007. http://www.nytimes.com/2007/03/08/books/08capt.html?_r=0. Accessed July 26, 2016.

Hardt, Michael, and Antonio Negri. *Multitude: War and Democracy in the Age of Empire*. London: Penguin Books, 2004.

Kübler-Ross, Elisabeth. *On Death and Dying*. New York: Scribner, 2011.

Loeb, Jeph (w), and John Cassaday (a). "Acceptance." *Fallen Son: The Death of Captain America, No. 5*. New York: Marvel Comics, August 2007.

Loeb, Jeph (w), and David Finch (a). "Depression." *Fallen Son: The Death of Captain America, No. 4*. New York: Marvel Comics, July 2007.

Loeb, Jeph (w), and Ed McGuiness (a). "Anger." *Fallen Son: The Death of Captain America, No. 2*. New York: Marvel Comics, June 2007.

Loeb, Jeph (w), and John Romita Jr. (a). "Bargaining." *Fallen Son: The Death of Captain America, No. 3*. New York: Marvel Comics, July 2007.

Loeb, Jeph (w), and Leinil Yu (a). "Denial." *Fallen Son: The Death of Captain America, No. 1*. New York: Marvel Comics, June 2007.

Millar, Mark (w), and Steve McNiven (a). *Civil War: A Marvel Comics Event*. New York: Marvel Comics, 2007.

Reynolds, Richard. *Superheroes: A Modern Mythology*. Jackson: University Press of Mississippi, 1992.

Sedgwick, Eve Kosofsky. *Touching Feeling: Affect, Pedagogy, Performativity*. Durham: Duke University Press, 2003.

Stewart, Kathryn. *Ordinary Affects*. Durham: Duke University Press, 2007.

Williams, Raymond. *Marxism and Literature*. London: Oxford University Press, 1977.

Wortman, Camille B., and Roxane Cohen Silver. "The Myths of Coping with Loss." *Journal of Consulting and Clinical Psychology* 57, no. 3 (1989): 349–57.

Chapter Fifteen

WILL EISNER

Master of Graphic Wisdom

LEONARD V. KAPLAN

WILL EISNER IS THE REPUTED GODFATHER OF GRAPHIC SEQUENTIAL ART in the United States. His work is necessary for any complete analysis of comic books and theology. However, Eisner deserves praise for more than being a central figure in legitimating comic books for scholarship. He contributed to the making of an important new artistic outlet that would provide other voices to the cultural brew. Indeed, his appropriation of what many considered "lowbrow" art is sufficiently rich to reward a conversation with one other Jewish thinker, Isaiah Berlin. For both Eisner and Berlin, the nexus of wisdom and Jewish thought interweave to provide new modes of engaging Jewish wisdom.

We can see this emerging category of Jewish wisdom in Eisner's most famous work, *A Contract with God* (1978). It opens with a midrash on the book of Job. That book, emanating from prebiblical wisdom, is paradigmatic for its harsh warning about human expectations. Eisner created parables and midrash, literary criticism and political commentary, to capture moments that reveal a culture to itself. Where Adorno examined astrological columns to illuminate the consciousness of the users of that medium, Eisner used an apparently lowbrow form and elevated it into illuminating literature. As a master cartoonist, he prided himself on creating and teaching technique. So too Berlin, who like Eisner probed the history, politics, and phenomenological limits of human consciousness. Berlin is the archetypical liberal to Eisner's prophetic literature. Yet both encompass positions on liberal theory, Enlightenment thought, Romanticism as art, and epistemology. And although Eisner was not a traditional philosopher, he situated his art in the kind of social space that evoked Berlin's theoretical world.

. . .

In his essay "Discovering Isaiah Berlin in Moses Hess's *Rome and Jerusalem*," Ken Koltun-Fromm celebrates Berlin, the man and his work, and designates him a Jewish wise man. However, he does not provide a genealogy for the category. Koltun-Fromm argues that Berlin stands for a distinctive liberalism and committed Zionism. He focuses on Berlin's rhetorical power as much as his analytics. Berlin's living voice expresses a Jewish humanism committed to protecting the uniqueness of each life, and his political status as public intellectual made him a significant force. Berlin was the master critic of idealized models of thought, and he championed a robust, liberal pluralism free from dogmatic essentialism as his central theoretical and political concern. He recognized that each mode of human thought requires its own method, and he was deeply suspicious of any grand theory that ran roughshod over the particularity of human lives. In this, both Berlin and Eisner share a good deal, for both recognized humanity in the streets, as it were. But where Berlin opened that life to philosophical reflection, Eisner drew it for us in gritty detail.

Indeed, Berlin has often been criticized as an abstract thinker. Zeev Sternhell, for example, claims that Berlin's talk about positive liberty itself was too idealized. Yet Berlin's distinction between the hedgehog and fox captures his epistemological worldview best and shows us how Eisner follows Berlin's lead to move abstract theory into human culture. The hedgehog believes that human complexity can be ordered by "the sheer force of conviction to unify the manifold particulars of any situation under a single commanding vision" (Sternhell 288). The fox, however, knows better: goods including values are not commensurable. Justice, fairness, and efficiency can each be prioritized for decision making. There is no axiological tiebreaker when fundamental values are in conflict. Berlin argued that pluralism in historical evaluations demands an understanding that cultures develop differently and that a good in one place differs from the good in another. Theory must develop in relation to the object of analysis, and scientific analysis must use tools different from historical work. When applied to history, Berlin's fox considers historical differences. Reading Berlin in this way, we can see how Eisner follows Berlin's lead to engage historical particulars, weaving sophisticated lines and textures into the lives of New York City Jews. Eisner's *A Contract with God* draws Berlin down into the art of human suffering and wisdom, the place where the book of Job finds its home too.

To understand the ethical concerns of Eisner's *Contract*, one needs to read it as a meditation on the book of Job. Now Job may be the oldest book in the Hebrew Bible, and it is paradigmatic of biblical wisdom literature. The book of Job makes clear that human beings are not central to creation. The wisdom literature in the Hebrew Bible outlines positive ways to live in an agricultural space dominated by shifting empires from Babylonia and Mesopotamia. Yet, just as importantly, it provides explicit limits for human knowledge and aspirations. This sense of physical and metaphysical limits lies at the core of Eisner's argument in *Contract*, for he continues the world of Job by depicting Jewish life in all of its struggles: we see poor Jews, orthodox Jews, social-climbing Jews, rich Jews. We see the mating game in all its crudeness and sentimentality. Eisner understands class and caste in America and the fluidity among classes predicated on intelligence, luck, and inheritance. He gives us gender differences and needs. In this work, he fills in what the embedded reality calls for: Eisner gives us Jewish social life in all its variety, nastiness, suffering, and interpersonal interactions.

But Eisner's work does not end with these engagements. He draws particularly Jewish books that act as critical interventions in the world. *The Plot: The Secret Story of the Protocols of the Elders of Zion* (2005) illustrates the reception of the virulent *Protocols* from its first propaganda use through its ugly history. *Fagin the Jew* (2003) presents Fagin criticizing his creator Dickens for unreflective stereotyping without empathy, and with no sense of what that stereotype means in an anti-Semitic world. In *Contract*, Eisner attends to the three levels of human existence that twentieth-century existential therapy designated as worthy of exploration: self, other, and God. A later story in the *Contract* trilogy, "A Life Force," gives us one view of Jewish life in New York City during the Depression: Jacob Shtarkah, a Jewish carpenter, has just completed a five-year project for his synagogue. When finished, he is told that there is no more work and that he should retire. Additionally, his work is credited to the name of the donor. Slumped over in an alley by his tenement, he watches a cockroach struggle and begins to talk to it about the meaning of life, God, and the differences between him and it. When someone tries to stomp on the cockroach, Shtarkah saves it and is beaten up. Shtarkah wrestles and loses to a thug, not an angel. Is this an absurd gesture? Eisner illuminates an individual worldview and its general incompatibility with most others. Yet Shtarkah expresses himself in this losing battle and affirms his being by resistance, even if it is through identification with a cockroach. Eisner also affirms his identification through the failed worker: Eisner's father, much like Shtarkah, experienced reality as a failed artist and businessman that labeled his life a failure. Shtarkah's story goes on in its own journey through small business, small crime, seduction outside marriage, and a sad end. This is Eisner's world; Jewish wisdom finds its place in the ordinary sacred, here and in *A Contract with God.*

. . .

Eisner's life contained similarities to that of Job. Eisner lost his only daughter to leukemia when she was sixteen, and like Job, he took the death personally. Perhaps more personally than did Job, who cried out to God only after excruciating pain added to the loss of his children, property, and the disbelief of his friends. In his biography of Eisner, Schumacher writes that Eisner felt as if he was punished for somehow not living an ethical life (157–58). We know about Eisner after the loss: he worked and lived, and he continued to live out the archetypical wisdom story. *Contract* rendered in illustration and word is as compact as the original Job narrative, and exceedingly short when compared to Jobean criticism. It is a comic Job for our time.

As with much recent Jewish commentary, Eisner adds little to a theodicy or apocalyptic interpretation of Job. The book of Job attempts to placate God with ritual and adherence to the good life. Eisner's protagonist in *Contract*, Frimme Hersh, is committed to do good and expects God to look out for him. Hersh is righteous and deeply admired in his community. He was very intelligent as a child, and he possesses a Jewish love and capacity for attempting to understand a rather difficult God. Indeed, many continue to believe that God will favor them if they are truly good. Eisner apparently felt some sense of this even though he was not an observant Jew. Certainly, he depicts his character as having that faith.

Hersh, the Job figure, is born into an East European shtetl community. He loses his parents at an early age, but he is a *yeshiva bocher*, another potential sage. His intellectual gifts are recognized by his community, and he becomes equipped to be a scholar of rare ability. Eisner did not have that experience, but he certainly understood the trope. Eisner's use of the contract motif fits well with the biblical notion of covenant, but it also suits Eisner, as he dealt with contracts in his professional life as a businessman. *Contract* fulfilled Eisner's ambition to create a graphic comic that would demand serious attention. Like Hersh, Eisner was a striver who had a healthy narcissism. He shared Hersh's God, but not his attitude toward people and the world.

Contract is inked with dialogue and exposition for mass consumption, yet art is central to the work. Comics were disposable, and so the art had to grab a reader's attention. Yet comics maintain an immediacy through their vulnerability. *Contract* opens with three adjacent tenement houses, with many other houses as backdrop—suggesting congested city towers that frame many of the stories. Eisner intimates the crowding of the tenements and the distant powerful skyscrapers that will become Dropsie Avenue, Eisner's terrain. The world he depicts, for Frimme Hersh and Jacob Shtarkah, is a world he knew. Eisner's very style produces clutter, and the reader's imagination provides density and intertextual allusiveness. Eisner absorbed that world from his father and from the movies, particularly film noir. Consider the central scene in which Hersh's adopted daughter is buried:

> All day
> the rain
> poured
> down on
> the Bronx
> without
> mercy.

These words are backed by lines mimicking a merciless rain. The sewers are overflowing and the waters rise over the street. Beneath the penciling, a slumped-over man walks through the puddles, gesturing the physical toll of depression. The facing page inks the address of the end journey of Hersh sloshing dejectedly through the tide, "like the ark of Noah" to number 55 Dropsie Avenue (4–5).

On the next page, the story is described on the left and our hero, about to step up to the tenement's entrance, is on the right. "Only the tears of ten thousand weeping angels could cause such a deluge! And come to think of it, maybe that is exactly what it was." The storyline is set, an abject man wading through rain, grief evidenced in both his sketched figure and in these few words—words that legitimize the actuality of Job for Hersh and for the reader: "after all, this was the day Frimme Hersh buried Rachele his daughter" (6–7). He is alone and abject, without God to call upon. On the next page we read: "Not so unusual a father brings up a child with care and love only to lose her . . . plucked, as it were, from his arms by the unseen hand—the hand of God. It happens to lots of people every day . . . to others maybe" (8–9). The gentile widow "Missis Kelly" is concerned and offers "a little nourishment," but she, just like the poor Jews on her block, is subject to the same pain as the others on 55 Dropsie Avenue. Pain, suffering, loss: these are elemental forces for Jews and non-Jews alike, in *Contract* and in the book of Job.

The contract between Frimme and his God, one in which Frimme demands that God reward him for good deeds, was inscribed on a fragmented stone, suggesting Moses's tablets. But what does it mean to establish a contract with God? Covenants are a core feature of biblical theology, and are critical to rabbinic commentary. But a contract is not a covenant, for to fulfill a contract there must be conversation, agreement between the parties, and the execution of the particulars of the agreement. Note, however, how Eisner depicts conversation between Frimme and his God: "And the old tenement trembled under the fury of the dialogue." Eisner draws flashes of lightning next to these words. And Frimme is enraged, with one hand clenched on a window curtain. He yells with fury, highlighted in bold by Eisner: **"If God requires that men honor their agreements** . . . then is not **God Also** so obligated??" The question marks are rendered to look like Hebrew lettering (25). Hersh is at the window, his head high, speaking to the unseen interlocutor. Hersh's enraged face is the face of defiance, the face of Job who feels rightfully aggrieved. In the bottom panel lightning is seen through the window and the curtain is rolled and disheveled, all sketched by Eisner with shades of black and white. Hersh's Jobean lament continues, and he asks, "Were the terms not clearly written [in the contract]?? . . . Did I ignore one tiny sentence—or perhaps a single comma?" Finally, he opens the window and a drawer, pulls out a jagged stone—presumably the recorded contract—and spits on it, his face enraged (26–28). He violently hurls the stone fragment through the window and it "clanks" to the pavement with rain pouring down relentlessly. This is a contract without a partner; this is a Job without his God.

Friends visit Frimme to console him, but all are met with "stony silence." What makes for consolation from ritual? Hersh lived that ritual. Was his participation facile? Or was his belief so personal and the trauma so deep that he has lost the capacity for community and consolation? Perhaps this brilliant man joined community, worked for it but in fact was never emotionally engaged with the diverse members of that community? Perhaps his very brilliance encouraged a narcissism that rendered him emotionally brittle? Still, after eight days of mourning (*shiva*), Hersh makes his morning prayer, shaves his beard, puts on a business suit and looks every bit like the prosperous businessman. He immediately turns to the bank on 186th Street, negotiates the buying of number 55 Dropsie Avenue by using pilfered bonds from the synagogue, and settles with a very gentile-looking banker. In the two pages that Eisner depicts this transaction, we see Frimme change guise several times. At first hat in hand, he looks like a poor supplicant; then expansive,

Figure 15.1. Frimme Hersh confronting God, *A Contract with God*, page 25, by Will Eisner. Copyright © 1978 Will Eisner. Used by permission of W.W. Norton & Company, Inc.

holding his lapels, he looks the prosperous businessman; and finally standing, shaking hands with the banker on the deal, he looks appropriately pleased. Two pages of black-and-white sketches establish his demeanor and it changes into what he is about to become—a slum landlord and a very wealthy man. The illustrations of Frimme Hersh as he transitions from observant Jew to incipient slum landlord capture a transformation of personality so immediate that Eisner need not include verbal description. They also capture class and class consciousness as Frimme realizes he can make his way in the secular, gentile world. Eisner shows that world of commercial interchange to be as hollow as the Frimme Hersh who becomes its new spokesman.

Frimme quickly assumes this despicable role. He raises the rents on 55 Dropsie Avenue by 10 percent, including that of Ms. Kelly, on a fixed widow's pension. "No exceptions," our new capitalist utters. Admiringly, an onlooker remarks, "Ach . . . These Jews . . . Yesterday a poor tenant, today the owner! . . . How do they do it?!" More quickly than possible in prose, Eisner shows us Frimme's real estate empire. He takes a "Shikse from Scranton, Pa." for a mistress but still returns to 55 Dropsie Avenue regularly "just to look at it," mistress by his side and chauffeur awaiting (34–38). This gentile consort, however, speaks truth to power: "Y'know, Frim, you got, like, a black hole inside o' you!" She tries to move Frimme to drink, but he will have none of it (39–40). Trenchantly, Eisner sums up the ubiquity of pervasive alienation: drink to fill the black hole. But the blackness remains, as it did for Job before him, and perhaps even for Eisner too. The black hole in the soul is thematic of Eisner's midrash. That black hole cannot be filled by theory, by Berlin, or even by Eisner himself.

Without any reason offered, Frimme Hersh finds himself walking from his penthouse to the old synagogue, where he asks the "wisest of the elders" to make a new contract with God for him. The request is pondered, with the appropriate recognition that such a demand is a juridical problem. But "on the other hand" (there is often such another hand, as Eisner well knows), "if not us—**WHO THEN?**" A second rabbi responds, "but, Rebbe, would it not be a blasphemy if we should **DEVIATE** from the law?" The response, a perfect kicker in all of Eisner's brilliance and irony: "We will not deviate! . . . We will **ABBREVIATE**!" (46–47). Generations of Jewish jurisprudence are embedded in Eisner's image/text abbreviation. Jewish jurisprudence thrived on dissenting opinions. The Rebbe and the elders are flummoxed. These are not wise men. They do want their communal resources restored, and they do not wish to destroy the law; they simply wish to abbreviate. Jewish law allows breach for reasons of health. But is there something that we can recognize as communal health? Eisner gently teases the Rebbe, the elders, and jurisprudence in general by marking the problem of the exception. I doubt that he knew of Carl Schmitt's work on how the exception could undermine an entire legal edifice. But he knew enough to mock jurisprudence in this case, as his bold lettering indicates. And in mocking legal order Eisner leaves the black hole open. Frimme cannot fill it through Jewish legal precedent or abbreviation. He cannot make it right. The black hole remains, and so does our modern-day Job.

This becomes all too clear when Frimme, with new contract in hand, returns home and immediately dies of a heart attack. He dies unfulfilled; the entire neighborhood is destroyed in the resultant storm, and 55 Dropsie Avenue stands alone. This is not a naturalist take on Job indicating failed belief or perhaps God's death. Hersh's death is marked by such force that the "old tenements seemed to tremble in the storm. It reminded the tenants of that day, years ago, when Frimme Hersh argued with GOD and terminated their contract." Blown by the storm, an outsized used newspaper page reads: "Real Estate Tycoon Dies" (54). God does not appear in a whirlwind, as in the book of Job, but in a raging fire that destroys everything but the site of Frimme Hersh's dwelling. Eisner calls this miraculous and in so doing situates this place as foundational, Jewish event alongside Mount Moriah (the site of Abraham's sacrifice of Isaac) and even Kishinev. Like a reverse Passover story, this passing over destroys an entire neighborhood, highlighting the force of place and capricious power. This is Frimme Hersh's Job story, and this is Eisner's midrash on Job.

In the epilogue Eisner shows us that Frimme is not the last modern Job. His is a type that continues, from generation through generation. Shloime Khreks, a new boy in the neighborhood, saves three children and old Ms. Kelly but is later attacked by "three toughs" who ridicule him and throw stones. After fighting back, Shloime finds the stone on which the contract is written, and he signs "his name below that of Frimme Hersh . . . thereby entering into a contract with GOD" (56–61). Eisner portrays Shloime as a modern, Hasidic Jew. Many nonobservant Jews recognize the Hasidim as keepers of the tradition, and here Eisner plays on this stereotype to highlight notions of continuity. The trajectory is clear, as I have argued in this chapter. It is a trajectory that travels from the biblical Job to Frimme Hersh, and now to Shloime Khreks: Frimme's "black hole" is not his alone.

. . .

If there is a form that might describe Eisner's *A Contract with God* other than an American version of the shtetl folktale, that form might be what Walter

Benjamin called the German Tragic Drama. In *The Origin of the German Tragic Drama*, Benjamin differentiated Greek tragedy from the German form that he located in the Baroque. The *Trauspiel*, or mourning play, is allegorical, ambiguous, a play of intrigue, delay, and catastrophe—in short, Hamlet as model. This form is characterized by excess: "A play wherein one man now enters and another exits; with tears it begins and with weeping ends. Yea after death itself, time with us still toys, when foul maggot and worm drill our putrid corpses" (37). This gets us close to what Eisner's *Contract* is all about: art does not freeze life but, as Benjamin shows, illuminates it whether it is from German Expressionism or a *Trauspiel*.

Samuel Weber argues that Benjamin's analysis of that form was itself dependent, ironically I would add, on Carl Schmitt's analysis of sovereignty. The Germany that produced this form lacked a solid basis for supporting the sovereign state. The lack of a solid sovereign enabled the creation of this mourning drama without a base to ground its imagination. Its over-the-top dimension collapses into a void without the sovereign support. But the story of Job rests on God as sovereign and so is anchored in the most stable sovereignty possible. Eisner has removed that security, and that ground, in his contemporary midrash on Job. The "black hole" remains because Eisner portrays in comic form a slice of narrative tragedy. Frimme Hersh, and Shloime Khreks after him, remain imprisoned in the shadows—as indeed the very last image in *Contract* suggests. Here, Shloime, much like Frimme before him, is slumped over on the staircase, apparently writing on the contract stone. The everyday forces us to attend to real misery and confront the nature of excessive human suffering. Yet even here, darkness is textured by light—a black hole opening to a distant future. The struggle to attain the messianic that informs Benjamin's work can be found here too in Eisner's *Contract*. It maintains the possibility of messianic hope, even in the everyday world of human suffering.

Eisner, Benjamin, and even Berlin each confronted the messianic mythos that has informed much of Jewish tradition. Benjamin blends his Marxist idealism in the messianic; Berlin eschews the mystical tradition altogether. Yet both Berlin and Benjamin challenged the established state roughly at the same time in history. Benjamin's illuminations captured events or moments that open to an inchoate theory pointing toward transformative politics. Berlin, to the contrary, was never convinced of the possibility for a transformative politics writ large.

Eisner's vision of transformative, messianic politics lies in the vicissitudes and battles of the everyday. His Frimme Hersh claims a higher demand on life even against history. His demands are more than Job's call for justice, for Job was forever anxious about his God. But Frimme Hersh is an actor in the world, a traveler in the mundane and everyday. His claim against God is no more, but certainly no less, than the common expectation of just deserts. He expects the everyday sacred to be his too.

The religious power of the everyday is the world Eisner traveled in too, one that cultivated transformation in the slow and sometimes frustrating work of worldly matters. Like Frimme Hersh, he was an actor in the world. Eisner taught the art of sequential drawing to generations of comic artists, including Art Spiegelman and Harvey Pekar. He was the start of an American genealogy of Jewish comic book writers in the United States. In doing all this, Eisner never lost his refined sense of irony. Frimme Hersh felt entitled, but Eisner knew entitlement was a narcissism that could well spell suffering to the self, and certainly to others. Work, love, and persistence: this is Eisner's legacy to us. Eisner's hope for a messianic politics is always tempered by the knowledge that we will fall short. Such is progress in the everyday sacred.

BIBLIOGRAPHY

Andelman, Bob. *Will Eisner: A Spirited Life*. Raleigh: TwoMorrows, 2015.

Bakan, David. *The Slaughter of the Innocents*. Boston: Beacon Press, 1972.

Benjamin, Walter. *The Origin of German Tragic Drama*. New York: Verso, 1985.

Berlin, Isaiah. "Political Ideas in the Twentieth Century." In *Liberty*, edited by Henry Hardy. Oxford: Oxford University Press, 2002.

Brownstein, Charles. *Eisner/Miller Interview*. Milwaukie, OR: Dark Horse Press, 2005.

Buhle, Paul (ed.). *Jews and American Comics: An Illustrated History of an American Art Form*. New York: New Press, 2008.

Eisner, Will. *A Contract with God Trilogy*. New York: W. W. Norton, 2006.

Eisner, Will. *Fagin the Jew*. Milwaukie, OR: Dark Horse Books, 2003.

Eisner, Will. "In His Own Words." *Comics Journal* no. 267, April/May 2005.

Eisner, Will. *Life, in Pictures: Autobiographical Stories*. New York: W. W. Norton, 2007.

Eisner, Will. *The Plot: The Secret Story of the Protocols of the Elders of Zion*. New York: W. W. Norton, 2005.

Eisner, Will. *Will Eisner's Shop Talk*. Milwaukie, OR: Dark Horse Press, 2001.

Feiffer, Jules. *The Great Comic Book Heroes*. Seattle: Fantagraphics Books, 2003.

Kaplan, Arie. *From Krakow to Krypton: Jews and Comic Books*. Philadelphia: Jewish Publication Society, 2008.

Koltun-Fromm, Ken. "Discovering Isaiah Berlin in Moses Hess's Rome and Jerusalem." In *Isaiah Berlin and the Enlightenment*, edited by Laurence Brockliss and Ritchie Robertson, 176–86. Oxford: Oxford University Press, 2016.

Levitt, Paul. *Will Eisner: Champion of the Graphic Novel*. New York: Abrams Comicarts, 2015.

Lewis, David. *American Comics, Literary Theory, and Religion*. London: Palgrave Macmillan, 2014.

Lowy, Michael. *On a Changing World: Essays in Political Philosophy from Karl Marx to Walter Benjamin*. Chicago: Haymarket Books, 1993.

McCloud, Scott. *Making Comics: Storytelling Secrets of Comics, Manga and Graphic Novels*. New York: HarperCollins, 2006.

McCloud, Scott. *Reinventing Comics: How Imagination and Technology Are Revolutionizing an ArtForm*. New York: William Morrow Paperbacks, 2000.

McCloud, Scott. *Understanding Comics: The Invisible Art*. New York: William Morrow Paperbacks, 1994.

Morgan, Michael L. *Interim Judaism: Jewish Thought in a Century of Crisis*. Bloomington: Indiana University Press, 2001.

Muffs, Yochanan. *Love & Joy: Law, Language and Religion in Ancient Israel*. New York: Jewish Theological Seminary of America, 1992.

Novak, David. *Covenantal Rights: A Study in Jewish Political Theory*. Princeton: Princeton University Press, 2000.

Rose, Gillian. *Judaism and Modernity: Philosophic Essays*. Oxford: Blackwell, 1993.

Schumaker, Michael. *Will Eisner: A Dreamer's Life in Comics*. New York: Bloomsbury, 2010.

Smith, Steven B. *Modernity and Its Discontents: Making and Unmaking the Bourgeois from Machiavelli to Bellow*. New Haven: Yale University Press, 2016.

Sternhell, Zeev. *The Anti-Enlightenment Tradition*. New Haven: Yale University Press, 2010.

Wildafsky, Aaron. *The Nursing Father: Moses as Political Leader*. Tuscaloosa: University of Alabama Press, 1984.

Waldron, Jeremy. *Political Theory*. Cambridge: Harvard University Press, 2016.

ABOUT THE CONTRIBUTORS

OFRA AMIHAY is a lecturer of Hebrew language and comparative literature at the University of California, Santa Barbara. She holds a PhD from NYU and has published articles on comics and graphic novels, Hebrew literature, children's literature, and photography. She is the coeditor of the volume *The Future of Text and Image* (Cambridge Scholars, 2012), and in 2015 she curated the photography exhibition "Text and the City" in the Museum of Contemporary Art in Zagreb, Croatia.

MADELINE BACKUS is a graduate of Bryn Mawr College with an AB in religion. Her interest in religious studies focuses on the material and visual dimensions of religion, and she has a love for comics, shrines, clothing, and art. Madeline spent her senior year as the advisee of Ken Koltun-Fromm exploring the ways religion is communicated through comics. She hails from Lawrence, Kansas, where she currently resides. This is her first coauthored and published piece.

SAMANTHA BASKIND, professor of art history at Cleveland State University, is the author or editor of six books, including *Raphael Soyer and the Search for Modern Jewish Art* (2004); a solely authored encyclopedia, *Encyclopedia of Jewish American Artists* (2007), which was named a *College and Research Libraries* Selected Reference Work; *Jewish Art: A Modern History* (2011); *Jewish Artists and the Bible in Twentieth-Century America* (2014); and most recently *The Warsaw Ghetto in American Art and Culture* (2018). She is also coeditor of the foundational volume *The Jewish Graphic Novel: Critical Approaches* (2008), served as editor for US art for the twenty-two-volume revised edition of the *Encyclopaedia Judaica*, and is currently series editor of *Dimyonot: Jews and the Cultural Imagination*, published by the Pennsylvania State University Press.

ELIZABETH RAE COODY directs the Writing Lab at the Iliff School of Theology in Denver, Colorado. Her own writing is often about the Bible and comics. As a trained biblical scholar whose PhD is in religious and theological studies with a concentration in biblical interpretation, she values the contributions to biblical interpretation that popular culture can make. Her 2015 dissertation project was on the way comics can help interpreters imagine the scandal of Jesus's death on the cross that is often domesticated by modern Christian sensibilities. Her work continues and expands themes of how popular culture can give insight into the Bible and how knowledge of the Bible can return the favor.

SCOTT S. ELLIOTT is associate professor in the Department of Philosophy and Religion at Adrian College in Adrian, Michigan. He received his PhD in New Testament and early Christianity from Drew University. He is author of *Reconfiguring Mark's Jesus: Narrative Criticism after Poststructuralism* (Sheffield Phoenix Press, 2011), and the chapter on "Graphic Bibles" in the forthcoming *Oxford Handbook to the Bible in American Popular Culture*, edited by Dan Clanton and Terry Clark. His research focuses on biblical literature, ancient Greek and Roman popular writings, and literary theory.

ASSAF GAMZOU is currently director of professional engagement at the International Koret School for Jewish Peoplehood, the Museum of the Jewish People, Beit Hatfutsot. Before that he worked as curator of the Israeli Cartoon Museum, where he has curated exhibitions, both local and international, on editorial cartoons, comics and graphic novels. Among his exhibitions: "Biblical Proportions: Stories from the Old Testament in Graphic Narratives," "Red Lines: Freedom of Expression in Israeli and International Cartooning," and "Culture Heroes: Cultural Leaders in the Yishuv and Their Cartoons (1970–1870)."

SUSAN HANDELMAN is professor of English literature at Bar-Ilan University. She is the author of numerous articles, including most recently "'Don't Forget the Potatoes': Imagining God through Food" (2016), "'Is Midrash Comics'? A Fish Story about Graphic Narrative, Visual Rhetoric and Rabbinic Hermeneutics" (2014), and the entry on "Judaism" for the *Cambridge Companion to Literature and Religion* (2016). She is also the author of six books, including *"Make Yourself a Teacher": Rabbinic Tales of Mentors and Disciples* (2011), *Fragments of Redemption: Jewish Thought and Literary Theory in Benjamin, Scholem, and Levinas* (1991), and *Slayers of Moses: The Emergence of Rabbinic Interpretation in Modern Literary Theory* (1982).

LEAH HOCHMAN is associate professor of Jewish thought and director of the Louchheim School for Judaic Studies at Hebrew Union College-Jewish Institute of Religion in Los Angeles. She received her BA from Pitzer College and her MA/PhD in religion and literature from Boston University. She has held fellowships at the Moses Mendelssohn Zentrum in Potsdam, the Oxford Centre for Hebrew and Jewish Studies, the Simon Dubnow Institute in Leipzig, and the Einstein Forum in Potsdam. She taught previously at the University of Florida and Boston University. Her book *The Ugliness of Moses Mendelssohn: Aesthetics, Religion and Morality in the Eighteenth Century* (Routledge, 2014) investigates the positive moral benefit of aesthetic ugliness. Her edited volume *Tastes of Faith: Jewish Eating in the United States* was published in December 2017.

LEONARD V. KAPLAN was the Mortimer Jackson Professor of Law and is now emeritus at the University of Wisconsin. He served as president of the International Academy of Law and Mental Health and has served on several editorial boards, including that of the *International Journal of Law and Psychiatry.* He has published numerous articles on law and mental health. He is currently book series editor with Lexington Press (Rowman & Littlefield), which he previously coedited with Andrew Weiner. He has coedited three books in the series Graven Images: *Theology and the Soul of the Liberal State* with Charles Cohen, *The Weimar Moment: Liberalism, Political Theology and Law* with Rudy Koshar, and *Imagining the Jewish God* with Ken Koltun-Fromm.

KEN KOLTUN-FROMM is Robert and Constance MacCrate Chair in Social Responsibility and professor of religion at Haverford College, where he teaches a wide range of courses in modern Jewish thought and culture, together with material studies in religion. His research focuses on Jewish conceptions of identity, authority, authenticity, and materiality. Koltun-Fromm has published four books—*Moses Hess and Modern Jewish Identity* (2001), *Abraham Geiger's Liberal Judaism: Personal Meaning and Religious Authority* (2006), *Material Culture and Jewish Thought in America* (2010), and *Imagining Jewish Authenticity: Vision and Text in American Jewish Thought* (2015)—and two edited volumes, *Thinking Jewish Culture in America* (2014), and *Imagining the Jewish God* (2016). He is currently working on a new manuscript, "The Ethics of Representation: Graphic Religious Narratives and the Moral Imagination."

SHIAMIN KWA is assistant professor of East Asian languages and cultures and comparative literature at Bryn Mawr College. She is the author of two books on Chinese literature, and a forthcoming book on the graphic narrative in the twenty-first century.

SAMANTHA LANGSDALE holds a PhD in the study of religions from SOAS, University of London. Her research interests include feminist philosophy, contemporary critical theory, visual culture, and religions. Her current work centers on theories of monstrosity and women in comics. She is lecturer in philosophy and religion at the University of North Texas and teaches a range of classes in Western philosophy, religious studies, and feminism and gender studies.

A. DAVID LEWIS holds a doctorate in religious studies from Boston University as well as a master's degree in English literature from Georgetown University. He has been producing comics studies scholarship since his undergraduate days at Brandeis University, and his 2014 *American Comics, Literary Theory, and Religion: The Superhero Afterlife* was nominated for an industry Eisner Award. Lewis is the founder of the nonprofit Comics for Youth Refugees Incorporated Collective (CYRIC) and is an award-winning graphic novelist, most recently writing the modern-day *Kismet, Man of Fate* adventures.

KARLINE MCLAIN is professor of religious studies at Bucknell University. She is the author of *India's Immortal Comic Books: Gods, Kings, and Other Heroes* (Indiana University Press, 2009) and *The Afterlife of Sai Baba: Competing Visions of a Global Saint* (University of Washington Press, 2016). Her latest research project is a study of the intentional communities, or ashrams, founded by Mahatma Gandhi in India and South Africa.

RANEN OMER-SHERMAN is the Jewish Heritage Fund for Excellence Endowed Chair in Judaic Studies at the University of Louisville. He is the coeditor of *Shofar* and the author or editor of five books, including *Diaspora and Zionism in Jewish American Literature* (2002), *Israel in Exile: Jewish Writing and the Desert* (2006), *The Jewish Graphic Novel: Critical Approaches* (2008), *Narratives of Dissent: War in Contemporary Israeli Arts and Culture* (2013), and most recently *Imagining Kibbutz: Visions of Utopia in Literature and Film* (2015), as well as numerous essays on Jewish writers from Israel and North America. He was a founder of a desert kibbutz, served as a combat soldier in the IDF, and worked for many years as a desert guide in Sinai and Israel.

JOSHUA PLENCNER is currently visiting assistant professor in the Department of Political Science at Union College. His teaching and research explore the intersection of American visual culture and the politics of identity, with special interest in racial formation, affect theory, comics studies, and American political development. His writing has appeared in both popular and scholarly outlets, including *Artists Against Police Brutality*, the website *The Middle Spaces*, and *Black Perspectives*.

JEFFREY L. RICHEY is professor of Asian studies at Berea College. Educated at the University of North Carolina at Greensboro, Harvard University, the University of California at Berkeley, and the Graduate Theological Union (PhD, 2000), he has published widely on a variety of topics related to his interests in early Chinese thought, Confucian and Daoist traditions, and the Japanese reception of classical Chinese culture. His books include *Confucius in East Asia: Confucianism's History in China, Korea, Japan, and Viet Nam* (Association for Asian Studies, 2013) and the edited volumes *Daoism in Japan: Chinese Traditions and Their Influence on Japanese Religious Culture* (Routledge, 2015), *The Sage Returns: Confucian Revival in Contemporary China* (coedited with Kenneth J. Hammond; State University of New York Press, 2015), and *Teaching Confucianism* (Oxford University Press, 2008). Since 2003, he has served as China Area Editor for the *Internet Encyclopedia of Philosophy* (http://www.iep.utm.edu/). He is a longtime fan of Marvel Comics' *Doctor Strange*.

INDEX

Page numbers in **bold** indicate illustrations.

CPSIA information can be obtained
at www.ICGtesting.com
Printed in the USA
FSHW010121190919
62153FS

9 781496 819475